# Student Learning in College Residence Halls

Gregory S. Blimling

Foreword by John H. Schuh

# Student Learning in College Residence Halls

## What Works, What Doesn't, and Why

**JB JOSSEY-BASS™**

A Wiley Brand

Cover design by Wiley

Cover image: © Robert Churchill | Thinkstock

Copyright © 2015 by John Wiley & Sons, Inc. All rights reserved.

Published by Jossey-Bass

A Wiley Brand

One Montgomery Street, Suite 1200, San Francisco, CA 94104-4594—www.wiley.com, www.josseybass.com/highereducation

Jossey-Bass books and products are available through most bookstores. To contact Jossey-Bass directly call our Customer Care Department within the U.S. at 800-956-7739, outside the U.S. at 317-572-3986, or fax 317-572-4002.

Wiley publishes in a variety of print and electronic formats and by print-on-demand. Some material included with standard print versions of this book may not be included in e-books or in print-on-demand. If this book refers to media such as a CD or DVD that is not included in the version you purchased, you may download this material at http://booksupport.wiley.com. For more information about Wiley products, visit www.wiley.com.

**Library of Congress Cataloging-in-Publication Data**
Blimling, Gregory S.
  Student learning in college residence halls : what works, what doesn't, and why / Gregory S. Blimling.
    1 online resource.
  Includes bibliographical references and index.
  Description based on print version record and CIP data provided by publisher; resource not viewed.
  ISBN 978-1-118-99239-5 (pdf) – ISBN 978-1-118-99240-1 (epub) – ISBN 978-1-118-55160-8 (hardback) 1.  Student housing. 2.  College students.
I. Title.
  LB3227
  378.1'9871–dc23                                                    2014043054

Printed in the United States of America

FIRST EDITION

HB Printing    10 9 8 7 6 5 4 3 2 1

The Jossey-Bass Higher and
Adult Education Series

# Contents

# List of Tables and Figures

## Tables

## Figures

# Foreword

I was delighted that Greg Blimling invited me to write a foreword to this volume. Greg's career and mine have followed similar paths over the years, and on a number of occasions we've had a chance to collaborate, beginning with our New Directions for Student Services volume, *Increasing the Educational Role of Residence Halls*, which was published in 1981. After that publication we collaborated several other times in writing about various aspects of residence hall administration, staff training, personnel roles, and the like. While our careers have taken divergent paths from time to time, his progressing to senior leadership in student affairs and mine moving to that of a full-time faculty member and then an academic administrator, I think both of us have always valued the foundational experiences we had as residence hall administrators, regardless of our professional assignment.

I would be remiss if I did not emphasize the powerful influence that our experiences at Indiana University had on each of us. Most significantly, it is important to acknowledge that Dr. Elizabeth A. (Betty) Greenleaf, the founding director of the Department of Residence Life at Indiana University, had a major effect on each of us. Both Greg and I were fortunate to have Betty as a colleague, mentor, and friend, and if any single person in history can be pointed to as accelerating the concept of residence education I nominate her as that person. She directed the Department of Residence Life at IU for a decade (1959–1969) (Hunter & Kuh, 1989) and then served as a faculty member there for another decade. Betty had a clear vision of the potential for residence halls to contribute to the education of college students, and her aim was to maximize that potential. Neither of us could ever adequately thank her for her contributions to our professional development or the field of student affairs education.

Greg has done a wonderful job in this book of tracing the development of residence education. I think it is important to emphasize what he has noted in this volume: Until Betty's leadership and that of a few other outstanding leaders such as Hal Riker at the University of Florida and Don Adams and Art Sandeen at Michigan State, residence halls mostly were regarded as convenient places for students to live and perhaps organize a social activity or two, but they were not thought of as having significant potential for adding to the potency of the student experience.

One publication that represents a change in thinking about the potential of residence halls to contribute to students' education worthy of note was the article by Dave DeCoster, Betty Greenleaf's successor at IU, and Hal Riker (1971) that presented a cohesive approach to residence hall operations and student learning. The article, as Greg points out in this volume, identified a series of building blocks that could be used to conceptualize the relationship between the provision of adequate facilities and financing for residence halls and the development of experiences that contribute to student learning. This article informed the work of housing and residence educators for years and in many ways is still contemporary. Its fingerprints, metaphorically, are all over Figure 1.1 and Table 1.1 of this volume, which do a splendid job of illustrating how the various elements of residence halls interact with and inform each other.

From the early 1970s moving forward, the emphasis on residence halls having the potential to contribute to student learning and growth has accelerated to the point where the contemporary residence hall is thought of as a living learning laboratory where, in the most advanced circles, students can learn and grow along such important dimensions as their leadership expertise, their community engagement skills, and their learning to contribute to the larger community. Of course, not all types of student housing have the same level of effect on students. As Greg points out in Table 4.1, some forms of student residences are more potent than others in terms of desired outcomes for the student experience. The effect of various forms of living circumstance ranges from virtually no influence on student learning (living at home) to a very potent influence on student learning (living learning centers). The table is particularly instructive because at one time the thinking was that living in a residence hall, regardless of whether or not a structured experience was provided, would result in student growth. That is not necessarily the case, as is emphasized in Table 8.2. A structured, intentional approach is likely to result in a far more powerful learning experience for students than simply assigning students to rooms and developing no structured experiences that are known to work.

This volume, like no other with which I am familiar, does a splendid job of providing the foundation for the development of residential experiences by including both theory and research to support the various assertions that are made. It makes a host of suggestions and recommendations in terms of what residence educators can do to provide a rich environment for the students who live in the residence halls under their oversight and then, finally, strongly emphasizes that contemporary programs and experiences need to be evaluated rigorously so that claims as to their effectiveness can be supported by systematic inquiry, in keeping with best contemporary practice.

This book is designed primarily for contemporary residence educators and, more specifically, directors of housing or directors of residential programs. In this way, not only can they be sure that they are up to date in their approaches toward student learning and growth in their residences, but, perhaps as importantly, they also can continue to develop, implement, and modify students' experiences so that they will always live in the most enriched environment possible. This point is crucial because our work with students needs to stay contemporary, using data to make sure that we do not get stuck repeating what we learned in graduate school years ago. Rather, a commitment to constant improvement, as we found in an in-depth project (Kuh, Kinzie, Schuh, & Whitt, 2010), serves students and our institutions particularly well. The book also is very appropriate for anyone who aspires to these positions because it provides a solid foundation on which they can build a professional career in residence education. Many of the ideas included in the work have no temporal bounds, so having a copy in their professional toolbox strikes me as a necessity.

I believe other audiences can benefit from reading this volume and implementing its suggestions. Senior student affairs leaders, who are looking for a lucid description of the learning that occurs in campus residences, will find this volume highly instructive as they communicate the work of their staff to various stakeholders such as parents, faculty, and other student affairs staff who may not be familiar with campus residence operations. Presidents or other senior officers can use the thinking represented by this book as the basis for informing their boards, graduates, and institutional friends about contemporary approaches to residence education, assuming what Greg has described is implemented in their campus residence halls. And if not, then some important questions should be asked as to why these approaches have not been implemented on their campuses.

Greg has built a masterpiece upon the shoulders of his own research, his rich administrative experience, and those who have influenced him for over 40 years. The resulting product includes timeless principles that are likely to be as contemporary in the future when our grandchildren go to college as they were when we learned from Betty Greenleaf. Happy reading (and learning)!

John H. Schuh
Director and Distinguished Professor
*School of Education, Iowa State University*

# Preface

Few students choose colleges based on the quality of residence hall programs, yet those who live on campus will spend more time in residence halls than classrooms and their residence hall experiences will significantly influence their success in college. Residence halls are the source of college friendships, informal orientation, role modeling, socializing, and emotional support. They are the first place students arrive when beginning college, and the last place they see when they leave for the summer. Residence halls are students' campus homes. The peer relationships they form there help them learn the informal knowledge of the campus culture that helps define them as students.

Residence halls offer students the opportunity to learn from peers and connect with the academic community. They open doors to involvement in campus activities and interaction with peers, faculty, and staff. Residence halls create and expand opportunities and experiences for student involvement and student learning.

Residence halls can be operated in ways that help students become successful, make friends, feel connected to the institution, and improve their chances of graduating from college. Alternatively, residence halls can be operated in ways that isolate students, frustrate them with institutional overregulation, and make them eager to leave the residence halls and perhaps the institution. What distinguishes these experiences from each other is the quality of housing and residence life programs and the knowledge, experience, skills, and attitudes of residence life professionals. Highly skilled and well-trained residence life professionals and resident assistants make the difference between educationally engaging residence halls that help students learn and ones in which students languish and grow restless and bored.

Although hiring great people to work with residential students is critical, it is not enough. Most entry-level professionals have limited formal training in residence life work, and much of what they know comes from experiences as resident assistants or graduate hall directors or both.

Much has changed in housing and residence life. Gone are the days when residence halls consisted of a series of rooms with steam heat, limited electrical systems, shared telephones, and a few fire extinguishers. Today's buildings have highly mechanized systems that help ensure fire safety, building security, energy efficiency, Internet access, emergency response, efficient water management, climate control, and access for students with disabilities. New residence halls are socially engineered to maximize learning opportunities for students and to promote the development of community.

Competition for students' time has never been greater. The Internet, social media, smartphones, texting, and a 24-hour-a-day news cycle that covers the world has made many of the traditional approaches to educational programming obsolete. Educational engagement through programming needs to do more than provide information students can get for themselves anytime and anywhere.

Today educators know more than ever about how to use the complex social systems of the residential peer environment to create positive learning experiences for students. This book is about how to use the tools available to residence life professionals to improve student learning.

## Purpose

This book examines the influence of contemporary college residence halls on the education of undergraduate students. Most of these students are between the ages of 18 and 24. Although graduate student housing and family housing are part of many housing and residence life programs, they are not the subject of this book. The book includes research on educational outcomes associated with living in residence halls and theories and research about student learning; however, the focus is on using this information to advance student learning. The book also includes a number of models and tables to illustrate relationships among the theories, research, and ideas discussed. The book does not preach an educational dogma; instead it focuses on what works and why.

## Intended Audiences

The primary audience for this book is residence life professionals, both within the United States and internationally. Residence life professionals constitute the largest segment of the student affairs profession, and many student affairs professionals and educators started their student affairs careers working in residence life.

A second audience for the book is graduate students who have assistantships in residence life or who may be interested in career opportunities in the student housing field. Universities that employ graduate students to help manage college residence halls often provide extensive in-service training programs. The book could serve as a source for in-service education, particularly for graduate students interested in entering the field of residence life as a full-time professional.

The book will also be of interest to higher educational administrators and faculty who work with students in living and learning programs and other educational enrichment programs that operate in residence halls. They will find in the book a useful review of studies that show how the experience of living in residence halls increases student learning and persistence.

Finally, senior student affairs officers responsible for housing and residence life programs will find this book useful. It will help them update their knowledge about student learning in residence halls and provide them with additional perspectives about the work of residence life professionals.

## Content Overview

The content of the book is a mixture of educational theory, research, and practical experience. The book begins with Chapter 1, "The Historical and Philosophical Foundations of Student Learning in Residence Halls." In Chapter 2, "How Biological and Psychological Development Influence Student Learning and Behavior," readers are introduced to neurobiological, psychosocial, and other research on late adolescent development that offers a fresh perspective on understanding the behavior of college students. Chapter 3, "How Students Learn in Residence Halls," discusses cognitive learning theory, experiential learning, forms of intelligence, and other factors that influence what and how students learn in residence halls.

Chapter 4, "How to Create Learning Environments in Residence Halls," reviews research on how residence life educators have structured the peer environment in residence halls to achieve positive learning outcomes with students. Chapter 5 is titled "Selecting and Developing Residence Life Staff to Advance Student Learning." Just as academic departments invest in faculty by recruiting and developing the best educators they can, so should housing and residence life departments invest in their professional staffs. This not only improves the quality of education but also is pragmatic. Highly qualified individuals with good judgment and a clear understanding of how to help students can make the difference between a minor conflict and a major crisis. This is an investment in both student learning and quality management of residence life programs.

Chapter 6, "How Residential Environments Influence Student Learning," examines the research on how the physical organization and layout of residence halls influence the social dynamics of interaction in those buildings. It also explores systemic change strategies for creating positive peer environments in residence halls. In Chapter 7, "How to Shape the Peer Environment in Residence Halls to Enhance Student Learning," the focus moves from the individual student to the student as a member of a peer group and the dynamic influence that peer associations have on student behavior and development.

Chapter 8, "Managing Student Life in Residence Halls to Support Student Learning," discusses a curriculum-based approach to residence education and explains a programming model using this approach. Chapter 9, "Assessing and Improving Residence Life Programs," outlines a process of systematic assessment focused on improving the quality of student life and learning in residence halls. Both qualitative and quantitative approaches are discussed, several assessment instruments are reviewed, and an assessment model is provided.

The book concludes with Chapter 10, "The Future of Residence Halls." It analyzes contemporary issues shaping how students will learn in residence halls and the administrative challenges residence life professionals face in maintaining quality educational experiences for students.

Residence hall research is often difficult to interpret because many studies are based on a single institution and the effects of residence hall environments are heavily influenced by contextual variables such as building design, size, program, and student composition. Universities and residence halls have personalities. Some are friendly and inviting places where students immediately feel at home and know many students; others are large, bureaucratic, and difficult to navigate. These differences affect the student experience. Add to these already diverse environments the regional variations in the political and religious climates, urban or rural settings, and various institutional missions, and determining exactly how residence halls influence students is challenging.

Therefore, throughout the book I made decisions about which studies to include. Some of these judgments are based on my own work in residence halls and experience as a senior student affairs officer. Some of it is based on my own reading of the research. I opted to include different points of view to represent the myriad approaches to research in this area and the variety of perspectives in the field.

Although the focus of this book concerns the work of residence life professionals, one should not assume that residence life professionals are more important to the success of a housing and residence life program than are housing professionals. Indeed, the foundation of any successful housing and residence life program begins with the effective and efficient management of residence hall facilities and finances. Without well-managed housing resources, residence hall programs could not exist, students would not want to live in residence halls, and institutions would be loath to support them.

Residence halls are filled with learning opportunities for students. They are in every way rich learning environments, but they are not without their challenges. Students' lives are on public display in residence halls, and sometimes the process of growing into adults spills over into the life of the campus. Student affairs work in residence halls is in large part about helping students navigate the challenges of growing into adulthood, giving students support, creating learning opportunities, guiding their development, and caring about them. The goal of this book is to provide research and practical information that residence life professionals can use to help students learn and become better adults.

# Acknowledgments

I became interested in college residence halls in part by living in one as an undergraduate but mostly by working in them as a hall director and later by supervising them as an assistant director of residence life and then as a senior student affairs officer. What made me invest time in understanding them better was the work of Betty Greenleaf at Indiana University and Larry Miltenberger at Western Illinois University. Betty was an early advocate of student learning in college residence halls and was instrumental in my decision to begin my career in student affairs by working in residence life. I could not have asked for a better grounding in the field of student affairs than serving as a hall director. It taught me more about student life than any other experience I have had in student affairs administration.

Larry taught me the practical side of residence hall administration. More important, he taught me about the compassion and ethic of caring that is necessary to do student affairs work. I count him as the model for what it means to be a student affairs professional. Much of what I know about residence halls and student affairs work I learned from Larry. I am indebted to both Betty and Larry for what they taught me about residence halls and students.

I am also indebted to the many residence life professionals with whom I have worked at Appalachian State University and Rutgers

University. Their dedication to students and the work of making residence halls educationally rich and engaging places for students is nothing less than inspirational. They have made a difference in the lives of students they serve.

The current book would not have been possible without John Schuh's advice and suggestions. His own work in residence life coupled with his strong scholarship made his comments about the book invaluable.

Leah Ross read early drafts of this book and contributed significant insightful comments, edits, feedback, and suggestions that greatly improved it. I cannot imagine how much longer it would have taken me to write the book without her great work on my early drafts. She brings a whole new meaning to the adage, "It's never a diamond until it's cut."

Most of all, I want to thank my wife, Sandra Kungle, who indulged my absence from family conversations and social engagements while I was working on the book and did more than her share of attending to family and household matters. Her academic background as a college professor gave her an appreciation for the time and focus it takes to write, which is just one of her many wonderful qualities. I also want to thank our children, Jenny and Paul, who understood the reasons for my unavailability and listened to me talk about the book even when they would rather have discussed something else.

# About the Author

Gregory Blimling is professor of college student affairs at the Rutgers University Graduate School of Education in the Department of Educational Psychology. He served as vice president for student affairs at Rutgers University, vice chancellor for student development, and professor of human development and psychological counseling at Appalachian State University in North Carolina and as dean of students at Louisiana State University, in addition to other administrative and teaching roles early in his career. He completed his bachelor's in sociology and speech and his master's degree in college student personnel administration at Indiana University. His Ph.D. in higher education is from Ohio State University.

Dr. Blimling is the author, coauthor, or editor of six books about college students and an extensive number of articles, essays, papers, and other scholarly contributions. His book written for resident assistants is now in its seventh edition and has been in continuous publication for over 30 years.

For nine years, Blimling was editor of the *Journal of College Student Development*, the leading scholarly journal in the field of college student affairs. He was a senior scholar with ACPA— College Student Affairs Educators International for six years and later was elected its national president.

Blimling's scholarship and administration have been recognized by many national organizations. He is the recipient of the NASPA Outstanding Contribution to Literature and Research Award, the ACPA Contribution to Knowledge Award, the Melvene Hardee Award for significant contributions to student affairs, and the NASPA Dissertation of the Year Award. In 2012, the faculty of the Rutgers Graduate School of Education awarded him the Distinguished Leader in Education Award, their national award for significant academic accomplishment in education. He has also received awards for his scholarship and administration in student affairs from Indiana University, Ohio State University, Bowling Green State University, Western Illinois University, and a number of regional professional associations and student groups.

Blimling's experience with college residence halls started as a graduate student responsible for a men's residence hall at Franklin College in Indiana. After completing his master's degree, Blimling went to Bowling Green State University as a residence hall director and then to Western Illinois University as assistant director of residence life. For his 22 years as a senior student affairs officer, Blimling was responsible for housing and residence life at Appalachian State University and then at Rutgers University. As vice president for student affairs at Rutgers, he was responsible for one of the nation's largest student housing programs with more than 16,000 students in over 140 buildings on the New Brunswick/Piscataway campus.

# Student Learning in College Residence Halls

# 1

# The Historical
# and Philosophical Foundations
# of Student Learning
# in Residence Halls

College residence halls (RHs) have a rich tradition that closely follows the history of higher education and the educational philosophies that guide it. The residential experience was part of the founding of American higher education, and for most of its history RHs have served as a vehicle to educate students. However, the educational role of RHs did not come without a struggle. The reason that RHs exist today is an interesting story and part of an educational debate about the purpose of a college education. At the core of this debate is the question of whether college should focus solely on a student's intellectual development or on educating the whole student, including his or her character, values, maturity, citizenship, and life skills (practical knowledge).

The title of this chapter implies a question often asked by those outside of the student affairs profession—why do student affairs professionals call traditional student housing RHs and not dormitories? The simplest answer to that question is that today's RHs are not anything like dormitories. The word *dormitory* comes from *dormant*, which means "to sleep"; a dormitory is literally a place of sleeping. The term was applied to American higher education in part when the early colonial colleges brought the practice of dormitory-style living from England's Oxford and Cambridge Universities. At one time, colleges and universities had large sleeping rooms known as dormitories; however, these facilities were abandoned many years ago. Today, occasionally a fraternity or a military academy will still have a dormitory room, but even these have become uncommon. Oxford and Cambridge abandoned dormitories, and the use of the term, more than a century ago. Now students at those institutions refer to college student housing as *halls of residence* or simply *halls*. Students living in college RHs in the United States are said to be living in college or simply living in.

Sleep is only one aspect of student life in RHs, which are often energetic spaces full of activity. Today they are centers of student life and places in which students learn from one another. RHs frequently house a variety of facilities to aid students in their studies and to facilitate community, such as study lounges, recreational spaces, computer labs, social lounges, student meeting rooms, and classrooms. Students in RHs make lifelong friends, form study groups, enjoy rich social lives, and pursue a host of recreational activities from sports to internet gaming.

In this chapter I review five historical periods that form the foundations for college RHs work and the philosophies under which they were operated: (1) collegiate; (2) impersonal; (3) holism; (4) student development; and (5) student learning. These five educational approaches parallel the changing student–institutional relationship from the earliest colonial colleges to that of contemporary residential colleges and universities. Although these five philosophies are the educational foundation of RHs, they do not tell the whole story. Housing and residence life professionals manage complex financial operations, build and maintain facilities, service bond debt obligations, market the use of facilities for summer conferences, and implement a wide range of institutional policies. Because of these administrative and management responsibilities, housing and residence life professionals straddle the teaching–learning mission of the university and the business management responsibilities necessary to sustain a financially self-sufficient and stable operation. Evolving educational and business management roles have shaped how RHs operate today, and in the final section of this chapter I discuss how these educational and business approaches in RHs coexist to support the dual mission of RHs as an environment for learning and as a revenue-generating capital asset of the residential colleges and universities.

## Collegiate Model

American higher education was founded under a collegiate model based on the educational traditions of Oxford and Cambridge, which the English brought with them when they colonized North America. All of the nine original colonial colleges (Harvard, William and Mary, Yale, Princeton, University of Pennsylvania, Columbia, Brown, Rutgers, and Dartmouth) were founded on the Oxford and Cambridge model of classical education using this collegiate model (Rudolph, 1962). Under this model, college was the place where young men (in the early years only men went to college) not only learned Latin, Greek, mathematics, philosophy, and religion but also developed character and learned values, manners, and deportment (conduct) of a gentleman.

The collegiate approach to higher education was organized to foster respectful and sometimes close relationships between faculty and students. Colleges were small communities, and students were generally from privileged backgrounds and shared a common social class. However, one should not mistake the intimacy between faculty and students as friendship. Often the relationship was one of paternalistic supervision that included the use of corporal punishment for student offenders of college policies as well as open rebellion by students against harsh or unpopular instructors (Thelin, 2004).

The idea that students learn in RHs by living together as communities under the guidance of tutors grew from the idea of liberal education shaped in post-Renaissance Europe. The goal of liberal education is the development of an educated person who is open-minded, knowledgeable of the Western canon, and trained as an independent thinker (Brubacher, 1977). Liberal education implies that the student acquired the values, ethics, and civic commitment to operate as an educated and informed citizen. William Cory (1861), a great Eton master of the 19th century, described some of the qualities of a liberally educated person:

> You go to a great school, not for knowledge so much as for arts and habits; for the habit of attention, for the art of expression, for the art of assuming at a moment's notice a new intellectual posture, for the art of entering quickly into another person's thoughts, for the habit of submitting to censure and refutation, for the art of indicating assent or dissent in graduated terms, for the habit of regarding minute points of accuracy, for the habit of working out what is possible in a given time, for taste, for discrimination, for mental courage and mental soberness. Above all, you go to a great school for self-knowledge. (p. 7)

Under the collegiate approach, a liberal education was accomplished through adherence to the classical curriculum and by close association with other students under the guidance of tutors. One of the strongest proponents of liberal education using the collegiate approach was Cardinal John Henry Newman (1933), who believed that living in a common residence under the supervision of tutors was an essential part of becoming a liberally educated person. He wrote:

> If I had to choose between a so-called University, which dispensed with residence and tutorial superintendence, and gave its degrees to any person who passed an examination in a wide range of subjects, and a University which had no professors or examinations at all, but merely brought a number of young men together for

three or four years, and then sent them away as the University of Oxford is said to have done some sixty years since, if I were asked which of these two methods was the better discipline of the intellect,—mind . . . if I must determine which of the two courses was the more successful in training, molding, enlarging the mind, which sent out men the more fitted for their secular duties, which produced better public men, men of the world, men whose names would descend to posterity, I have no hesitation in giving the preference to that University which did nothing, over that which exacted of its members an acquaintance with every science under the sun. (p. 137)

## Impersonal Approach

During the 1800s, a large number of American faculty members completed their advanced academic work in continental Europe and learned under a philosophy of rationalism, which is based on a system of deductive and intellectual reasoning. Students who attended universities in continental Europe lived outside of the university in private homes, boarding houses, and similar accommodations. Although many of the universities there provided student housing early in their histories, by the early 1800s most had abandoned the practice (Cowley, 1934). The Germans abandoned the practice of housing students following the Protestant Reformation (1517–1648) because the facilities (Bursen) too closely resembled the monkish cloisters of Catholic monasteries, which were antithetical to the ideals of the Reformation. The French abandoned student housing after the French Revolution (1789–1799) because students could not afford to pay for the accommodations.

American faculty members educated in Continental Europe (usually Germany) adopted the view that the European system worked well and that American colleges should focus exclusively on the creation and dissemination of knowledge, as was common in Germany (Rudolph, 1962). The role of faculty was to educate the mind; society, family, and church were responsible for the character and conduct of the student. Williamson and Sarbin (1940) observed that "the single greatest force that changed the old student-centered college [collegiate approach] was the growing emphasis on specialized scientific research and scholarship—particularly of the German pattern" (p. 6). The result of this change in philosophical orientation was that professors were appointed to faculty posts based on their research skills and their association with German universities, whether or not they had any interest in students. West (1907) described the ideal faculty member during this time as a "man dedicated to specialized learning who put research first, teaching second, and his personal care of students last" (p. 109).

A manifestation of the shift away from the British approach of student-centered collegiate learning to the German approach of content-centered (impersonal) learning was that faculty became increasing devoted to the creation and specialization of knowledge. Consistent with this change was the development of specialized courses of study that reflected faculty members' interests. So pervasive was the specialization of knowledge and the independent research interests of faculty that in 1869 Charles W. Eliot, president of Harvard University, proposed dropping Harvard's classical liberal arts curriculum and replacing it with an elective system of courses. Harvard implemented the new elective system with the senior class in 1872 and with other classes in successive years (Rudolph, 1962). "By 1897 the prescribed course of study at Harvard had been reduced to a year of freshmen rhetoric" (Rudolph, p. 294).

The new system of electives allowed for increased specialization of knowledge and eventually gave rise to departmentalization of faculty into academic disciplines. As the Harvard model was adopted throughout colleges and universities in the United States, faculty became increasingly interested in knowledge specialization and much less interested in students. Faculty considered students to be adults and left them alone to resolve their personal problems. An educational philosophy focused on knowledge content and impersonal relationships with students became pervasive in American higher education. Faculty, who in past years were intimately involved in the lives of students, abandoned those roles and limited their functions to teaching, discipline, remedial education, and mentoring (Lloyd-Jones, 1952).

Students filled the void left by the impersonal approach with clubs, athletics, and student activities. Many college fraternities and sororities, which provided housing for students, were formed at this time, and debating teams, sports teams, and literary societies were born on many college campuses as well. The first intercollegiate boat race occurred between Harvard and Yale (Harvard won) in 1852, the first intercollegiate football game occurred in 1869 between Princeton and Rutgers (Rutgers won 6–4) (Cowley, 1934), and the first intercollegiate baseball game occurred in 1859 between Amherst and Williams (Amherst won) (Williams, 2009).

When universities adopted more impersonal relationships with students, faculty and administrators began to question the value of providing student housing. Many members of the faculty thought that the resources needed to build and maintain RHs could be put to better use in building classrooms, laboratories, and libraries. The presidents of the University of Michigan, Brown University, and Columbia University, among others, expressed harsh criticism of college RHs and the raucous behavior of the young men who lived in them. Henry Tappen, president of the University of Michigan, offered the following explanation for closing a RH and converting it to classrooms in 1852: "The dormitory system is objectionable in itself. By withdrawing young men from the influence of domestic circles and separating them from the community, they are often led to contract evil habits and are prone to fall into disorderly conduct" (as cited in Shay, 1964, p. 181).

In 1888, a faculty committee at the University of Minnesota that was formed to recommend reorganization of the University rejected any investment in student housing because RHs were associated with the old-fashioned American college. Committee members believed that investment in student housing would interfere with the "intellectual training" of students. Except for the students studying agriculture who lived on campus to provide labor at the university farms, the committee believed that students should find their own lodging with families in Minneapolis (Williamson & Sarbin, 1940). This recommendation created a problem for women students because off-campus housing was usually unchaperoned, but the committee defended its position by declaring that there was no system "so detrimental to sound morals and a healthy sentiment as this shutting young women up in cloistered dormitories away from common society" (as cited in Williamson & Sarbin, p. 5).

## Holism Period

By the beginning of the 20th century, parents and some of the faculty who had continued to maintain personal relationships with students mounted an effort to make colleges and universities less impersonal and more focused on the needs and interests of students. The problems associated with student behavior in the mid-1800s had mellowed into funny stories and remembrances of days long since passed. People missed the sense of community they associated with the collegiate system and began to question the educational philosophy that separated what students were taught from who they became as a result of their educations. Educational philosophers such as John Dewey argued against educating only the intellect of students while ignoring their emotional and affective development. He advocated for an emphasis on the individual student and attention to the overall educational experience. This holistic philosophy promoted the idea that people function as complex systems and that they must be viewed as a whole and not simply as a collection of independent parts. Dewey (1922) expressed that "the separation of warm emotion from cool intellect is the greatest moral tragedy" (p. 258).

Among the defenders of the educational values of college RHs during this time was Charles Franklin Thwing, who served as president of Western Reserve College and Adelbert College. Thwing (1920) explained the educational value of dormitory life:

> The advantages of dormitory life are not hard to distinguish. One of the most inherent advantages lies in the tendency of this life to intensify academic atmosphere. The student is apart from his home. The building he occupies is made for the college; he lives with other students. Within he spends happy days and happier nights. The community is academic and of it he is an individual part. . . . His talk, his fun, his tricks, his friendships, are all academic; he takes the academic bath. The worth of such absorption is great. At the altars of good fellowship and of opportunity, as well as at the shrine of scholarship, it is worthwhile to burn incense. (p. 393)

College RHs also continued to exist in part out of housing necessity. The development of land-grant colleges under the 1862 and 1890 Morrill Acts established campuses in some less populated regions of the United States and required the construction of student housing so that students would have a place to live. Women's colleges also played an important role in the rebirth of college residence halls. Vassar, Smith, and Mount Holyoke Colleges were founded in the 1800s and were strictly residential.

Where colleges did not provide student housing, students were expected to either commute from home or find lodging off-campus. However, off-campus housing was often inadequate, particularly for women. In unchaperoned off-campus housing, women had no place to receive callers except in their rooms, which Victorian morality could not permit. This situation was unacceptable and required a change. It was one thing to let a group of young men fend for themselves in the community but quite another to abandon young women in unsupervised environments. Colleges came to accept the responsibility of educating young women and protecting their good reputations. Marion Talbot, dean of women at the University of Chicago, supported the need to provide student housing and believed that RHs also helped young women "acquire the power of expression, the facility in social intercourse, the ability to meet situations of an unusual or unexpected character, with dignity and poise" (Talbot, 1909, p. 45).

Although many educators supported the idea of educating the whole student, some thought less of the idea. Robert Maynard Hutchins, president of the University of Chicago, commented on the concept of educating the "whole person" in his exclamation "of all the meaningless phrases in education, this is the prize" (1943, p. 36).

Despite some opposition, a commitment to the education of the whole student began to emerge in the late 19th century, and with it a renewed commitment to student housing and a return to some components of the Oxford style of collegiate education. In 1907, Woodrow Wilson, as president of Princeton University, established the residential quadrangle plan; in 1929, Lawrence Lowell, president of Harvard University, established the Harvard House plan; and in 1931, James Angell, president of Yale University, established Yale residential colleges (Duke, 1996). Cooperatives (housing in which students share responsibility for the operation and maintenance of a rooming facility) were present on many land-grant campuses that operated under the student housing principles issued by the U.S. Department of Agriculture (Nowotny, Julian, & Beaty, 1938). Traditional-style RHs were constructed to house increased enrollments at many universities. Rooming houses for off-campus students were still used, and deans of men took an interest in how they should be controlled and monitored to provide adequate supervision for students living off-campus (Clark, 1920).

The rejection of having impersonal relations with students, renewed interest in returning to the collegiate model, concern over the poor state of student housing, safeguarding the reputation of female students, and a commitment to educating the whole student gave birth to the personnel and guidance movement in higher education. However, faculty had no interest in retreating from their scholarship and teaching to embrace a new commitment to undergraduate life. At most colleges, faculty continued with research and teaching; select faculty members and others who had friendly relationships with students were appointed to positions in which they could care for undergraduates. In 1890, LeBarron Russell Briggs was appointed the first dean of students at Harvard College; in 1892, Alice Freeman Palmer was appointed the first dean of women at the University of Chicago; in 1916, the first graduate program to educate deans of women was established at Teachers College Columbia; in 1917, the National Association of Deans of Women was established (1917); and in 1918, the National Association of Deans of Men was established.

The debate about the purpose of education and the rejection of the impersonal approach to working with students were the foundations of the establishment of the core principles of student affairs' commitment to the whole student. On April 16, 1937, 19 educators appointed by the American Council on Education (ACE) came together and unanimously adopted a report on the philosophy and development of student personnel work in colleges and universities. *The Student Personnel Point of View* (SPPV) (ACE, 1937) called for colleges and universities to focus on the education of the whole student and not just the intellect of students. The report advanced a philosophy for the development of the student as an individual and imposed on institutions an obligation to consider a student's intellectual capacity, emotional makeup, physical condition, social relationships, vocational aptitudes and skills, moral and religious values, economic resources, and aesthetic appreciations. The *SPPV* rejected the idea that the purpose of a college education was only the development of the intellect as reflected by the completion of a set of college courses. It placed the student at the center of learning and made it the responsibility of colleges to develop the individual student. However, neither this document nor anything else happening in higher education at that time brought faculty out of their laboratories and classrooms to engage students in their personal growth and development. Faculty continued their commitment to teaching and research and left other aspects of students' lives to student affairs professionals (Williamson & Sarbin, 1940).

Although some educators (Hand, 1938) advanced the belief that the benefits of college living groups were the most important influence on learning in college, exactly how to achieve the development of the whole student was open to interpretation. For female students, Orme (1950) proposed these goals:

> Help every resident to develop the social skills which make for happier human relations; provide conditions conducive to study and suitable facilities for wholesome recreation; encourage the development of intellectual interests, aesthetic appreciation, and ethical values; give opportunity for the growth of leadership ability and social responsibility through participation in self-government; offer living conditions which foster physical and mental health; and help the student to manage her life with intelligence and self-discipline. In brief, a dormitory should contribute to the student's all around development, that she may become a socially competent, intelligent, well-balanced person, having concern for the welfare of others. (p. 3)

On many college campuses until the early 1970s, RHs were run by housemothers who acted in loco parentis. They were female faculty, faculty widows, deans of women, and other mature female adults with good judgment who could be entrusted with the supervision of housing for students (Reich, 1964). They became the confidants of students and surrogate parents who not only chaperoned students' daily activities but also provided guidance on manners, conduct, and courtesies. Although RHs for women always had house-mothers, not all RHs for men had houseparents. For example, during this time period land-grant colleges were required to operate Reserve Officer Training Corp (ROTC) programs, in which male students participated mandatorily for at least one year. It was common for first- and second-year male students to live in RHs supervised by military personnel and cadres of student officers from the corps of cadets.

People who performed student affairs functions on college campuses relied on what they knew from their own college experiences and from colleges' lists of rules and regulations. These rules covered everything from what time students needed to be in their RHs (curfew) to dress codes for various campus activities. A commitment to the development of the whole student may have been the operating philosophy, but it was implemented by student affairs staff assuming a paternalistic responsibility for controlling students' behavior. Students rebelled against these paternalistic rules during the 1960s. Peterson (1968) observed that student protests against college policies—the ones enforced by student affairs administrators—accounted for the second greatest number of student protests in 1967–1968 after those against the Vietnam War. As a result of student dissatisfaction, college administrators began to question the value of archaic paternalistic college rules, and student affairs professionals started to rethink their duties and search for a more coherent educational mission.

## The Student Development Approach

Closely linked to the work of guidance and counseling, where student affairs work found a home in the 1950s, a new counseling approach based in humanism emerged that was consistent with the values of student affairs work. Humanistic psychology is based on a holistic approach to working with individuals. It advances the belief that people are essentially good and that people who experience emotional problems are deviating from their natural tendency to be good. Personal growth, self-actualization, creativity, and individuality are driving forces in the lives of individuals, and guidance and counseling can help people overcome obstacles that inhibit these driving forces in people's lives. Humanistic psychology also accepts the importance of environmental factors in shaping people's personalities and behaviors. The work of humanists such as Abraham Maslow (1954) and Carl Rogers (1969) became required readings for student affairs administrators in the 1960s and 1970s.

Riker (1965) explained how the humanist approach came to infuse the work of residence life professionals:

> Roadblocks to learning exist in a student's preoccupations with his vocational future, sex relations, home problems, finances, or physical condition and appearance. If these preoccupations are not reduced or removed as roadblocks, the student will fail and drop out. . . . Many institutions employ counselors and other personnel specialist to improve students' chances of learning. As part of this team, housing staff performs an invaluable function in identifying roadblocks, helping students to clear them away, or referring students where remedial action can be initiated rapidly. (p. 6)

Humanism offered a strong philosophical base for the work of student affairs professionals but lacked a clear articulation of what should result from students' growth and development as they matured. It also needed a theoretical base that defined work with students and a clear connection to the academic mission of universities.

The American College Personnel Association (ACPA) recognized that the philosophy of in loco parentis was dead and
offered a new direction for student affairs work that Parker (1978)
described as *student development*. In 1968, ACPA launched the
Tomorrow's Higher Education (T.H.E.) Project, which began as a
strategic plan to address the rapidly changing college environment and offered a vehicle for the revitalization of student affairs
work. Although the original committee never released a workable
document, a number of papers were written to address the need
for change. One of the best known of these publications was a
monograph written by Robert Brown (1972), who identified five
key concepts to serve as a framework for defining student
development and the work of student affairs administrators
(pp. 33–36):

1. Student characteristics when they enter college have a
   significant impact on how students are affected by their college
   experience.

2. The collegiate years are the period for many individual
   students when significant developmental changes occur.

3. There are opportunities within the collegiate program for it to
   have a significant impact on student development.

4. The environmental factors that hold the most promise for
   affecting student developmental patterns include the peer
   group, the living unit, the faculty, and the classroom
   experience.

5. Developmental changes in students are the result of the
   interaction of initial characteristics and the press of the
   environment.

Miller and Prince (1976) further elaborated on the T.H.E.
Project and how the work of student development could be realized
through programs on university campuses. Although the ACPA

project advanced the thinking of student affairs professionals about their role within colleges and universities, "what was not accomplished in the ACPA project was a careful examination, identification, or elaboration of psychosocial, developmental theories which can be used to guide practitioners who work with students" (Parker, 1978, p. 9).

A substantive body of literature in the field of developmental psychology provided a theoretical basis for student development in the areas of cognitive development, psychosocial development, and person–environmental interaction. The works of Nevitt Sanford (1962), Arthur Chickering (1974), William Perry (1970), and Lawrence Kohlberg (1969) were instrumental in establishing a theoretical core for the emergence of the student development approach to working with college students. DeCoster and Mable (1974) saw the role of residence life professionals under this new student development approach as more than holding programs or creating activities—residence life professionals should help students develop their full potential by involving them in meaningful ways and by constructing shared educational experiences that allow them to learn from fellow students, faculty, and staff. These experiences, DeCoster and Mable believed, would assist students in their psychosocial development and help them master important interpersonal skills.

Student development was the dominant philosophical approach to student affairs work for more than 25 years. Virtually all master's degree programs in the field of college student affairs required coursework in the psychosocial and cognitive development of students, and student affairs professionals began to define themselves as experts in the development of students. The ACPA *Journal of College Student Personnel* changed its name to the *Journal of College Student Development* in 1988, and many universities began using titles like *vice president for student development* for the senior student affairs officer. Student development theories provided a common theoretical base for student affairs work and helped inform the professional standards for the field (Mable, 1991). Interaction with peers, educational programming, and the guidance of residence life staff who understood and applied student development principles to helping students grow and develop occupied the mission and purpose of most housing and residence life programs in the United States through much of the 1980s.

## Student Learning Approach

Beginning sometime in the mid-1980s, educators in many fields began questioning how institutions of higher education were delivering education to undergraduates. Institutional pressure for increased research funding kept faculty from focusing their attention on teaching or mentoring undergraduates. On many campuses, low graduation rates, large class sizes, and extensive use of graduate assistants and part-time lecturers were sources of widespread criticism. More than two dozen reports published during this time scrutinized higher education for its failure to provide better undergraduate education (Gamson, 1987).

As the reform movement in higher education shifted toward greater attention to undergraduate education, student affairs professionals questioned whether they were doing all they could to help students learn. Among those who expressed concern that the student development approach was not well suited as an operating philosophy for student affairs were Boland, Stamatakos, and Rogers (1994). They challenged the student development approach and argued that the idea of student affairs professionals becoming experts on student development drew them away from the core university mission of teaching and learning. Their argument was not about whether student development theory was useful but that student development theories had limited utility in their application to the daily practice of student affairs work. They advocated for a return to the humanistic ideals embodied in the 1949 version of the *SPPV* (ACE, 1949).

In 1993, the Wingspread Group on Higher Education issued a report that called for a return to an emphasis on student learning as the focus of higher education. As president of ACPA, Charles Schroeder responded to this call by organizing a group of senior scholars and practitioners in student affairs to discuss the relationship of student affairs to the student learning mission of higher education. The Student Learning Imperative (SLI; ACPA, 1996) resulted from that meeting as a response to how student affairs organizations could fit into a renewed emphasis on undergraduate student learning. The introduction of the SLI stimulated a debate over the fundamental mission of student affairs, encompassing issues such as student development, student services, student learning, and principles advanced in the SPPV. The authors of the SLI argued that a student learning approach was more inclusive than a student development approach and that the SLI incorporated all of the developmental concepts on which student affairs professionals had come to rely. In the student learning approach, student affairs administrators were focused on the creation of learning experiences that connected students to the overall educational mission of the university rather than on the individual development of students, as was the case with the student development approach.

The SLI led to a reexamination of the mission of student affairs. It focused more effort on engaging students in active learning and shifted more emphasis to coupling student affairs with the learning mission of the university. In 1997, the two national professional associations in student affairs, ACPA and the National Association of Student Personnel Administrators (NASPA), adopted seven principles of good practice for student affairs based on the student learning approach (ACPA & NASPA, 1997). The principles operationalized the student learning approach into actionable steps that could be used by student affairs administrators to focus on and to advance student learning by (1) engaging students in active learning, (2) helping students develop coherent values and ethical standards, (3) setting and communicating high expectations for student learning, (4) using systemic inquiry to improve student and institutional performance, (5) using resources effectively to achieve institutional missions and goals, (6) forging educational partnerships that advance student learning, and (7) building supportive and inclusive communities.

Although the SLI addressed the issue of bifurcating student learning into academic instruction and development by stating that learning included development, two subsequent documents focused more attention on thinking about student learning as inclusive of both academic instruction and development. *Learning Reconsidered* (Keeling, 2004) and *Learning Reconsidered 2* (Keeling, 2006) emphasized that intellectual development and affective development are interlinked, integrated, and mutually dependent and that the idea of separating the two makes no sense from the perspective of student affairs work. Student affairs professionals should be engaged in advancing student learning, as a process and even more so as an outcome.

## Administrative and Business Approaches

The five philosophical approaches form the core of student affairs work in RHs from an educational perspective. However, housing and residence life (HRL) professionals play a somewhat unique role in higher education. Although they focus on providing an educational experience for students by engaging them in experiences that facilitate positive educational outcomes, HRL professionals are also administrators with budgetary control, organizational demands, management duties, and policy enforcement responsibilities.

The management and administrative responsibilities encompassed in the duties of HRL are significant. RHs are capital investments that generate revenue from leasing rooms to students, and those funds are used to cover operating expenses of the RHs, including personnel and debt service on the buildings. HRL professionals are often among the best business managers on a college campus. They have to be. They run multimillion-dollar enterprises and are responsible for the lives, safety, and education of students during many hours of each day. They are also charged with the fiscal health and operational quality of a significant budgetary unit of universities.

Because of this dual role, some HRL professionals have adopted a business management philosophy as their primary way of operating RHs. Emerging from this business management responsibility are two communities of practice in student affairs that emphasize a business approach to residence life and housing: student services and student administration.

### Student Services

The student services approach is grounded in the student consumerism movement from the early 1980s, the business reform movement of the late 1980s, and the emergence of a practical-minded business orientation that has been a recurrent theme for those demanding greater business-like accountability in higher education (Blimling, 2001). The focus of this approach is to provide high-quality student services that are cost-effective and that result in higher levels of student satisfaction. Interest in student services as an approach to operating student housing and other student affairs organizations has been a continuing theme in higher education administration. However, in the early 1990s the American business community developed a fascination with the Japanese management style, based largely on the work of Deming (1982). The application of this approach included the adoption of programs such as total quality management, continuous quality improvement, and benchmarking. This management approach stresses student satisfaction based on evaluation of how well programs serve the needs of students. The quality of service becomes an end in itself, and student satisfaction is the primary measure of success.

### Student Administration

The student administration approach is based on a philosophical orientation that views student affairs administration as an exercise in management and leadership (Blimling, 2001). The goal of this approach is to effectively and efficiently manage the resources available to students. Those who practice this approach are focused heavily on procedures, policies, and processes. Legal issues frame much of the conversation about interaction with students and play heavily into this organizational philosophy.

## What Works, What Doesn't, and Why

Four communities of practice continue to operate on college campuses today: (1) student development approach; (2) student learning approach; (3) student administration approach; and (4) student services approach. Table 1.1 provides a comparison. Although they are presented as discrete approaches, effective student affairs professionals possess skills in each of these areas. However, the question is not about skills as much as it is about a philosophical orientation to working with students in RHs and how these communities of practice inform work with students. Each of the four communities has a strong philosophical base and reason to exist.

To manage the challenges of an HRL program, professionals need to have both business and educational skills. However, one of these approaches comes to dominate the philosophical orientation of an RH program. It is possible to administer RHs under a business-only philosophy or simply to contract the management of RHs to a private for-profit corporation commercial specializing in property management of college housing. That approach works reasonably well if the primary objective of an HRL program is to lease rooms to students and earn a profit. Building managers with the help of housekeeping and maintenance personnel can maintain the buildings and respond to students' basic needs. Essentially, this is the type

Table 1.1 Communities of Practice in Student Affairs

| | Student Learning | Student Development | Student Learning | Student Administration |
|---|---|---|---|---|
| **Purpose of Student Affairs** | Student affairs as an active partner in the learning mission | Student affairs as equals in the education of students focused on personal growth and development | Student affairs as supporting the academic mission | Student affairs as managers of institutional resources to support students |
| **Student Metaphor** / **Student Affairs Metaphor** | Student as learners / Student affairs as educators | Students as clients / Student affairs as human development experts | Students as customers / Student affairs as managers | Students as participants / Student affairs as administrators |
| **Process** | Engage students in active learning | Assist students with life stage growth and development | Improve the quality and efficiency of services | Manage resources and policies to advance the quality of student life |
| **Goal** | Student learning, skill development, personal growth, and involvement | Greater self-knowledge and maturity | Student satisfaction | Organizational efficiency and effectiveness |

| | | | | |
|---|---|---|---|---|
| **Theory Bases** | Learning theory, involvement theory, other educational theories | Human development theories; cognitive development theories | Customer services and management theories | Leadership and organizational theories, legal and policy analysis |
| **Examples of Theories and Models** | SLI; principles of good practice in student affairs | T.H.E. Project; Chickering and Reisser (1993); Perry (1970); Kohlberg (1969) | Total quality management; continuous quality improvement; benchmarking | Court cases; federal laws and regulations; systemic change theory; leadership trait theory; management theory |
| **Assessment Examples** | Tests, CSEQ, CAAP, NSSE | SDTLA, DIT, MJI | Satisfaction surveys | Graduation rates, employee evaluations, program usage analysis |

*Notes:* SLI, student learning imperative; CSEQ, College Student Experience Questionnaire; CAAP, Collegiate Assessment of Academic Proficiency; NSSE, National Survey of Student Engagement; T.H.E., Tomorrow's Higher Education; SDTLA, Student Development Task and Lifestyle Assessment; DIT, Defining Issues Test; MJI, Moral Judgment Interview.

Adapted from Blimling (2001).

of program in operation by most off-campus landlords. They usually rent apartments and leave students alone.

This business-only philosophy does not work particularly well if the university expects RHs to engage students in active learning and build supportive inclusive communities. However, to operate a student housing program that was not grounded in a strong business model or that was not interested in providing quality student services to students who resided there would be a disservice to students and the university. Similarly, student housing programs would miss a significant opportunity to advance the educational mission of the university if they did not actively engage students in ways that helped them learn.

Regardless of the multiple skills that HRL administrators need in each of the four approaches, there emerges an overarching operating philosophy about how they do their work and the purposes of their work. If a person develops an administrative and student services orientation, the approach she uses is a principled decision-making mode about the creation of environments for students, the policies that operate to support students, and how facilities and programs are evaluated. Similarly, if a person has a student learning or student development orientation, that orientation tends to drive decision making in his work with students. The question about residence philosophies is not one of either–or. It is a question about which philosophy guides decision making. If an administrator's primary orientation is business, where success is measured by profits, decisions about the management of RHs will be made to advance that goal above other goals. In contrast, if an administrator's orientation is educational, where success is measured in terms of the best educational interests of students, the goal will guide decision making over other goals. These philosophical orientations are at the heart of many HRL decisions.

All four approaches can work on a college campus; my own view is that students need different types of housing at different stages of their development in college and that different stages may be best served by different philosophical emphases. In the first year of college, I believe that traditional-aged undergraduates benefit most from living in traditional residence halls, not in apartments. As I discuss in later chapters, the evidence of the educational value of living in traditional residence halls is overwhelming (Blimling, 1993, 1998; Kuh, Kinsey, Buckley, et al., 2006; Pascarella & Terenzini, 1991, 2005).

Although the emphasis may change slightly with the type of housing provided and the maturity of students, students are served by HRL operations grounded in a student learning philosophy, followed by a strong commitment to effective business management grounded in a student services philosophy. Administrative skills, leadership, operational policies, and student development theories are used to advance student learning. They are means to an end but are not ends in and of themselves. What I believe works best is a commitment to students individually and as a group. The tools in this process include quality student services, knowledgeable and well-applied institutional policies, highly trained staff members, an ethic of caring, and a deep commitment to enriching the lives of students.

Although a student learning approach may work best for working with undergraduates in conventional RHs, a student services approach may work better for housing upper-division students, graduate students, and families in apartments and other forms of independent living. Quality of facilities, availability of programs, ease of access, affordability, and help when needed reflect more the expectations and needs of students in these types of housing facilities.

How these philosophies combine to form a comprehensive HRL program that meets the needs of students, the educational objectives of the university, and the business demands of a financially independent unit of a university is a big challenge. In 1971, Riker and DeCoster developed a model that described the relationship between educational objectives and management functions in student housing. They identified five objectives and arranged them in a hierarchy with level five at the top of the hierarchy as the most important (Riker & DeCoster, p. 6):

Level V: Opportunities for individual growth and development

Level IV: Development of an interpersonal environment that reflects responsible citizenship and a concern for others as well as an atmosphere conducive to learning

Level III: Establishment of guidelines that provide structure for compatible and cooperative community living

Level II: Adequate care and maintenance of the physical facilities

Level I: Provision of a satisfactory physical environment through new construction and renovation

The model was plotted along a continuum that started at the bottom of the hierarchy with attention to the facilities-oriented physical environment and proceeded to the top of the hierarchy (level V) with a student-oriented interpersonal environment. The model recognized the need for both management and educational functions in RHs and that the management of residential facilities ultimately served a higher educational objective, namely, the creation of a student-oriented interpersonal environment.

Riker and DeCoster's (1971) model incorporates many of the observations covered in this chapter and demonstrates how management and educational programs must be integrated into an overall student housing philosophy reflected in an HRL program. When they developed their model, residence life work was based on a humanistic approach that eventually transitioned into the student development approach discussed earlier. Since Riker and DeCoster developed their model, thinking about the role, scope, and mission of HRL has moved to more fully embrace student development and student learning. Using the four communities of

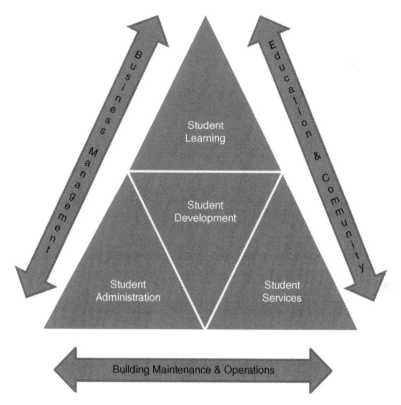

**Figure 1.1    Model of Goals and Objectives for Housing and Residence Life**

practice identified earlier, I have constructed a student housing model (Figure 1.1) that incorporates the housing fiscal and facilities management functions with the four educational program functions of student services, student administration, student development, and student learning.

> Student learning: Active engagement of students in experiential programs in residence hall settings that result in measurable student learning outcomes
>
> Student development: Structuring the peer environment in residence halls and providing residence life professionals

to support the psychosocial and cognitive development of students

Student administration: Policies and systems for the management of student housing that respect the rights of students, that support community living, and that most students accept as fair and equitable

Student services: Quality residential facilities that are clean, well maintained, and nicely appointed

Education and community: Efforts to advance student learning and build community among students

Building maintenance and operations: Quality facilities that are well maintained and efficiently managed for the welfare of students

Business management: Use of sound business practices and fiscally responsible decision making

The premise of this model, like the Riker and DeCoster (1971) model, is that the social and physical environment influence student behavior and that successful student housing programs are built on a foundation of good facilities that are well maintained and managed in a financially responsible way. The environment in which students learn influences their development by accelerating it or limiting it. This model is also based on a philosophy that student learning is a dynamic process that includes active engagement of students in experiences designed to create both functionally transferable skills and self-knowledge.

To realize these goals, HRL professionals need to understand why college students do what they do. The answer to that question involves an understanding of the neurobiological development of college students in late adolescence and how they change, grow, and develop during the traditional college years. These are topics for the next chapter.

# 2

# How Biological and Psychological Development Influence Student Learning and Behavior

The behavior of traditional-age college students (ages 18 to 24) has puzzled adults for many years. Why do some students learn quickly and others struggle to concentrate? Why do some students engage in high-risk behaviors, lack good judgment, and fail to consider the consequences of their actions? Why do they engage in a period of hedonistic behavior characterized by sexual adventurism, binge drinking, and drug experimentation? Why do men seem to overperform in these areas compared with women, and why do many of these behaviors seem to stop at around the age of twenty-five?

To better understand students' behavior and how they learn, we need a broad understanding of late adolescent development, including biology, neuroscience, psychology, and sociology. The scope of these topics exceeds what we can reasonably review in one chapter. Therefore, this chapter focuses on some of the critical areas that appear to have the greatest influence on student behavior, including new research in the evolutionary basis of adolescent behavior, neurobiological development of the brain during late adolescence, psychosocial development, sleep behavior, sexual behavior, psychological health, physical health, and alcohol use. The next chapter addresses cognitive development and the student learning process in residence halls (RHs).

After covering these topics, the chapter reviews difficulties that some students experience in adjusting to college and common adjustment difficulties of traditional-age college students. The chapter concludes with a discussion about the advantages of using a philosophy based on student learning to work with college students in RHs.

## Evolutionary Basis of Adolescent Behavior

Based on research into adolescent neurobiological development, the U.S. Department of Health & Human Services (2013) divides adolescence into three stages: early (ages 11 to 13), middle (ages 14 to 18), and late (ages 19 to 24). Most full-time undergraduates enter college directly after high school (approximately age 18), which is the transition time from middle to late adolescence, with late adolescence continuing throughout the undergraduate years.

The evolutionary function of adolescence is the transition period between childhood and adulthood. Ellis and colleagues (2012) suggested that from an evolutionary perspective the primary function of adolescence and young adulthood is "to attain reproductive status—to develop the physical and social competencies needed to gain access to a new highly contested biological resource: sex and, ultimately, reproduction" (p. 601). Greater risk-taking, impulsivity, independence, and sensation seeking during adolescence are age-related traits human beings develop to ensure access to suitable mates and opportunities for reproduction. What differentiates adolescents from children is puberty, and what differentiates adolescents from adults is physical and social development coupled with social status (Ellis et al.). The drive for greater independence, the desire to seek new sensations, the willingness to accept greater risks, and the impulsivity of decision making are manifestations of this basic biological transition that facilitates the steps necessary to find a mate outside of the nuclear family or community group.

Peers are influential during this period because of the emotional support they offer and the opportunities afforded for testing social skills related to hierarchical social status. Peers also offer a way to learn social skills related to friendship, group interaction, leadership, and participation within a social community. When all of these genetic, biological, and neurological factors are combined, the effect on the behavior of college students, particularly male college students, is nothing short of remarkable.

Although college administrators try to control the hedonistic adventurism, foolish judgments, alcohol and drug experimentation, and impulsive behavior of undergraduates, the neurobiological and evolutionary processes of maturing into adulthood propels college students into behaviors that often put them on collision courses with institutional policies and sometimes the law. This biological predisposition to be independent and adventurist during adolescence worked well for primitive social groups. However, the same adolescent traits that promoted the survival of the human race and propagated almost every inhabitable region of the world does not always work well in modern society where adolescence is prolonged and appropriate social behavior is well defined (Ellis et al., 2012; Weisfeld & Coleman, 2005).

## Neurobiological Development in College Students

Until recently, scientists believed that the brain was fully developed by the age of 18. Advances in magnetic resonance imaging and functional magnetic resonance imaging led to the discovery that the human brain continues to change throughout life (Blakemore, 2012). One area of the brain that experiences dramatic changes during the traditional college years is the prefrontal cortex (PFC), which does not fully develop structurally or functionally until about the age of 25. Some neurocognitive experts estimate that the brain is not fully mature until approximately age 30 (Weinberger, Elvevag, & Giedd, 2005).

During late adolescence, the brain undergoes dynamic changes that include the development of some of the most complex neurological processes it experiences, and the PFC plays a leading role. It regulates executive functions that control risk-taking, perseverance, decision making, sensation seeking, and understanding other people's emotions and perspectives. Development in this region of the brain inhibits socially inappropriate behavior, controls social decision making, and gives rise to self-awareness and identity. All of these higher-level executive functions help students develop their personality, emotional maturity, self-control, and self-concept (Amen, 1998; Blakemore & Frith, 2005).

Beginning at the time of puberty and lasting until approximately age 24, the brain undergoes a process of dramatic change. The synaptic connections contained in the brain's gray matter are pruned, and a myelination process occurs to protect neurological connections and increase the speed of neurological processing that prepares the brain for complex functions (Blakemore, 2012). The completion of this process is closely linked to the age at which the brain becomes fully mature. Many of the most important functions for complex problem solving, abstract thinking, and applying learning and memory skills to the accomplishments of goal-directed tasks are developed late in the cycle of myelination.

Another developmental change in the PFC that occurs during late adolescence is the remodeling of the relationship between the amounts of dopamine (a neurotransmitter) produced in the limbic system (which controls emotions) and the number of receptors in the PFC to process the dopamine (Steinberg, 2008). Dopamine is associated with sensation seeking and emotional well-being and is critical for focusing attention, resolving conflicts, and mature judgment. As the brain matures, the relationship between the amounts of dopamine produced and the number of receptors in the PFC to process it becomes more balanced. With maturity, this remodeling creates better coordination between emotions and cognition and results in improved emotional regulation (Steinberg). However, during adolescence there is an imbalance in this transmission process that contributes to the urge for students in late adolescence to seek greater sensation, take greater risks, and act impulsively (Gardner & Steinberg, 2005; Steinberg, 2009).

College students in late adolescence also struggle with the ability to accurately interpret the mental states of other people. Burnett et al. (2009) report on a series of studies conducted at universities across the world on the brain activity of people from childhood to full adulthood. The studies used different problems to identify areas of the brain involved in mentalization tasks, such as understanding irony, examining one's own intentions, interpreting sarcasm or sincerity, and thinking about emotions like guilt or shame. In each of these studies, adolescents showed greater neural activities in the medial PFC area of the brain than adults and were less accurate in their perceptions of other people's emotions. Blakemore (2012) suggests that the differences between adolescents and adults are the result of using different cognitive strategies or neuro-anatomical changes that occur between adolescence and adulthood.

Our brains have the unique ability to create connections and make assumptions based on our past experiences. Consider a two-dimensional painting of a landscape that depicts shadows, color, perspective, and texture. Our minds create a three-dimensional image by associating what we see in the painting with what we know from our life experiences. This transmutation occurs because our minds fill in the gaps and make assumptions about what the painting represents (Kandel, 2013). Other examples of how our brains make these connections include perception puzzles in which some people see a vase and other people see silhouettes of people facing each other. Our minds make sense out of these visual images based on our experiences and how we have learned to attend to certain features (Kandel). This same process happens when reading emotions in people's verbal and nonverbal cues.

Adolescents do not have as much experience processing this information as adults or as much feedback in social situations and therefore struggle to accurately interpret the feeling and emotions of others. This explains, in part, why adolescents might say or do something that makes a relationship conflict worse or why they may misread the intentions of other people and overreact (Amen, 1998).

Despite how compelling new neuroscience research is, the brain is not the mind. People are more than neurons. They think, feel, love, hope, and dream. Neuroimaging studies reveal significant amounts of information about what happens in various regions of the brain. However, each region performs more than one function, and mental tasks may activate several areas of the brain at one time. Satel and Lilienfeld (2013) warn that although it is seductive, neuroscience does not answer all of the questions about how people think, feel, and act. Like most scientific research, it has value and limitations. The challenge is to place this research in context.

## Risk-Taking and Sensation-Seeking Behavior

When individuals make decisions about potentially dangerous and risky situations, both the emotional center of the brain (limbic system) and the PFC are involved in the process. When confronted with high-risk and potentially thrilling situations, such as bungee jumping, dopamine and other stimulating chemicals flood the limbic system and increase feelings of excitement in anticipation of the reward of engaging in the activity (Gardner & Steinberg, 2005; Steinberg, 2008). For adolescents, this reward could be peer approval or a new sensation or experience. Because men produce higher levels of certain chemical stimulants (e.g., dopamine) than women and because estrogen and testosterone have different effects on how rapidly these stimulants are processed in the PFC, males are more likely than females to take greater risks, seek greater rewards, and act impulsively (Casey, Jones, & Hare, 2008).

The inability to accurately assess social-emotional situations and risks in the pursuit of new sensations should not be confused with lack of intellectual ability. Steinberg (2008) estimates that adolescents acquire the cognitive capacity for significant intellectual accomplishment by the age of 16. What teenagers lack is the capacity to control their behaviors in ways that are consistent with their intellectual abilities. Even though they possess the intelligence to use logical reasoning to make decisions, their lack of experience has not yet allowed them to complete the neuro-cognitive network that will one day make the process of adult decision making the preferred method for evaluating risks (Steinberg). Instead, college students in late adolescence rely more on gut-level emotional impulse to act without weighing all relevant factors in decision making.

One explanation for why adolescent decision making is different from that of adults is that adolescents are still in the process of learning how to act through a process of trial and error. Sensation seeking and risk-taking are means of testing limits and seeking new information about themselves and social environments. As they experience their environments, they act out adult roles and experience the consequences of their actions. This experiential learning helps to create neural pathways and strengthens existing ones. The process, called *neuroplasticity*, allows repeated experiences to strengthen the neurological processing of information related to those experiences (Fredrickson, 2001). It also explains why dramatic emotional experiences can cause posttraumatic stress and how we learn common responses to social experiences, such as expressions of approval or disapproval. These socially programed responses are spontaneous because our neural pathways rapidly respond to environmental stimuli with appropriate social reactions (Blakemore, 2012; Blakemore & Frith, 2005).

Genetics may play a role in risk-taking behavior. One particular gene, labeled COMT, has been shown to influence how people respond to real physical stress, such as cliff diving, and to perceived stress, such as test taking (Bronson & Marryman, 2013). The COMT gene has an assembly code that clears dopamine from the PFC responsible for executive functions such as making decisions, planning, resolving conflicts, and considering consequences of actions. Dopamine regulates the speed at which neurons fire. The more dopamine produced, the greater the rate at which the neurons fire. The COMT gene helps regulate the amount of dopamine in the brain, but it has both a slow-acting (methionine) variant and fast-acting (valine) variant (Stein et al., 2006). About 50 percent of people have both genes, 25 percent have the slow-acting variant, and 25 percent have the fast-acting variant.

Under normal conditions, the slow-acting COMT gene is an advantage because it allows dopamine to heighten awareness and increase focus, which is useful in performing executive functions associated with college-level academic work. However, under times of significant stress, the fast-acting COMT gene more rapidly clears excessive dopamine and reduces the debilitating effects of excessive anxiety (Bronson & Marryman, 2013; Stein et al., 2006). People with the fast-acting gene are at their best in high-risk situations, such as base jumping, freestyle rock climbing, cave diving, and combat. The thrill and intensity of the experience helps them shine and feel fulfilled. Bronson and Merryman refer to people with the rapid-acting variant as *warriors* and those with slow-acting variant as *worriers*. They observe that both warriors and worriers have an evolutionary place in the historic survival of the human tribe—the warriors defend the community and the worriers plan, anticipate, and strategize.

Although the COMT gene appears to be normally distributed among men and women, women appear to have higher baseline levels of dopamine that are controlled, in part, by increased estrogen levels (Diamond, 2007). In turn, this has a moderating effect on those with the warrior gene and possibly accentuates the effects of those with the worrier gene (Diamond).

One cautionary note about genes should be considered. Although there are associations between genes and behaviors, genes are not a good way to predict a person's behavior. A large international study that included more than 126,000 participants did not find any genes related to academic achievement, motivation, or degree attainment (Benjamine et al., 2013). Social-environmental variables, age, and life circumstances that influence behavior in significant ways may be better predictors of behavior than genes.

## Psychosocial Development in College Students

Research about neurobiological development in adolescence and the evolutionary basis of adolescent behavior is relatively recent. Prior to this research, psychologists observed human behavior and constructed theories about how psychosocial and cognitive development occurs during the traditional college years. Most student affairs professionals are introduced to these theories in graduate school, and other authors (Evans et al., 2010; Jones & Abes, 2013) provide a good review. However, some characteristics of psychosocial development are relevant to understanding why college students do what they do. Also, parallels between neurological and psychosocial maturation in late adolescence deserve mention.

Based on an analysis by Widick and Simpson (1978), we know that psychosocial development is a continuous process; it is not a particular state of being we reach and then stop developing. This development takes time and is dependent on the types and quality of interaction in the social environment. Without social interaction, psychosocial development would not occur. A person isolated from others during the formative years of psychosocial growth would have arrested development.

Psychosocial development has order, but the order is fluid. Some development tasks need to be resolved before others, but the sequence is not invariant. Therefore, same-aged students may be in the midst of resolving different developmental issues. Although development is related to age, some individuals progress faster than others depending on the variety and quality of their social interactions and human relations skills.

Erikson (1968) used the term *epigenesis* to describe a type of internal time clock that moves people through psychosocial and personality development. Heredity, neurobiology, evolutionary urges, and the social environment all have roles to play in the pace and manner in which development occurs.

To illustrate how psychosocial development parallels neurobiological development during the college years, we can consider Chickering and Reisser's (1993) theory of the psychosocial development of college students, which spans ages 18 to 24. This theory is among the most widely used theories in the field of student affairs and paints a big picture of some of the developmental tasks students confront during late adolescence. What is particularly compelling about Chickering and Reisser's theory is how closely it follows neurobiological development during late adolescence.

Briefly, Chickering and Reisser (1993) identified seven developmental vectors occurring during the traditional college years: (1) developing competence; (2) managing emotions; (3) moving through autonomy toward interdependence; (4) developing mature interpersonal relationships; (5) establishing identity; (6) developing purpose; and (7) developing integrity. The first five vectors involve development occurring in the PFC and its relationship to the limbic system, including the development of social competence in the first vector, which is a PFC executive function. Managing emotions, the second vector, is a function associated with the development of the limbic system and the capability of the PFC to manage the emotional stimulation and sensation-seeking behavior associated with it. As Amen (1998) explains, it is the PFC that translates "the workings of the limbic system into recognizable feelings, emotions, and words, such as love, passion, or hate" (p. 114).

Chickering and Reisser's (1993) third vector—moving through autonomy toward independence—results from neurobiological changes in the PFC as it remodels its relationship to other areas of the brain. Casey et al. (2008) attribute this drive for increased autonomy and independence to a biological imbalance between an increased desire for novel and positive sensation experiences and an immature self-regulatory control system not yet fully capable of inhibiting inappropriate behavior. With time, experience, and better coordination between the PFC and the limbic system, this imbalance corrects itself.

Developing mature interpersonal relationships, the fourth vector, involves the development of the socioemotional regions of the brain and the PFC's increasing capacity to correctly interpret the feelings of others, develop empathy, and respond appropriately. The fifth vector is establishing identity. It concerns self-acceptance and the integration of internal and external self-perceptions. Self-understanding and one's relationship to others are part of the development of the PFC influenced by socioenvironmental and life experiences. Self-awareness is an extension of this development that requires physical maturation of the PFC.

Chickering and Reisser (1993) recognized that students move through these seven vectors in different ways and that environment plays a prominent role in how developmental tasks get resolved. Their vectors are not invariant or necessarily sequential, except that some developmental tasks need to be resolved before other tasks can be undertaken. All of the vectors contribute to an evolving sense of identity that closely parallels the development and integration of structural and functional elements of maturity in the PFC.

Not all students move through development at the same pace or follow exactly the sequence Chickering and Reisser (1993) identified. Men and women confront aspects of their development in different ways. Hosts of factors influence identity development. An extensive literature describes the development issues that help students define racial identity, ethnic identity, multiracial identity, sexual identity, and gender identity (see Evans et al., 2010; Jones & Abes, 2013). Although there are commonalities among these theories, one version of psychosocial development does not fit everyone. The common themes are development and neuro-biological maturation by gender.

## Music and Adolescent Behavior

On most college campuses, it is common to see students walking or sitting alone while plugged into earphones. Perhaps more than any other time in life, adolescents are tuned in to the contemporary music of the day, and it has been that way since students first appeared on college campuses with record players. Why, during this time of life, does music play such an important role? Of course, one answer is that contemporary music is a medium of adolescent conversation in the same way that sports is for many people. Music provides a topic of conversation, common interests, and shared experiences, and students who are particularly knowledgeable about contemporary music acquire a certain status among their peers.

However, it does not answer the question of why it is important during adolescence. Neuroimaging studies show that emotionally meaningful music activates the subcortical nuclei in the brain associated with reward, emotion, and motivation (Salimpoor et al., 2011; Zatorre, 2012; Zatorre & Salimpoor, 2013). Anticipation and the occurrence of peak moments in music stimulate the release of the neurotransmitter dopamine in the striatum. This area of the brain also responds to other rewarding stimuli such as food, sex, and certain recreational drugs. Because the production of dopamine and its processing are in transition during adolescence, adolescents are more sensitive to its effects. The remodeling of dopamine processing in the brain causes adolescents to exhibit more sensation-seeking and risk-taking behaviors than adults. Music that produces the release of dopamine is particularly rewarding and may explain why adolescents can listen to the same song repeatedly.

## Sleeping Behavior in College Students

Social interaction among students in RHs is at its peak in the late evening, and on most college campuses parties do not start much before 11:00 pm. Even though students have some control over their academic schedules, few have the luxury of avoiding morning classes even after they have been awake much of the night. Circadian rhythm (a natural biological process that regulates sleeping, waking, appetite, body temperature, and hormonal changes) begins changing at the time of puberty and continues throughout adolescence. Environmental conditions, such as daylight, affect circadian rhythms (American Academy of Sleep Medicine, 2008). However, the most disruptive effects on the circadian cycle come as a result of hormonal and psychophysiological changes that occur during adolescence and early adulthood. Even if first-year college students want to go to bed at 10:00 pm, many find it difficult to sleep.

Receiving sufficient sleep is very important during adolescence and early adulthood because the brain is still maturing. Sleep provides the time required to process information and social experiences. It relieves stress and allows human growth hormone to make the physical and biological changes necessary for adolescents to reach maturity. Circadian cycles regulate these sleeping patterns, and disruptions interfere with the quality and quantity of sleep needed for optimum functioning.

Sleep deprivation research shows that inadequate sleep negatively influences behavioral control, emotional regulation, memory, and mental focus (Dahl & Lewin, 2002). All of these functions are critical to academic performance and to the development of appropriate social interaction skills. Inadequate sleep also presents health risks, such as increased risk of substance abuse, challenges with self-regulatory behaviors, tension, depression, irritability, confusion, and dissatisfaction (Pilcher, Ginter, & Sadowsky, 1997). Sleep deprivation is also associated with a number of other physical problems including challenges with metabolism, weight control, immune function, disease resistance, mood, heart disease, and attention deficit disorder (Brody, 2013).

Both the amount of sleep and the quality of sleep are important. Even students who sleep eight hours per night, but have changes in the sleep-wake cycle of as little as two hours show increased signs of depression and diminished concentration. When students do not get enough sleep during the academic week, they frequently try to compensate by sleeping longer on the weekends. Although this offers some help, the change in the sleep schedule reduces the quality of sleep and results in a gradual slowing of concentration and an increase in irritability and depression (Taub, 1978).

Erratic sleep patterns, low-quality sleep, and inadequate sleep contribute to reduced academic performance and behavioral problems in college students. Trockel, Barnes, and Egget (2000) studied a random sample of 200 first-year students living in on-campus RHs at a large private university. The researchers wanted to determine the effects of various lifestyle and health-related behaviors on students' grade point averages (GPAs). Among the variables they examined were sleep, exercise, eating habits, mood states, time management, perceived stress, social support, number of hours worked per week, gender, and age. Of all of these variables, sleep, particularly as it relates to the time a student woke up, accounted for the largest amount of variance in GPA. Lower academic performance was associated with later wake-up times during weekdays and weekends. The researchers concluded that the quality of the sleep and irregularity of the sleeping patterns were more likely the source of the lowered academic performance than the actual amount of sleep students received. These findings on the quality of sleep are consistent with earlier studies (Lack, 1986; Pilcher & Walters, 1997; Pilcher et al., 1997) that showed adverse effects from erratic sleep habits in college students (Lund et al., 2010).

Many college students exhibit inconsistent sleep patterns. In one study, 1,125 students aged 17 to 24 completed a series of sleep study questionnaires designed to evaluate sleep patterns, academic performance, physical health, and use of psychoactive drugs (Lund et al., 2010). The study showed that over 60 percent of students experienced poor quality sleep with disruptive bedtimes and rise times, and they frequently used prescription, over-the-counter, and recreational drugs that alter sleep and wakefulness. Students classified as poor-quality sleepers reported significantly more problems with psychological and physical health than did students classified as good-quality sleepers. Overwhelmingly the students reported that stress was a major contributor to sleep disruption, accounting for 24 percent of the variance in sleep quality. Exercise, alcohol, and caffeine consumption were not consistent predictors of poor sleep. In an earlier study, Buboltz, Brown, and Soper (2001) found that most students experienced sleep deprivation and that women reported more sleep disturbances than men.

Although sleep deprivation impairs many cognitive functions, such as mood and academic performance, the effects can be reversed with improved sleep quality and quantity. In a study of traditional-aged students, a spectral analysis of electroencephalogram results was used to measure brain function during sleep (Mander et al., 2010). The researchers learned that recovery sleep improved performance because of changes in brain functioning in areas such as the PFC and that this recovery was due ostensibly to the restorative effects of slow-wave sleep (deep sleep).

Although at one time colleges controlled student sleep times with curfews and lights-out rules, those days have long since passed. What works now is providing information to students about the importance of sleep, the effect more sleep has on academic performance and mood, and ways to improve sleep. The good news is that sleep problems can be corrected with more sleep, a normal pattern of sleep, exercise, less caffeine and alcohol near bedtime, and management of the physical environment. Some students ignore this information, but others use it to improve their sleep in attempts to do better academically.

## Sexual Behavior of College Students

The majority of college-aged men (54 percent) and women (58 percent) report having sex by the age of 18, and 65 percent of males and 70 percent of females report having sex by the age of 19 (Abma et al., 2004). According to data from the Centers for Disease Control and Prevention National Center for Health Statistics, 68 percent of 18- to 19-year-old males and 84 percent of 20–24-year-old males reported having at least one sexual partner within the previous 12 months (Mosher, Chandra, & Jones, 2005). For females, 72 percent of 18- to 19-year-olds and 86 percent of 20- to 24-year-olds reported having at least one sexual partner within the previous 12 months (Mosher et al.). Although many students are sexually active in college, they tend to be monogamous. Approximately 70 percent of sexually active students reported having had only one partner within the past 12 months; however, almost half of all graduating seniors reported having hooked up for casual sex at least once in college (Levine & Dean, 2012).

The self-identified lesbian, gay, bisexual, and transgender (LGBT) community constitutes approximately 4 percent of the U.S. population (Gates, 2012). In 2012, Gallup surveyed 120,000 adults in the United States and found that 3 percent of adults identified as LGBT, 92 percent identified as heterosexual, and 4 percent did not identify (Gates & Newport, 2012). However, there is a difference between identifying as a member of the LGBT community and sexual behavior. Sexuality is best understood as a continuum: (1) exclusively heterosexual; (2) predominantly heterosexual and only incidentally homosexual; (3) predominantly heterosexual but more than incidentally homosexual; (4) equally heterosexual and homosexual; (5) predominantly homosexual but more than incidentally heterosexual; (6) predominantly homosexual and only incidentally heterosexual; (7) exclusively homosexual; and (8) no sociosexual contacts or reactions (Kinsey Institute, 2014). Gates (2012) estimated that about 8 percent of adults have engaged in same-sex sexual behavior at some point since the age of 18, and of that group approximately 5 percent identify as heterosexual. College students report their sexual identity as 91.2 percent heterosexual, 3 percent gay or lesbian, 3.9 percent bisexual, and 1.9 percent unsure (American College Health Association, 2012).

## Physical Health of College Students

Results from the National College Health Assessment (American College Health Association, 2012) of over 98,000 college students at 157 institutions showed that approximately 7 percent of college students reported being diagnosed or treated with attention deficit disorder, 5 percent with a chronic illness, 4 percent with a learning disability, and 6 percent with a psychiatric condition. The factors that students reported as having the most negative effect on their academic performance included anxiety (20 percent), sleep difficulties (21 percent), and stress (29 percent). Approximately 20 percent of college students reported never having used alcohol, and approximately 68 percent report never having used cigarettes. On average, approximately 63 percent of college students reported not having used marijuana, and approximately 65 percent of college students report not having used any other drugs. In all cases, there was a higher frequency of males using alcohol, marijuana, cigarettes, and other drugs than females. Approximately 34 percent of students reported being overweight or obese, with male students reporting a greater likelihood of being overweight than female students.

## Psychological Health of College Students

Surveys of college counseling centers show that each year approximately 10 percent of students seek counseling from college counseling centers (Barr et al., 2011). Of that number, approximately 25 percent of students take some form of psychotropic medication. The most common diagnosis for students seen in college counseling centers is anxiety (41 percent), followed by depression (37 percent) and suicidal thoughts or behavior (16 percent) (Barr et al.).

In 2010, counseling directors reported 133 student suicides, 79 percent of which were male, 88 percent undergraduates, 83 percent white, 7 percent Asian or Pacific Islander, and 4 percent African American. Most of the suicides (81 percent) happened off-campus (Gallagher, 2010). Most counseling center directors (91 percent) believe that the severity of student mental health problems has increased in recent years (Gallagher).

First-year students' self-ratings on the 2010 Cooperative Institutional Research Survey (CIRP) Freshmen Survey showed that only 52 percent rated their emotional health in the highest 10 percent, a drop of more than 3 percent from the previous year (Higher Education Research Institute, 2010). Women were less likely than men to report high levels of emotional health.

The University of Minnesota asked students from 14 Minnesota colleges and universities to complete the 2007 College Student Health Survey, which tracks a range of student health-related behaviors (Boyton Health Services, 2007). From the almost 10,000 students who completed the survey, the study revealed that approximately 27 percent of students received treatment for mental health-related issues at some point in their lifetimes, and 16 percent received mental health-related diagnoses within the previous year. Depression and anxiety were the two most often cited mental health concerns that occurred during a student's lifetime, and anxiety was the most frequently cited mental health concern during the past 12 months in college.

## Alcohol Use by College Students

College student drinking has long been a concern of college administrators because of its close association with reduced inhibitions, disruptive behavior, and irresponsible conduct. The health concerns associated with excessive alcohol consumption center on binge drinking and the potential that this behavior could lead to alcohol poisoning and possible death. Although occasionally people might attempt to link excessive use of alcohol during college to the disease of alcoholism, there is no strong evidence for this association.

What we know about alcohol use in college is that the heaviest and most problematic drinking occurs during the earliest part of college between the ages of 18 and 22 (O'Malley, 2004–2005). Thereafter, drinking behavior stabilizes and gradually declines until it reaches levels consistent with overall adult use around the age of 24. Educational efforts to curtail excessive student drinking have included programs geared at responsible drinking, social renorming of information about how much drinking occurs rather than what students think occurs, and no-tolerance programs focused on rigorous enforcement and heavy disciplinary penalties. None of these efforts has been very successful. More recently, the goals for many college campuses have been to enforce policies against underage drinking, enforce rules about alcohol at social events and college bars, use educational interventions to attempt to change student behavior, include parents in the conversation about alcohol use, and do everything possible to curb excessive drinking with the hope of preventing students from accidentally dying as a result of excessive consumption.

Recent neurobiological research has raised new questions about whether this approach is enough. Alcohol appears to affect the adolescent brain differently than adult brains, and it may cause long-term cognitive damage (Butler, 2006). Heavy drinking affects neuropsychological performance of the brain by interfering with memory functions, blood flow, and electrical signals, and it interrupts growth of some neurological structures (Tapert, Caldwell, & Burke, 2004–2005). Studies of animals show that the brain is uniquely susceptible to the effects of alcohol during adolescence. Adolescent animals are more sensitive than adult animals to the negative effects of alcohol on learning and memory but less sensitive to the effects of alcohol on motor skills coordination and sedation (Hiller-Sturmhofel & Swartzwelder, 2004–2005).

The reduced sensitivity to alcohol on motor skills coordination and the lessened effects of sedation contribute to a higher tolerance for alcohol among adolescents. Impaired motor skills and sedation provide natural protection against alcohol poisoning. As alcohol impairs the body, the body makes it more difficult for a person to drink by affecting motor skills and making the person sleepy. These body defense mechanisms make it harder for a person to consume a lethal amount of alcohol before falling asleep. Because of the greater tolerance for alcohol, adolescent mammals are able to withstand larger amounts of alcohol than adult mammals, making them more vulnerable to the negative effects of alcohol on memory and learning and increasing the risk of blackouts (Hiller-Sturmhofel & Swartzwelder, 2004–2005).

Emerging adults in late adolescence can consume more alcohol than adults before they feel the effects. As a result, they run a greater risk of damage to the PFC, cognitive impairment, and blackouts caused by excessive consumption (Butler, 2006). Alcohol consumption reduces blood flow and electrical signals in the PFC region of the brain, causing impaired judgment, low impulse control, and an inability to focus. Because the PFC is the area of the brain that regulates behavior, when it is impaired by alcohol a person is more likely to act directly on emotions such as anger or sadness without normal regulatory controls provided by the PFC.

College students experience more violence during the college years than at any other time in their lives. Leonard, Quigley, and Collins (2002) found that 33 percent of male and 22 percent of female college students reported experiencing physical aggression during the 12 months preceding their study. Most of the violence college-aged men experienced occurred in bars and clubs; college-aged females were more likely to experience violence in their apartments or residence hall rooms. The circumstances that provoke intoxicated aggression appear to arise from personality differences among people and from characteristics of the situations. People who are generally angry, impulsive, and less agreeable are more likely to engage in intoxicated aggression (Quigley & Leonard, 2004–2005).

To learn where students were most likely to drink, how they drink, and the age and gender variables influencing drinking behavior, Paschall and Saltz (2007) surveyed undergraduate students at 14 of California's public universities. The 10,152 responses highlighted off-campus parties (75 percent), bars (68 percent), RHs (38 percent), and fraternity parties (36 percent) as the places students were most likely to drink. Underage drinkers (younger than 21) were more likely to drink in residence halls, at fraternity parties, and at off-campus parties than students of legal age, who were more likely to drink in bars. In all settings, men were more likely than women to drink heavily.

Paschall and Saltz (2007) found that drinking location influenced the amount of alcohol consumed. Regardless of underage or legal age status, drinking in a bar was associated with the highest level of alcohol consumption. On most college campuses, drinking occurs throughout the typical week, but party nights usually include Thursdays (56 percent), Fridays (85 percent), and Saturdays (88 percent) (Levine & Dean, 2012). During the course of one of these days, students may drink in multiple locations—all of which contribute to the level of alcohol intoxication.

Underage drinkers consumed more drinks before going to social events or bars than students of legal age did, and female students consumed more alcohol than males before social events or bars, Paschall and Saltz's (2007) study also revealed. Their research lends support to the hypothesis that being of legal age reduces the amount of alcohol students consume. A study by Wagenaar and Toomey (2002) supports this and shows a strong association between legal drinking status and a reduction in overall alcohol consumption.

## Pragmatism in College Students

Today students express greater anxiety about the job market and are more vocationally orientated than students of some past generations. Prior to 2006, the major reason students gave for pursuit of college educations was to learn about things that interested them (Higher Education Research Institute, 2012). Since that time, students have become more career focused. Today, the most frequent answer to that question is to get a better job (Higher Education Research Institute). Students' anxiety about career issues was reflected in Levine and Dean's (2012) study of students and senior student affairs officers. The senior student affairs officers observed that students were more stressed and anxious than past generations and described them as more academically driven, more career focused, and intent on completing their degrees in the shortest amounts of time. The surveys with students confirmed these observations.

As one example of this new pragmatism, students have moved away from majoring in the humanities to more vocational fields. In 2010, only 7 percent of college students nationally majored in humanities, compared with 21 percent in 1966 (Levitz & Belkin, 2013). Part of the reason for this may be the rates of unemployment among humanities majors. Carnevale and Cheah (2013) used unemployment data on college graduates from 2010 and 2011 to compare unemployment rates among recent college graduates by major. They found that the lowest unemployment rates, approximately 5 to 6 percent, were among students who graduated with degrees in nursing, elementary education, physical fitness/recreation, chemistry, and finance. The Bureau of Labor Statistics (2013) data show that for employment of recent college graduates ages 20 to 29, based on data from October 2011, 20 percent were in educational services, 18 percent were in health care/social assistance, 14 percent were in professional and business services, and 14 percent were in leisure/hospitality.

## Student Adjustment Issues in College

College adjustment difficulties depend on a number of factors, such as age, year in college, financial security, parental relationships, body image, dating relationships, campus involvement, personality, academic proficiency, and physical and mental health. Members of the general public and some educators often have unrealistic views of college life. They believe that full-time students are actively engaged in scholarship and free from many of the daily pressures of the world outside of the university. When not in class, many people believe that students are studying, engaged in campus activities, or partying with friends. This image of college students is reminiscent of the 1950s and ignores that the majority of college students work at least part-time while in college and struggle with personal finances and that many are coping with physical, mental health, or learning issues. Others have disruptive family situations. A long-term romantic relationship that comes to an end or a roommate conflict can disorient a student and take a monumental amount of time to resolve. Students lead highly complex lives with multiple demands. Despite universities' egalitarian approaches to students and the desire of students to complete their degrees, the socioeconomic disparities and life circumstances of students make college easier for some than for others.

### Common Adjustment Issues

Adjustment to college is multidimensional. Students may adjust well in some areas, such as academics, but not in others, such as social. The first year of college is important to students' success. Students' adjustment to college is strongly associated with both academic performance and retention. Credé and Niehorster (2012) performed a meta-analysis on 237 studies published before 2010 that used the Student Adaptation to College Questionnaire (Baker & Siryk, 1999), which measures college adjustment. They found that college adjustment was a strong predictor of grades and college retention and was associated with individual traits, social support, and students' relationships with their parents.

Credé and Niehorster (2012) also discovered that social support strongly and positively correlates with adjustment to college and that support from peers, more than any other group, was important to this adjustment. Social support from faculty and the institution was positively associated with academic adjustment and institutional attachment. The trait factors they found that helped with adjustment to college included conscientiousness, self-efficacy, an internal locus of control, and positive self-esteem. Similarly, affective state variables such as positive emotionality, low negative emotionality, and low depression were also associated with adjustment.

Elsewhere I identified common adjustment difficulties students frequently experience in college (Blimling, 2010). In the first year of college, these adjustment difficulties often include issues related to the transition to college, time management, break in the child–parent relationship, homesickness, roommate conflicts, body image, self-esteem, academic adjustment, and romantic relationships. Common adjustment issues in the sophomore and junior years include general stress, emotional expression, clarification of their values including their religious beliefs, and an increasing drive for greater independence, which is frequently demonstrated through the desire to leave RHs and move into apartments or off-campus houses. The senior year brings about increased anxiety centered on completing college degree requirements and questions about what will happen after college—jobs or graduate school. Students also commonly experience a sense of loss about leaving their college friends and relationships and recognize that the completion of college marks an important life transition. Nostalgic feelings about the college experience merge with satisfaction about completing degrees and apprehension about what lies ahead.

**Adjustment Issues for Selected Student Groups**

First-generation college students experience more adjustment challenges than do their non–first-generation peers. Demographic changes predict that the number of students from underrepresented groups will increase significantly by 2021 whereas the number of white students as a percentage of enrolled students will decrease and Hispanic student enrollment will increase by 20 percent—faster than any other student group (NCES, 2012b). Compared with students who had one or both parents attend college, first-generation students start college later, have lower educational expectations, are less academically prepared, have greater financial difficulties in college, are less likely to graduate, and are more likely to live off-campus (Choy, 2001; Eagle, 2007; Saenz et al., 2007).

First-generation students enter college with more academic, cultural, and social challenges than their non–first-generation peers, and they have more difficulty adjusting to college (Padgett, Johnson, & Pascarella, 2012). Using longitudinal data from the Wabash National Study of Liberal Arts Education, Padgett et al. found that first-generation students derive significantly less value from faculty interaction than do their non–first-generation peers. Regardless of the quality of teaching or the type of interaction, first-generation students were underprepared to interact with faculty compared with students who had one or both parents attend college. However, first-generation students showed greater gains in psychosocial development (moral development, intercultural effectiveness, and psychological well-being) from their peer interactions than did non–first-generation students. The researchers attribute these differences to first-generation students struggling with issues of social attainment differences (social capital) between themselves and faculty and the greater psychosocial developmental work that first-generation students do to catch up to their non–first-generational peers who had richer academic and development experiences prior to college.

To help first-generation students with the transitional adjustment to college, Padgett et al. (2012) suggested assigning first-generation and non–first-generation students as roommates in RHs. Both the residential environment and the peer interaction should assist first-generation students in learning the adaptive skills necessary to adjust sooner and fully engage their college experience.

Another area of increasing concerns is the number of students with attention deficit hyperactivity disorder (ADHD). Approximately 2 to 8 percent of college students report clinically significant levels of ADHD, and about 25 percent of students with reported disabilities in college have ADHD, with this number continuing to increase (DuPaul et al., 2009). ADHD diagnoses in the United States increased at an average rate of 5 percent per year from 2003 to 2011 (CDC, 2013). Most ADHD diagnoses occur around the age of 7; as of 2011, approximately 6.4 million children under the age of 17 were diagnosed with ADHD (CDC). Males are more likely than females to be diagnosed with hyperactivity and treated for ADHD (Hasson & Fine, 2012).

Norwalk, Norvilitis, and MacLean (2009) investigated the effects of ADHD on college adjustment using a questionnaire to examine ADHD symptoms. Their analysis of the results showed a significant relationship between higher levels of ADHD symptoms and lower levels of career decision-making, self-efficacy, academic adjustment, study skills, and grade point average. However, only the cluster of symptoms that identified inattention was a significant predictor of career decision-making, self-efficacy, academic adjustment, and study skills.

College adjustment issues can manifest themselves in RHs through interpersonal conflicts, anxiety, low self-esteem, frustration, and feeling of failure. Sometimes students act out these feeling through disruptive conduct. Students who struggle to manage the college experience need the support of residence life professionals and their peers to succeed. Some of these students may need more time and more attention, but they too can succeed if given the support and resources they need.

## Implications for Student Learning in RHs

Starting in the late 1800s with the progressive movement in higher education, a new attitude emerged about college students. One of the ideas behind it was that students should be given more responsibility for learning and that part of what they needed to learn was democratic values and civic responsibility. To accomplish this, students needed hands-on experience with student government and student judicial boards. Although many universities had student governments, the proliferation of these bodies emerged in the early 20th century as an extension of the idea that students would learn democratic values from the experience. Both progressive educational philosophy and student self-governance led to the general belief that students should be treated as adults when they entered the university. If treated like adults, educators hoped that students would behave like adults. This idea was further supported by court decisions such as *Dixon v. Alabama*, which eroded in loco parentis policies, the Family Educational Rights and Privacy Act of 1974, which granted 18-year-old students control over the privacy of their student records, and the 26th Amendment to the U.S. Constitution in 1971, which gave 18-year-olds the right to vote (Kaplin & Lee, 2009). Despite these laws and the educational philosophy that supports them, biology has its own schedule for adulthood, and it does not begin at 18.

Gap years in the United States are not common, and college has become the "de facto maturing experience for adolescents who have no interest in joining the military. Colleges weren't designed with that task in mind" (Selingo, 2013, p. 164). Higher education in the United States has attempted to address this lack of maturity in two ways: first by encouraging students to take a gap year (Harvard University is among this idea's supporters); and second by establishing first-year college experience programs that help first-year students make the transition to college and facilitate their involvement and integration into the university community (Gardner &

Jewler, 1989; Upcraft, Gardner, & Associates, 1989). This transition year is important because it allows additional time for neurobiological development and more time for students to adjust to the academic and social demands of a more complex social-cultural environment than high school. Part of that first-year experience should include a provision for first-year RHs that offer additional services and support for students. A better option, although one that many universities will not adopt for financial reasons, is to encourage high school students to do a gap year. A quick check of the Internet will locate dozens of organizations and companies providing gap year options for graduating high school students, though only approximately 1 percent of graduating high school students in the United States take a gap year (James, 2012).

### Assisting Students in Growth toward Adulthood

A review of the issues in this chapter shows the challenges faced by college students in the normal process of growing into adulthood in a complex global society. The question posed here is: Given what we know about students, how can we best aid them in their growth and development?

We know from the research that college students during late adolescence have strong drives for independence and autonomy, have urges to seek new experiences and sensations, and are inclined to take risks without considering in advance the consequences of their actions. We also know that students tend to be impulsive, are heavily influenced by peers, are developing abilities to accurately read the emotions of others, are sexually active, are relatively healthy, and get less sleep than they need. They are not adverse to casual sexual encounters, but they tend to be monogamous over the course of a year by building relationships with one partner at a time. We also know that today's students are more likely to seek counseling, use psychotropic drugs to assist them with emotional problems, and report being under greater stress than past generations of students. They are more career oriented and more driven than some past generations. Most drink alcohol, too many are binge drinkers, and it takes them longer than adults to lose motor skill coordination and get sleepy after consuming alcohol—contributing to overdrinking and increasing the risk of alcohol poisoning and blackouts. They tend to express their gut emotions and are therefore more likely to act out feelings, overreact to situations, and take action before thinking. Despite these neurobiological and social psychological issues, students have the intellectual capacity for significant scholarly accomplishment, and each day they interact in the college environment they mature, develop better social interaction skills, and advance toward full adulthood, which occurs somewhere between the ages of 24 and 30.

In Chapter 1, four dominant student affairs philosophies were identified: (1) student affairs administration; (2) student services; (3) student development; and (4) student learning. Any of these philosophies can be used to guide students during the traditional college years; however, only two of these approaches incorporate what we know about the neurological and psychosocial development of students. The student affairs administration approach can work, but it does not use what we know about students. This administrative philosophy is governed by adherence to policies and focuses on the execution and enforcement of the process of administering policy.

The student services approach focuses on giving consumers what they want. Here, one of two attitudes could prevail. The goals are student satisfaction and repeat business, represented by students returning to live in the RHs the subsequent year. The student service approach would likely focus on the quality and efficiency of the processes in place to improve the quality of the residential experience. If the students are satisfied with the process, the objectives of the program are being met, regardless of the outcome.

In contrast, the student development and student learning approaches consider the developmental needs of students. They include considering students' neurobiological, psychosocial, and cognitive development and engaging students where they are developmentally. With the student development approach, the emphasis is on helping students understand the ramifications of their choices and helping them make more mature decisions.

The student learning approach incorporates many of the same basic premises about growth and development found in the student development approach. There is an appreciation for the neuro-biological maturity of students and an understanding of how students make impulsive decisions, how peers influence those decisions, and other issues of importance in the developmental context in which students make decisions. Learning through active engagement that calls on students to commit effort and energy to their own learning experiences is the hallmark of a successful student learning approach.

Residence life professionals face challenges in educating increasing numbers of first-generation students, who have more adjustments to make in adapting to college life than do their non–first-generation peers. They also face challenges addressing high-risk student behaviors that are a normal part of adolescence development, and they face special challenges in helping an increasing number of students who have ADHD or a mental health concern. Residence life professionals can approach these challenges as educators invested in helping students succeed or as administrators interested in order, organization, and control. In my judgment, an education approach focused on learning and development is the only approach likely to help the most number of students succeed.

The traditional college years are a dynamic and highly complex period of adolescence when students are rapidly changing neurologically, biologically, psychologically, and socially. Nurtured in an academic environment dedicated to helping students gain knowledge and mature into better adults, most students leave college ready to enter young adulthood. College RHs can aid in that process by structuring the peer environment in ways that facilitate the growth, development, and learning of students. How that learning happens through the experience of living in an RH is the subject of the next chapter.

# 3

# How Students Learn in Residence Halls

Social science research provides evidence that students who live in residence halls (RHs) learn more and are more likely to remain in college and to graduate than students who have never lived in an RH (Blimling, 1993; Gellin, 2003; Pascarella & Terenzini, 1991, 2005; Pelter, Laden, & Matranga, 1999; Schudde, 2011; Terenzini, Pascarella, & Blimling, 1996). However, most of this research also shows that the effects of RHs are indirect—meaning that learning occurs as a result of student interaction and the greater access RH students have to faculty, student clubs, and campus facilities (Pascarella & Terenzini, 1991, 2005). Unlike academic courses, RHs are not usually organized to teach content-based knowledge. Instead, the intermediate peer environment of RHs is structured to create conditions that engage students in active learning. It is through student interactions in this environment that students learn. Although some special assignment programs in RHs are designed to produce specific student learning outcomes, which are addressed in the next chapter, traditional RHs create conditions that facilitate student learning.

What is it about RHs that creates the conditions for student learning? How do students learn in RHs? Moreover, what information do residence life professionals need to improve student learning in RHs? This chapter addresses these questions.

The chapter starts with a discussion about how students learn and the different forms of intelligence people possess. A critical factor in how students learn in RHs is how they connect with other students to form social groups. Research about social group formation and the power to influence people provides insight into how intermediate peer environments in RHs affect student learning, which is discussed next. Cognitive capacity and human development play a role in student learning. Dozens of theories (Evans et al., 2010) about the psychosocial and cognitive development of students provide insight about how, when, and what students learn through RHs; this chapter examines several of the theories and explores how they inform an understanding of student learning. The influence that roommates, other peers, and residence life professionals have on student learning is discussed next. The chapter concludes with an examination of the social ecology of RHs, and together with cognitive capacity, psychosocial development, social group identity, and knowledge domains it answers the question of how students learn in RHs.

## How Learning Occurs

Learning starts with information received from the environment and retained in the working memory. The working memory has a limited capacity and retains information for a short time (Cowan, 2001). Too much information or highly complex information overwhelms the working memory, and information is lost or the brain fails to process it (Sweller, 2010). Working memory connects with long-term memory to form schemas or connections that, through repetition or sensory significance, are stored for later use in the long-term memory. Lee and Kalyuga (2014) explain, "Learning is a process of active reconstruction of existing schemas. During learning, relevant schemas stored in long-term memory are activated and integrated with incoming information in working memory resulting in the construction of more advanced knowledge and skills" (p. 32).

Frequent recall of information from the long-term memory increases retention by strengthening the neurocognitive pathways through a process known as long-term potentiation (Ratey, 2001). New information is harder to learn because the brain must create a new network of connections and does not yet know if the information needs to be retained. Doyle and Zakrajsek (2013) use the analogy of blazing a trail to explain how the learning and retention process works: "Establishing connections is like blazing a trail, which requires a great deal of work. But every time the trail is used, it becomes more established and easier to use" (p. 6). Repeated use of the neurological trail results in stronger neurological connections that improve retention and recall.

Learning is enhanced by frequent recall and also by elaboration—that is, when information is used in more ways with more physical senses employed. This process creates more connections in the brain that make the information easier to retrieve (Schacter, 2002). Consider a student who has seen pictures of roller coasters, has heard about them, and has read about them but has never ridden one. All of the information the student collected about roller coasters is helpful to understand them. However, riding a roller coaster involves more of the student's physical senses, and the lived knowledge of roller coasters is therefore likely to be retained longer than only reading about them. Similarly, if the student explained roller coasters to a friend, lectured on them in a class, wrote a story about them for a blog, and built a model of one, the multiple applications of the knowledge would increase the likelihood of retention and improve the student's depth of knowledge on the topic.

Applying information also creates increased opportunities for the acquisition of new and related information in a scaffolding process (Askell-Williams, Lawson, & Skrzypiec, 2012). For example, learning to play the cello starts with learning to read music, positioning fingers on a fingerboard, and using a bow to create notes. It progresses through playing musical scales and songs and improves with feedback and instruction on technique, dexterity, musicality, and sightreading music. The more students practice, the better they become. Learning to play less complicated music lays the foundation for playing more complex music.

This same scaffolding process can be applied to student learning through social interactions in RHs. Repeated social interactions, shared experiences, and feedback increase the complexity and sophistication of communications by building on past social encounters that change neurological connections in the brain to improve social interaction. Siegel (2012) explains that "human connections shape neural connections, and each contributes to mind. Relationships and neural linkages together shape the mind . . . [by] altering both the activity and the structure of the connections between neurons," resulting in learning (pp. 3–4).

Learning also involves skills, beliefs, prior knowledge, and intelligence. Ambrose and Lovett (2014, p. 8) define four forms of learning:

1. *Content-specific knowledge* involves knowing what, when, how, and why in a particular domain.

2. *Intellectual skills* are the vehicle by which students express, apply, and demonstrate their content knowledge.

3. *Epistemological beliefs* focus on the nature of knowledge and learning.

4. *Metacognition* encompasses a student's ability to reflect on and direct his or her own thinking and learning.

Content-specific knowledge, such as calculus, is retained information that can be recalled and used to inform decision making or to provide information. This type of knowledge involves knowing information (facts), how to apply it (skills), when to apply it (conditions), and why to apply it (relationship connections). Intellectual skills include the ability to communicate information, reason, analyze data, evaluate ideas, develop conclusions, and make informed judgments (Ambrose & Lovett, 2014; Pascarella & Terenzini, 2005).

Students have epistemological beliefs about their own learning abilities that change over time with experience and maturity (Baxter Magolda, 1992). These ideas influence how students think about knowledge. Beliefs such as all knowledge is uncertain, or that there are absolute right and wrong answers to all questions, are only one aspect of beliefs students have about knowledge. Students also have beliefs about their learning capabilities and their skills managing their own learning processes. These metacognitive skills include the ability to recognize their learning strengths and weaknesses and to plan their learning (Dunning, 2007). Without related metacognitive skills, such as practice and effort, students may not be able to apply information retained in the long-term memory when needed (Ambrose & Lovett, 2014). For example, students who know cognitively how to play the cello but do not have the metacognitive skills of self-discipline to practice and organize their learning will find it difficult to apply their knowledge when asked to play the instrument. Procrastination and time management—two metacognitive issues—are frequent problems for first- and second-year students who are still in the process of developing these executive functions in the prefrontal cortex (Misra & McKean, 2000; Rabin, Fogel, & Nutter-Upham, 2011). These difficulties manifest themselves in RHs during exam times when many students exhibit signs of anxiety and stress and act out their feelings through disruptive behaviors or episodic emotional events.

## Forms of Intelligence

Most universities offer admission to students who demonstrate linguistic intelligence, logical/mathematical intelligence, and analytical (existential) intelligence. Common standardized tests used in the college admission process, such as the SAT and the ACT, assess students' knowledge in these areas. Also, the core curricula of most colleges emphasize increasing students' knowledge in these areas. Yet being knowledgeable and being intelligent are not the same.

Being knowledgeable generally refers to having access to information and facts as well as the ability to recall it. Intelligence usually refers to a person's ability to reason, solve problems, think critically, comprehend subject matter, use language to communicate effectively, construct relationships, employ logic, and manipulate numbers (Gardner, 1999). College students are not either intelligent or not intelligent; instead, they are likely to be better at some learning tasks than others.

### Forms of Intelligence

Gardner (1999) refers to these varying degrees of proficiency as forms of intelligence. He identified nine forms of intelligence that people use to create something new, solve life's problems, or find a solution to a complex physical, structural, or biological problem:

1. *Linguistic intelligence* is the ability to use language and express oneself orally and in writing.

2. *Logical/mathematical intelligence* is the ability to understand mathematical logic and use the principles of mathematics to manipulate numbers, quantities, and mathematical operations.

3. *Musical rhythmic intelligence* is the ability to think in music, hear musical patterns, manipulate patterns, feel the music, and reproduce it in an ascetically pleasing way.

4. *Bodily/kinesthetic intelligence* is the physical ability to use one's body to solve a problem, create something (dance or act), or accomplish something (speed or endurance).

5. *Spatial intelligence* is the ability to perceive spatial relationships, or employ this intelligence to create something, navigate somewhere, solve a chess problem, or accurately sculpt something.

6. *Naturalist intelligence* is the ability to understand and differentiate among elements of the physical/natural world—the type of

intelligence seen in those skilled at farming, hunting, herbal medicine, botany, and environmentalism.

7. *Intrapersonal intelligence* is the ability to understand self and what one can and cannot do well, how to react and how to avoid conflict, and how to accept personal responsibility for self-direction.

8. *Interpersonal intelligence* is the ability to correctly interpret social interactions and to understand other people.

9. *Existential intelligence* is the capacity for deep reflective thinking about complex questions concerning reality, life, death, and cosmology.

Individuals possess all nine forms of intelligence, but to varying degrees. Cultures and occupations use and value forms of intelligence differently. The ability to navigate in open seas without a global positioning satellite (GPS) device requires spatial-relationship intelligence. This was highly prized among Polynesian people who navigated among small islands in the Pacific Ocean and is also valued among architects, artists, and chess players. However, universities do not normally assess this form of intelligence when selecting students for admission, even though certain curricula help students develop it for some occupations.

Merely living in a traditional RH does not directly increase students' abilities in the first six of these forms of intelligence. A student does not become better at calculus or composition by living in a RH. Although it is possible to advance learning in these areas by constructing a special residential learning environment, it does not happen without organizing the peer environment to specifically facilitate that form of learning. Most forms of learning in RHs occur through the intermediate peer environment of conversation, social encounters, intentional and unintentional experiences, and opportunities to explore interests. Students might become better chess players by living in RHs because they find other students who enjoy playing the game and a nightly chess match becomes recreation. Over time, the experience of playing chess might improve students' spatial relationship intelligence, but most RHs are not designed to increase chess skills or spatial intelligence. Learning of this type takes place because RHs create environments in which students of common interest live, interact, connect, and engage with each other in activities that result in learning.

### Intrapersonal Intelligence

RHs have the most direct effect on intrapersonal, interpersonal, and existential intelligence. Intrapersonal intelligence is concerned with self-knowledge including self-awareness, self-motivation, introspection, and appreciating the conditions of others (Gardner, 1999). Because students live together in RHs, they are confronted by multiple social and academic situations that require them to think about themselves in relationship to their peers. Students quickly learn what they do well and what others do better. Living with other students creates friendships that compel disclosure of personal information that, in turn, allows students to better articulate aspects of their identities. In return, these students benefit from similar disclosures about the life experiences and beliefs of their peers. These social interactions enhance intrapersonal skills by allowing students to gauge their own self-knowledge against that of other students. Consistent with exposure to intrapersonal sharing is the psychosocial and neurobiological developmental process that creates the capacity to engage the experience of self-reflection and learn from it (Siegel, 2012). Students improve these skills through practice and by being placed in increasingly more complex social situations (Bronfenbrenner & Morris, 2006; Chickering & Reisser, 1993; Lee & Kalyuga, 2014).

### Interpersonal Intelligence

RHs also facilitate the development of interpersonal intelligence. The simple act of group living requires the development of knowledge and skills for collective coexistence. Students learn to understand the motives of other people, how to communicate, and how to perceive and understand the feelings and expressions of others. Some students have strong interpersonal skills, and they thrive in RHs. Other students struggle with what to say, how to say it, how to engage others, and how to make friends. RHs facilitate the development of social knowledge and skills in this area by exposing students to other students, some of whom serve as models of highly skilled interpersonal intelligence. In other circumstances, students learn through the process of trial and error. Learning to relate to others in a group can happen only in part by observation. At some point, students need to engage others, and in doing so they receive positive and sometimes negative feedback about those interactions. "Interpersonal experiences directly influence how we mentally construct reality," and the pattern of those relationships "directly affect the development of the brain" (Siegel, 2012, p. 9).

**Emotional Expression**

One type of interpersonal skill students learn is how to interpret and express emotions in socially appropriate ways. Neurobiological research shows that emotional intelligence in late adolescence is still under development; it is still being processed in the medial prefrontal cortex instead of the dorsolateral cortex area of the brain used by adults (Blakemore, 2012; Burnett et al., 2009). Traditional-age students are in the process of learning to understand and accurately interpret the emotions of others and to adapt their emotional expressions to conform to adult expectations.

People have access to the same basic emotions; however, they must learn how to express them. Plutchik (1980) identifies eight basic human emotions that serve as mechanisms for human survival and social group living. He believes that these basic emotions were learned as part of evolutionary human experience. Although there are many ways to express emotions, Plutchik believes that only eight are prototype emotions common to all people: trust, fear, surprise, sadness, disgust, anger, anticipation, and joy. Emotions are psycho-physiological reactions to experiences expressed with different degrees of intensity defined by social/emotional circumstances. This fits with Siegel's (2012) assertion that emotions serve as a "central organizing process within the brain . . . [that] directly shapes the ability of the mind to integrate experience and to adapt to future stressors" (p. 9).

Learning how to express emotions within a social system is knowledge acquired through social interaction governed by the rules and customs of the culture. One culture may encourage open and intense expression of emotional feelings, whereas another may see that same behavior as inappropriate. The exception is primal emotions, such as fear when confronted by a predator. Emotional expression is a matter of how much or the degree to which one expresses an emotion. Plutchik's (1980) eight basic emotions include continuums from extreme to minimal expression:

Trust: acceptance to admiration

Fear: timidity to terror

Surprise: uncertainty to amazement

Sadness: gloominess to grief

Disgust: dislike to loathing

Anger: annoyance to fury

Anticipation: interest to vigilance

Joy: serenity to ecstasy

Combinations of these basic emotions create other forms of expressions. For example, the combination of the emotions joy and trust produce love, while the combination of the emotions anticipation and anger produce aggression (Plutchik, 1980).

Social interactions in RHs establish expectations for emotional expression and provide students with peers who model emotionally mature responses as well as those who do not. Emotional expression is tied to gender and is reinforced through interactions with members of the same gender. In her longitudinal study of young males, Way (2013) observed a significant change in the manner in which young men expressed emotions as they entered late adolescence. The young men decreased their use of vulnerable words such as *love* and *sadness* and increased words related to frustration and anger. She attributes this change in emotional expression to the "mainstream perception in the United States . . . that autonomy, independence, and emotional stoicism are the most important aspects of maturity" for men (p. 210). Eliot's (2009) research on neuroplasticity, emotions, and cognition shows that women are not naturally more emotional than men. She found that social and cultural influences are responsible for shaping gender-related stereotypes that discourage emotional expression in men and support it in women. The social interpersonal environment in RHs tends to reinforce gender stereotypes for fulfilling adult role expectations consistent with commonly held notions of how adult males and females are expected to behave.

## Sociocultural Acumen

Another form of interpersonal intelligence is the ability to understand and learn from interactions with people from other racial, ethnic, and cultural backgrounds. Crisp and Turner (2011) argue that experiencing social cultural diversity, such as what students are likely to encounter in RHs, challenges stereotypes and has long-term positive consequences on cognitive processes that positively influence other domains of thinking and reasoning. Experiencing diversity challenges expectations not only by increasing acceptance of different cultural, ethnic, and racial groups but also by enhancing students' overall psychological functioning (Crisp & Turner, 2011). Pascarella (1996) reached a similar conclusion from the national study of student learning that found that diversity experiences in the first year of college had long-term positive effects on critical thinking throughout college, particularly for white students.

Interpersonal intelligence and other cognitive skills increase as a result of living in RHs because RHs bring together students from different racial, ethnic, cultural, and social class groups during a time of their lives when they are predisposed to learn, connecting with peers, engaged in a common pursuit (college), and open to new experiences. Students who live at home with parents and commute to college are less likely to have these opportunities.

## Existential Intelligence

Living in a RH offers ample opportunity for students to engage and challenge each other about complex moral and religious issues concerning the purpose of life and personal goals. Such questions are the subject of reflective thought with others who may share divergent opinions about these questions. However, each question requires students to construct cogent arguments to offer other students in discussions. If their arguments are weak or dogmatic, peers are likely to challenge them and force greater reflective thinking and more coherent reasoning.

In situations where students live together and take one or more academic course together, RHs create opportunities for cognitive elaboration by using information discussed in class in out-of-class-room conversations. It is easy to imagine how a group of students in a world history class who live together in an RH might enter into a conversation about the morality of war or whether atomic bombs should have been dropped on Hiroshima and Nagasaki in World War II. If the residents participating in that discussion include both American and international students, the conversation could open a wide range of political, social, moral, religious, and racial issues that challenge the students to restructure previously held beliefs and alter cognitive schema to accommodate more complex ways of understanding the inherent issues. This is exactly the type of synergistic learning that RHs offer. However, these experiences do not necessarily occur by programmatic design. Instead, they occur indirectly by virtue of the collective experience of students living together and interacting.

It is highly likely that most students experience some of these intellectual engagements in RHs (Cullum & Harton, 2007). Yet students do not experience the same conversations on the same subjects or engage other students in discussions of deep moral and social issues in the same way. As a result, RHs have different effects on different students, and the degree of learning that takes place with students is partially idiosyncratic to students' individual experiences.

RH research does not attempt to detail what each student learns. Instead, it explores the collective learning experience compared with students in different living situations. This generalization or averaging of what most students learn maybe useful for describing common learning outcomes, but it misses the individuality of student learning through the experience of RH living. Attempts to capture the quality of students' individual experiences are best gained through qualitative and ethnographic research that adds depth and dimension often missing in quantitative research (Moffatt, 1989; Nathan, 2005; Seaman, 2005).

## Experiential Learning

Some learning in RHs may increase the mastery of content-specific information, such as an educational program or workshop on a topic of interest. Other forms of learning are experiential, such as participating in RH student government, organizing an educational program or field trip, volunteering, and serving as a resident assistant (RA). These experiences teach functionally transferable skills such as organization, working within policy structures, civic engagement, cultural awareness, and management skills.

Experiential learning creates cognitive understanding and information retention through the transformative process of experience (Kolb, 1984; Kolb, Boyatzis, & Mainemelis, 1999). Siegel (2012) explains that the transformative process of learning through experience "directly shapes the [neurological] circuits responsible for such processes as memory, emotion, and self-awareness . . . [by] altering both the activity and the structure of the connections between neurons" (p. 9).

Kolb (1984) outlines four stages of experiential learning: (1) concert experience; (2) reflective observation; (3) abstract conceptualization; and (4) active experimentation. Students can start anywhere in the process but return to test their understandings and modify them based on experience. For example, a student could experience giving a speech at an RH student government meeting (concert experience), consider how well she did (reflective observation), make certain generalizations about the experience to previous speeches (abstract conceptualization), and based on this process modify her speaking style in future speeches (active experimentation). Students' choices about where to start in the experiential learning cycle are based on their epistemological beliefs about their own learning strength and weaknesses.

Students must take the initiative to learn by engaging other students and participating in formal learning opportunities, such as programs and workshops offered in RHs. When students struggle with how to learn or process experiences on their own, RAs and residence life professionals are available to help them translate their experiences into learning though advising, feedback, and counseling.

## Learning as a Function of Social Group Identity

The need to associate and establish bonds with other people is basic to the quality of people's emotional lives (Holt-Lunstad, Smith, & Layton, 2010; Siegel, 2012; Way, 2013). As social beings, people care about what others think and feel about them (Way). Evolutionary psychologists attribute the reasons for this to the basic human instinct for survival and reproduction (Ellis et al., 2012;

Harris, 1998; Hawley, 2011; Wright, 1994). Humans needed to be part of social groups to protect themselves from predators, to find food, and to reproduce.

Assimilation is the psychoevolutionary process by which people connect with a social group and become more like other members of the group (Harris, 1998). Initially, group members reduce the social distance between them by becoming more alike in dress, language, hairstyle, and gestures. Groups also differentiate themselves from other groups by forming social boundaries of inclusion and exclusion. Social rules, customs, and taboos define the group's behavioral norms that establish social boundaries for group membership (Hogg & Vaughan, 2002).

Leaving home to attend college and live in an RH is a transitional experience marked by leaving one social structure—family and high school friends—and transitioning to a new social structure. For most full-time students, the transition experience occurs in late adolescence when they are driven by a desire for increased autonomy and new experiences, yet remain closely identified with the adolescent peer culture. Group approval during this stage of life is important because of the psychosocial need to define identity, which is accomplished in part by receiving feedback, emulating the behaviors of other people, and comparing one's behavior to that of other people (Erikson, 1968). The focus on external validation and group approval during adolescence is the locus of control for decision making. As students mature into adulthood, locus of control shifts from the need for external validation from peers and others to an internal decision-making process consistent with a person's ethics, values, and identity (Chickering & Reisser, 1993).

Students who enter RHs as strangers begin to form social groups or cliques shortly after they arrive. Frequency of contact—such as living in adjoining rooms, using the same restroom facility, playing on the same RH intramural team, or taking the same classes—or having some prior association such as hometown, nationality, or ethnic or racial identity often becomes the catalyst for these cliques to form. As these social groups emerge in RHs and students share more common experiences, the social groups gain emotional power. Members are rewarded through inclusion, positive laughter, emotional connections, feelings of closeness, and trust; members are punished through ridicule, embarrassment, humiliation, shame, and ostracism.

Student learning in RHs is tied closely to how social groups function. If a student happens to be located in an RH where most of the first-year students are interested in affiliating with a fraternity or sorority, chance are good that the environmental press of that RH will lead to a higher percentage of students participating in the Greek life recruitment and selection process than if most of the students in the building shunned social fraternities and sororities (Sacerdote, 2001). The social pressure to join fraternities or sororities compels students who want to retain the support of their social groups to follow their friends and explore opportunities in Greek life.

Group differentiation defines the social boundaries of a group and distinguishes the conditions and dimensions of group membership. The process of differentiation begins with categorizing group commonalities and differences with competing groups (Harris, 1998). The process of identifying and categorizing these differences strengthens group cohesion in a process that focuses on commonly shared traits or characteristics that distinguish one group from another. A good example of the natural process of differentiation and group conformity is portrayed in the well-known novel *Lord of the Flies* by the Nobel prize-winning author William Golding (1954). The story is about a group of English schoolboys who are stranded on a deserted island with no adult supervision. The story is an allegory about human nature, civilization, and social group dynamics. At one point in the novel, the boys divide into two groups. Each group develops distinctive characteristics, and the boys in each group organize themselves around a different set of beliefs and ways of treating their members. At the most basic level, this division illustrates the process of differentiation and the formation of group social identity. Although *Lord of the Flies* is fictional, several classic studies confirm the basic human need to associate, form groups, identify common traits, and defend territory (Ash, 1987; Sherif et al., 1961; Tajfel, 1970).

Among college students, the process of differentiation and assimilation occurs in many groups but may be most evident among social fraternities and sororities. To the casual observer, traditional fraternities and sororities appear similar. When compared with the general student population of nonmembers, characteristics such as social status, wealth, social skills, and lack of racial diversity might be defining features of membership for many of these Greek letter organizations. However, students within the fraternity and sorority system sort the organizations with granular specificity that differentiate one group from another (Kimmel, 2008). On a large campus, one fraternity might be described as the athletic fraternity (jocks), the best looking (face men), wealthiest (rich boys), most politically connected (connected), or best partiers (party people). A similar demarcation exists among sororities focused on exclusivity, social reputation, wealth, philanthropy, academics, student leadership, and sociability. Over time, these attributes can become self-fulfilling as groups seek to select new members who are most similar to themselves and reinforce their differentiation from other groups.

Special assignment programs such as living and learning centers, honors housing, and special interest groups create differentiation from other RH groups through the process of categorization. The act of socially engineering students into RHs defines distinguishing features of the group. Making living assignments based on specific traits increases the frequency of interaction about the common topic of interest and triggers the normal adaptive process of group assimilation and differentiation from other groups (Blimling, 1993; Pascarella & Terenzini, 2005). Once individuals identify with a group, they come to prefer that association and often disparage other groups. Turner et al. (1987) attribute this process to an instinctive motivation to maintain a positive self-concept. Believing that the group with whom one is identified is better than another group increases self-esteem and may be a motivating factor in assimilation and differentiation (Turner & Reynolds, 2003).

The value students place on their association with a group gives that group the power to influence students' social identities (Hogg & Vaughan, 2002). Social identity is different from personal identity in that personal identity concerns self-knowledge individuals discern from their unique experiences and attributes; social identity is the public expression of identity—or what students want other people to perceive about them.

One of the ways social groups influence students is through how students spend their time, which can impact academic performance. As part of an analysis on the causal effects of studying, Stinebrickner and Stinebrickner (2008) found that students whose roommates brought video games with them to RHs received lower grades than students whose roommates did not have video games. They attributed the grade decline to a reduction in study effort that accompanied the amount of time the students spent game playing. Although some of how students spend their time and what they learn from their RH peers may be inconsistent with the learning objects of RHs, this learning may serve other important socializing needs consistent with age-related interests and social status within peer groups.

In their study of contemporary college students, Levine and Dean (2012) identified a number of current generational characteristics, opinions, and attitudes that differ from past generations. They described today's undergraduates as digital natives who are more diverse, connected to one another through social media, globally conscious, isolated interpersonally, career oriented, immature, dependent, and more entitled than past generations. The Pew Research Center (2014) identified similar commonalities—primarily that current students are ideologically more liberal and politically independent than students in past generations. Students favor same-sex marriages, legalization of marijuana, and legal status with a path to citizenship for undocumented immigrants. Both of these studies show generational similarities in student attitudes and opinions that may be attributable to various unique social and cultural events that hold special significance for them (Levine & Dean, 2012). Peer influences in RHs reinforce shared generational attitudes and opinions and create an environmental press to conform to or consider adopting the opinions and attitudes of the dominant group (Cullum & Harton, 2007). In this way, the peer environment in RHs serves to teach contemporary peer culture on a wide range of issues.

## Learning from Roommates and Other Peers

RHs provide unique environments in which many students live outside of their families of origin for the first time and often share space with other students. Students spend a considerable amount of time with roommates. Stinebrickner and Stinebrickner (2006) found that on average students spent more time with roommates per week than with non-roommates. A total of 47 percent of the over 300 students in their sample indicated that they spent more time with their roommate than with other friends, even though only 37 percent categorized their roommates as one of their four best friends. In a survey of over 1,200 students living in four RHs, Cullum and Harton (2007) found that 33 percent of students' friends live in their living units, which was higher than the number of friends who are in the same RH (18 percent), who are in a different RH (27 percent), or who lived off-campus (22 percent). Most student conversations in RHs (87 percent) were face to face, and room proximity was a significant predictor of students' interactions.

Researchers have studied how roommates influence behavior. Kremer and Levy (2008) studied the peer effects of randomly assigned roommates on alcohol use and academic performance.

They found that on average males who had roommates who reported drinking in high school received one quarter-point lower grade point averages (GPAs) than those assigned to nondrinking roommates in the first year of college; this negative effect persisted into the second year. Also, the negative effect on academic performance is larger for students who drank alcohol themselves during high school. GPAs of female students were not influenced by roommates' drinking prior to college. Roommates' past high school grades, admission test scores, and family backgrounds did not affect the other roommates' academic performances. The authors observe that offering substance-free RHs would segregate the drinking students and increase the likelihood that they would have lower GPAs.

Eisenberg, Golberstein, and Whitlock (2014) found that roommates influenced binge drinking but had little effect on other behaviors, such as smoking, illicit drug use, suicidal ideation, and nonsuicidal self-injury. Similarly, Duncan et al. (2005) found that roommates had no effect on marijuana use or the number of sexual partners but that they did influence the frequency of binge drinking. Eisenberg et al. (2013) found no significant overall effects of roommate influence on happiness and only modest evidence that roommate anxiety and depression affects the other person's mental health. They also found that similarity of baseline mental health was a good predictor of closeness of roommate relationships. Overall, their results show little influence that the mental health (happiness, anxiety, depression) of one roommate significantly influences the mental health of the other roommate outside of a specific context. After controlling for high school GPA and SAT scores, Foster (2006) found no significant peer effects (defined as all students residing in rooms that were on the same wing of an RH floor) on semester GPA.

The decision to join a fraternity may be influenced by a roommate. Sacerdote (2001) found that randomly assigned first-year roommates were more likely to join a fraternity if their roommate was joining. Sacerdote also found that living in a residence hall with a high percentage of students who were drinking was positively and significantly correlated with joining a fraternity (men) or sorority (women).

Roommates can increase students' feelings of acceptance and may influence academic performance. In two studies (Shook & Fazio, 2008; Shook & Clay, 2012) researchers found that African American students randomly assigned to white roommates reported an increased sense of belonging at the university and received higher GPAs than African Americans assigned to roommates of the same race. Shook and Clay suggest that sense of belonging was a mediating factor in the academic performance of the African American students.

Van Laar et al. (2005) examined the effect of randomly assigned interracial roommate pairs of white, Asian American, Latino, or African American students on affective, cognitive, and behavioral indicators of prejudice. After controlling for preexisting racial attitudes in the first year of college, the researchers examined the effects of voluntary roommate contact during the second and third years of college on fourth-year prejudice. Both randomly assigned and voluntary contact was associated with decreased prejudice, and the decrease in prejudice was generalized to other groups, particularly from African American roommates to Latinos and vice versa.

Gender may be a factor in the degree of influence that roommates and other peers have on students. Ficano (2012) discovered strong evidence for male peer influence on GPA but found no similar effect for female students. One reason may be a stronger need for adolescent males to identify with their peers and acquire new friends when entering college. Way (2013) found that while adolescent males often had intimate male friendships during early and middle adolescence, they lost them as they transitioned to late adolescence around the age of 18. This happened even though young men continued to desire close male friends and needed their emotional support. Way attributes this loss in close male friendships to a misguided notion of masculinity that drives young men away from intimate childhood friendships to become mature men "who are autonomous, emotionally stoic, and isolated" (p. 205). In contrast, women experience a change in best friend emotional attachments much earlier, around the age of 12 or 13 (Brown & Gilligan, 1992).

One conclusion to draw from these findings is that personal decisions, such as using drugs, gambling, smoking, or having multiple sexual partners, are value-based decisions that are not influenced significantly by roommates or other peers. However, social group decisions and behaviors, such as binge drinking and joining a fraternity, are more likely to be associated with social group identification. Eisenberg et al. (2014) observe that "binge drinking is more likely to exhibit large peer effects, because in college settings drinking frequently takes place in social contexts with many peers [and] . . . heavy drinking has relatively low stigma in college-age populations" (p. 127). Foster (2006) makes a similar observation, noting that conventional peer effects on academic performance may not exist but that peers may have more influence on social outcomes, such as drinking and fraternity membership. Therefore, it is the influence of the social force of the group rather than a particular individual that has the greatest power to influence student behavior and learning in social situations.

### Learning as a Function of Cognitive Capacity

College students aged 18 to 24 are in the midst of important neurobiological changes to the prefrontal cortex that influence their capacity for cognitive development (Blakemore, 2012). Although students' abilities to master content-specific knowledge is well advanced by the time they enter college, their intellectual skills, epistemological beliefs, and metacognitive skills are in early stages of development. A number of researchers have studied the stages of cognitive growth in college students (Baxter Magolda, 1992; King & Kitchener, 1994; Perry, 1970), and their theories share several common observations about cognitive development. Among these are that cognitive processes move from simple to more complex and that reasoning is an integrative process. Students use increasingly complex forms of reasoning to determine the credibility of information and to evaluate the sources of information. These theories assume that mastery of lower-order developmental tasks allows students to scaffold reasoning into increasingly complex cognitive schema facilitated by psychosocial, intellectual, maturational, and neurobiological processes. Information mastery, comprehension, understanding, cognitive complexity, and application are the desired outcomes of cognitive development.

Baxter Magolda (1992) organizes the growing cognitive capacity of college students into four stages: (1) absolute knowing; (2) transitional knowing; (3) independent knowing; and (4) contextual knowing. King and Kitchener (1994) have seven stages clustered into three periods: (1) prereflective thinking; (2) quasi-reflective thinking; and (3) reflective thinking. Finally, Perry (1970) has nine positions he organizes into four periods: (1) duality; (2) multiplicity; (3) relativism; and (4) commitment to relativism. All of these theories start with college students categorizing information into right or wrong, knowable or unknowable, and absolute or conditional. They all end with a form of contextualized knowing in which knowledge and behavior is based on reasoning, evidence, context, personal experience, values, and self-concept.

Baxter Magolda (2001) also proposed that the interrelationship of psychosocial and cognitive development creates a psychological process of self-authorship that evolves throughout life and changes with experience and age. In her theory of self-authorship, Baxter Magolda proposes four phases she labels as (1) following formulas, (2) crossroads, (3) becoming the author of one's life, and (4) internal foundations. These phases can be understood as allowing others to define a person, finding and establishing a direction consistent with interests and experiences, choosing a self-direction and affirming one's personal beliefs, and grounding those beliefs in a system of self-determination and experience consistent with who the person has become.

It is important to note that because a theory proposes multiple stages of cognitive development, it does not mean that students complete all stages by the time they leave college. Indeed, most full-time undergraduate students complete college before they have developed commitments to mature internal decision making based primarily on reason, ethics, and values. Students who live in a traditional RH for one or two years before moving into an apartment are most likely to be in the early stages of cognitive development, such as prereflective or quasi-reflective reasoning in the King and Kitchener (1994) theory.

## Learning from Residence Life Professionals

Feedback from residence life professionals is a student learning advantage that is often overlooked. Faced with the fundamental problems of understanding and controlling their worlds in ways that make them more predictable and easier to transition into adulthood, students sometimes struggle, make poor decisions, and need feedback and support that helps them move forward with their development. Feedback allows students to gauge their progress in meeting their goals by allowing them to measure where they are in their learning and development in relation to those goals. The role of feedback is in part to assure students that there are paths to academic and personal success.

Feedback has been widely studied as a learning strategy in classroom instruction. This research shows that feedback makes a significant difference in the amount of information students learn, in some cases doubling the rate of learning (Hattie & Timperley, 2007; Shute, 2008). Residence life professionals routinely give feedback to students about matters such as study habits, relationship building, involvement in campus life, emotional maturity, parental relationships, roommate disputes, personal conduct, and the need to seek support services such as counseling or financial aid. Although students often have the basic knowledge they need to resolve problems, they frequently need help in evaluating the options and circumstances objectively. Students also need reassurance that inferences they made are accurate and affirmation that their plans to resolve matters of concern are workable.

Sometimes students seek feedback from residence life professionals, and at other times residence life professionals initiate the feedback. Residence life professionals might give students feedback about well-executed RH programs or make suggestions about how to better conduct RH student government meetings. Students' personal conduct sometimes becomes the reason for feedback about behavior, maturity, institutional expectations, or seeking mental health assistance. Feedback is most powerful when it engages students at, or just above, their current levels of functioning and challenges them to invest effort in moving forward (Hattie & Yates, 2014). To the extent that residence life professionals can validate what students have already learned and connect that learning with areas in which they still need to grow, students are more likely to view the feedback as constructive.

Feedback provides guideposts to help students learn. Its effectiveness can be difficult to assess because it resides in what students perceive and how they interpret it rather than in what the educator believes has taken place (Hattie & Yates, 2014). In RHs, where students' lives are on open display, residence life professionals see students at their best and at their worst. These encounters provide opportunities to engage students about issues that might otherwise go unnoticed if the students did not live in the RH. Both positive and negative feedback about how students are progressing offers students information they can use to grow, change, develop, and learn.

Student learning also happens in RHs as a function of the environmental milieu created by the intellectual atmosphere among students, the demeanor of the residence life staff, and the quality of the facilities available for learning. By providing the organizational structure, advising, feedback, and support students need, residence life professionals—in concert with residents—are able to create environments in which student learning is expected and occurs both formally and informally.

## Learning as an Integrative Process

Student learning in RHs can be understood as a dynamic process through which psychosocial, neurobiological, and cognitive development occur within the context of an adolescent peer culture defined by the unique character of the interpersonal dynamics of the RH and college campus. Bronfenbrenner (1989) offers an integrative ecology theory for understanding how human development interacts within an environmental context like an RH. Renn and Arnold (2003) provide an explanation of the application of Bronfenbrenner's theory to the college peer culture, and Renn (2003) demonstrates its utility for exploring the racial identities of students.

Bronfenbrenner (1989) proposes that human development can be understood only within the context of people's life experiences as influenced by multiple social and cultural forces. He identifies four elements for understanding human development: (1) person (individual traits, abilities, and experiences); (2) process (interaction effects with the environment); (3) context (interactions in the immediate environment); and (4) time (development over time resulting from social and cultural influences). Bronfenbrenner and Morris (2006) believe that development is interactive and is in a constant state of change resulting from people interacting within various environmental and cultural systems. They call this a proximal process and define it as "progressively more complex reciprocal interaction between an active, evolving biopsychological human organism and the persons, objects, and symbols in its immediate external environment [sustained] . . . on a fairly regular basis over extended periods of time" (p. 797).

For development to occur, the person must engage the environment, and for that interaction to be effective, it must be sustained over a period of time. The reason for the sustained interaction is that the developmental challenges need to become increasingly more complex. Although most of these interactions occur through social interaction, physical structures and objects, such as art, can also have an interactive influence causing a person to react.

Because each person brings a unique set of life experiences into any interaction, the interactions affect people differently. Renn and Arnold (2003) observe that Bronfenbrenner's (1989) work encompasses Astin's (1984) idea of involvement and Sanford's (1962) concept of challenge and support in that people must engage the social environment and be challenged by the interaction to learn from it.

Of course, people do not operate in a single social environment. Bronfenbrenner's (1989) theory accounts for this by identifying overlapping spheres of influence that he describes as microsystems, mesosystems, ecosystems, and macrosystems. Renn and Arnold (2003) explain that for a traditional-age college student, the microsystem might include "a residence hall or apartment with roommate, a science laboratory section, a student organization, an athletic team or a campus job" (p. 270). Each one of these environmental contexts presents its own set of conditions that define interaction in that environment. In one place, a student might be a leader, and in another, a follower. Although the microsystems may serve the same functions, the social dynamics of how they operate might be very different. For example, students in RHs, fraternities/sororities, and service clubs may wish to raise funds to support a dance marathon charity event; however, the social dynamics operating in each group might dictate different ways of raising the funds based on how the social system of each group functioned.

Renn and Arnold (2003) place roommates, friendship groups, classes, and jobs in the mesosystem; financial aid policies, immigration policies, faculty curriculum committees, and parents/spouse/

workplace are placed in the ecosystem. The macrosystem includes the larger cultural context of interactions including historical trends, social forces, and cultural expectations. Interaction in these systems is a continuous part of development. Over time, both people and environments change, resulting in an evolving set of knowledge and experiences that define people and influence their perceptions and interactions.

Bronfenbrenner's (1989) theory provides a way to understand the dynamic nature of student learning in RHs. Students come from many backgrounds, bringing with them their unique sets of intellectual skills and life experiences to form a community defined by those experiences, the university's academic climate, the RH facility, and institutional policies. The physical structure of the building and the university's room assignment process influence the likelihood that students will meet and form associations. The amount of time students spend with each other provides the opportunity for sustained learning and increasingly more complex relationships to form. In this way, every unit in every RH provides a unique social environment.

Students' personalities and conditions of interaction make a difference in what and how much students learn in RHs. Students who do not engage the social environment are likely to learn little from it, while students who opt to engage are likely to be changed by it and will, in turn, influence that social environment. The microsystem of a particular RH living unit is defined by student relationships and changes as their life experiences change. The absence of a student who serves as a catalyst for various forms of social interaction in a living unit changes the nature of the social encounters in that unit. If an important member of the social group has a family crisis, becomes ill, is assaulted, or joins a Greek letter organization, the social dynamics of the group change, and what students learn from each other is affected as a result.

Social group attachment forms an emotional bond that students want and need to maintain for their emotional health. These attachments anchor students in the institutional environment and allow them to connect with the greater university culture by serving as places of security and acceptance. In this way, RH social groups serve as bridges to greater institutional involvement. Students want to maintain the emotional connections of peer relationships and are reluctant to leave the university in part because of these connections. Indeed, students grieve when removed from RHs for misconduct or when leaving college prematurely for academic reasons in large part because of the loss of the friendships formed in their living environments.

## Conclusions

What students learn in an RH depends on how students, residence life staff, and the building interact together. Each RH community has unique properties, much like individual personalities. Social dynamics in a building change as students change and as the RH community grows together throughout the academic year. Learning in RHs is in part a function of this evolving social dynamic of student interaction and guidance from residence life professionals. Some of what students learn in RHs is lagniappe and circumstantial.

However, not all learning in RHs is random. Students who engage their peers are challenged to increase their interpersonal, intrapersonal, and existential reasoning skills to secure positions of respect within social groups and benefit from the emotional support that groups offer. What makes this growth possible are seven agents of change operating within RHs: (1) power of social groups; (2) influence of peers during late adolescence; (3) shared stages of neurobiological development; (4) shared psychosocial/cognitive developmental tasks; (5) feedback and guidance from residence life educators and student staff; (6) common commitment to pursue a college degree; and (7) how personal relationships change neurological functioning.

While students bring different life experiences and types of intelligence with them to RHs, they share common age-related neurobiological, psychosocial, and cognitive developmental tasks that provide a medium for interaction and engagement that changes neurological pathways in the brain. Add to this the media-driven cultural influences that define popular music, fashion, visual media, social networks, technology, language, and humor, and RHs become a milieu of shared opinions and experiences defined by multiple forces that together draw students into common learning experiences and produce changes that are not only different from those of students who have not lived in RHs, but different based on the campus culture and personality of individual RHs.

If residence life professionals did nothing but assigned students to RHs and left students alone, students would still learn from each other. What they learned, how much they learned, and how safe the environments might be is open to conjecture. The question about student learning in RHs is not whether students learn. They will learn. It is about how to create an environment that maximizes the opportunities presented when these forces of change come together.

The question that residence life educators must ask themselves is how to organize the peer environment in RHs to maximize student learning. One answer to this question is addressed in the next chapter. Special assignment programs that use classification systems to assign students based on academic merit, intellectual ability, academic discipline, or personal interest enhance student learning consistent with the organizing feature of the special assignment unit (Blimling, 1993). Chapter 4 provides a host of examples. The results of these educational efforts are the creation of living and learning centers (LLCs), first-year interest groups (FIGS), cooperatives, academic living units, and special lifestyle housing.

# 4

# How to Create
# Learning Environments
# in Residence Halls

Residence life professionals have experimented with many ways
to structure the peer environment in residence halls (RHs) to
achieve positive educational outcomes for students. This chapter
presents some of the research about these attempts and identifies
programmatic interventions that have been successful in enhancing
student learning, the quality of student life, and the social climate in
RHs. In examining the influence of conventional RHs, we look at
the research that demonstrates the advantages of living in RHs.

The educationally purposeful programs that operate in college
RHs are very diverse. They range from homogeneous assignment
programs by academic discipline to living and learning centers
(LLCs) based on the Oxford model (Duke, 1996). The National
Study of Living-Learning Programs (Inkelas & Associates, 2007)
uses the term *live-learn programs* (LLPs) to identify the large set of
educational programs designed to structure the residential experience for students to increase student learning. Soldner and Szelenyi
(2008) studied the NSLLP database and found 613 LLPs in the
United States consisting of a variety of residential units, models, and
experiences. The median size of the programs was 52 students, and
the modal size was 50 students. Only 11 programs enrolled 1,000 or
more students. The LLPs that existed for 15 years or more had the
greatest number of faculty involved and had more formal policies

and regulations to guide the selection, structure, and involvement of the students in the programs.

Because of the volume of literature and the diversity of programs, the first part of this chapter is devoted to presenting a typology for student housing. I then review the research in each of the eight areas identified in the typology. The chapter concludes with a summary of how RHs influence students, why they have an impact, and the policy implications of this research.

## Typology of Student Housing

In 2002, Zeller, James, and Klippenstein identified five general types of residential-based educational programs used to varying degrees throughout the United States: (1) residential colleges; (2) LLPs; (3) theme housing; (4) residential learning communities; and (5) freshman-year experiences. These five types of programs focused on integrating the academic interests of students into the residential experience to enhance student learning. Inkelas and Associates (2007) developed a typology for special educational programs that they described as LLPs. They analyzed 611 of the LLPs in the NSLLP database and classified them into 17 types: (1) civic/social leadership; (2) cultural; (3) disciplinary; (4) fine and creative arts; (5) general academic; (6) honors; (7) leisure; (8) political interest; (9) research; (10) ROTC; (11) residential college; (12) sophomore; (13) transition; (14) umbrella; (15) upper division; (16) wellness; and (17) women's.

The Zeller et al. (2002) and Inkelas and Associates (2007) typologies provide useful ways to describe and understand the variety of special educational enrichment programs universities have developed to enhance student learning. However, student housing is much broader than the living units that house students in special programs. Conventional RHs and apartments are the dominant form of student housing on most campuses. The student housing typology outlined herein focuses on student housing types and incorporates the enrichment programs that are the subject of the aforementioned typologies.

A review of the literature on student housing reveals eight general types of university-controlled student housing: conventional RHs, LLCs, homogenous assignment programs, theme housing, cooperative housing, independent living programs, special housing programs, and transitional housing. Although it is possible to identify these common types of RHs and programs, no typology can adequately capture the contextual influences that institutional missions, size, history, location, and regional influences have on RHs. In addition, typologies in housing and residence life all suffer from a nomenclature problem. Residence life professionals frequently use the same term to describe different programs. Depending on the institution, a first-year interest group (FIG) might be a first-year program for students who share a common interest such as environmental preservation, or it could mean that students took most of their first-year courses together and lived in the same RH. Sometimes students in living units homogeneously assigned by academic discipline are referenced as LLCs, and at other times they may be referenced as FIGs or theme housing. Although it is possible to identify common type elements for a typology, the types are not discrete. They overlap and function more like a category than a classification. Therefore, this typology is categorical, and individual campus variations exist.

## Conventional Residence Halls

Conventional RHs provide enriched residential experiences that usually include educational programming planned collaboratively between residents and residence life staff, some form of RH government, and student support provided by resident assistants (RAs) and hall directors (full-time professionals or graduate students). This type of housing constitutes the majority of housing offered on college campuses and can be coed or single gender.

Pascarella and Terenzini (1991, 2005) analyzed most of the published research on the influence of college on students between 1960 and 2004. They were interested to learn which college characteristics and experiences were associated with specific changes in students. Place of residence was one variable considered in how the college environment influences students. Pascarella and Terenzini (2005) found that "living on campus has statistically significant, positive impacts on increases in aesthetic, cultural, and intellectual values; liberalization of social, political, and religious values and attitudes; development of more tolerance, empathy, and ability to relate to others; and the use of principled reasoning to judge moral issues" (p. 603).

Pascarella and Terenzini (1991, 2005) also found that the impact of college RHs was stronger in LLCs than in conventional RHs because of the greater focus placed on academic issues and the opportunities to interact with peers and faculty on educationally meaningful topics. Most of the research reviewed by Pascarella and Terenzini shows that the influence of college RHs is indirect rather than direct. The indirect effect comes from living on campus, which increases the likelihood of student involvement in cocurricular activities, interaction with peers and faculty, and supporting a positive perception of the campus social climate and the overall college experience.

In 1993, I (Blimling, 1993) reviewed the RH literature published between 1966 and 1993. This research showed that RHs had the greatest influence on enhancing nonintellectual areas, such as psychosocial development, persistence in college, participation in cocurricular activities, student satisfaction, and the overall quality of the undergraduate experience. It also demonstrated that where and with whom students live has a significant influence on college friendships, participation in co-curricular activities, and the quality of students' overall college experience. Other reviews of the RH research (including Feldman & Newcomb, 1969; Flanagan, 1975; Pascarella, Terenzini, & Blimling, 1994, 1996; Scherer, 1969; and

Williams & Reilly, 1972, 1974) conclude that living on campus in an RH for at least one year has a positive influence on students, particularly in areas of psychosocial development, satisfaction, retention, graduation, and involvement. The literature presents significant evidence that conventional RHs provide residential students significant advantages over commuter students. There is less agreement, however, about which RH experiences produce what changes in students and what factors influence those outcomes.

In a meta-analysis of the effects of student involvement in clubs and organizations on critical thinking in undergraduates, Gellin (2003) observed that RH students had greater gains in critical thinking than other students. He suggested that the greater gains in critical thinking were explainable by greater opportunities that RH students had for involvement in clubs and organizations and the greater peer interaction that living in RH afforded them. Difference in level of involvement occurs as early as the second semester of the first year. In a study conducted at York University in Canada, Grayson (1997) found that first-year students who lived in RHs had involvement scores that were approximately 22 percent higher than those of students living at home with their families. One of the results of less campus involvement by commuter students is that they often have fewer relationships with peers and less interaction with faculty and staff. RHs offer students more opportunities to engage peers and faculty through the RH experience and through proximity to on-campus student activities and organizations. The more students engage in these activities, the more they learn, persist, and graduate (Kuh et al., 2008).

Banning and Kuk (2011) examined 47 dissertations that addressed issues of student housing published from 2003 through 2008. They wanted to understand better the research methods, theories, and topics of current interest among educators completing their doctoral degrees in areas of interest to residence life professionals and others. After studying these dissertations, Banning and Kuk observed that "the residential housing experience continues to have a positive impact on student success, satisfaction, and persistence in their college experience, and special housing environments like learning communities are especially helpful" (p. 97).

One of the most often cited benefits of living in an RH is the influence it has on student retention and graduation (Tinto, 1993). In 1977, Astin found that living in an RH compared with living with parents or in a private room "adds about 12% to the student's chances of finishing college" (p. 109). More recent research confirms Astin's finding that RHs have a positive influence on students' chances of graduating by increasing first-year student retention. Using combined data from the Educational Longitudinal Study (NCES, 2009a) and the Integrated Postsecondary Education Data System (NCES, 2009b), Schudde (2011) created a national sample of students who lived on and off-campus. After controlling for variables that might account for difference between these two groups, she compared first-year retention rates and found that students' who lived in RHs in their first year in college had a 3.3 percent higher rate of persistence than students who lived off-campus. She concludes that the evidence from her study "provides causal support for the notion that campus residency improves retention" (p. 599). Other studies have confirmed higher rates of persistence and graduation for RH students (Huhn, 2006; Noble et al., 2007) and found that students living in RHs were significantly more likely to engage in cocurricular activities, interact with students from diverse backgrounds, and exhibit greater academic effort, compared with students who lived-off campus (LaNasa, Olson, & Alleman, 2007).

In 2014, Gallup conducted a Web-based survey with a random sample of approximately 30,000 college graduates to determine what factors in college made a difference in level of engagement in work, overall well-being, and emotional attachment to their alma mater. Findings show that having a person such as a faculty member take an interest in them, being actively involved in cocurricular activities and organizations, and having an internship or campus job that allowed them to learn played a significant role in students' level of work engagement, overall well-being, and alumni loyalty after college. Living on campus was the best predictor of institutional attachment (24 percent), followed by fraternity/sorority membership (22 percent), and participation in a club (21 percent).

Before reviewing educational outcomes associated with various types of student housing, a comment about coed and single-sex housing is appropriate. I have not identified coed housing as a type of student housing in the typology offered earlier in this chapter. I would have 20 years ago. At one time housing men and women in the same RH was controversial, but on most college campuses that debate has long since passed. Today most institutions offer coed housing, and on many campuses nearly all of the housing is coed (Willoughby et al., 2009). Therefore, most contemporary research references gender only in the case of single-gender RHs. For those interested in this subject, I address it in an earlier review of the literature (Blimling, 1993), and some additional research is available (Willoughby & Carroll, 2009; Willoughby et al.).

## Living and Learning Centers

Living and learning centers (LLCs) are academic communities that include (1) significant faculty involvement, (2) at least one course (credit or non-credit) taken in common by students in the LLC, (3) some form of selection or application process, and (4) a clearly defined mission. Residential colleges are one form of an LLC.

The idea behind LLCs is that having students live together in a community of scholarship, enriched by high levels of faculty participation, academic engagement, and cultural programs, produces greater student learning. Furthermore, it brings about closer integration of what students learn from formal instruction with where they learn it and how it is shared with peers in the living unit. Instead of separating these environments, LLCs merge them to focus the residential experience on intellectual issues.

LLCs intensify the academic experience, and for most educational criteria LLCs are more beneficial to students than conventional RHs. Compared with students living in conventional RHs, students in LLCs often perform better academically (Edwards & McKelfresh, 2002; Pasque & Murphy, 2005; Rohli & Rogge, 2012; Stassen, 2003; Taylor et al., 2003), have more interaction with faculty (Garrett & Zabriskie, 2003; Inkelas, 2000) and perceive the intellectual atmosphere of their living environment to be more academic (Inkelas, Vogt, et al., 2006; Pasque & Murphy, 2005; Rohli & Rogge, 2012; Taylor et al., 2003). Students in LLCs report higher levels of involvement and engagement in their community than other students do (Inkelas & Weisman, 2003; Pike, 1999; Pike, Schroeder, & Berry, 1997). Some studies show that LLC students have greater gains in critical thinking (Kohl, 2009; Pascarella et al., 1993); other studies found no significant differences in critical thinking associated with the LLC experience (Borst, 2011; Inman & Pascarella, 1998). Similarly, research on academic performance is mixed. Some studies show marginally higher grade point averages (GPAs) associated with LLC participation (Pasque & Murphy, 2005; Rice & Lightsey, 2001), and others have not (Chafin, 2006; Johnson, 2001; Pike, Schroeder, & Berry, 1997; Logan, Salisbury-Glennon, & Spence, 2000). Researchers also have found no significant differences in perception of intellectual growth (Inkelas et al., 2006), or emotional intelligence (Chafin, 2006) attributable to the LLC experience.

Most studies comparing the social climates of LLCs and conventional RHs show LLCs to have more positive social climates (Henry & Schein, 1998; Inkelas & Weisman, 2003; Pike, 1999; Schein, 2005; Taylor et al., 2003; Wawrzynski et al., 2009) and students to exhibit stronger feelings of institutional belonging (Schussler & Fierros, 2008). LLC students also report better personal adjustment, a greater sense of well-being, stronger intellectual growth, and more enriched academic experiences (Pasque & Murphy, 2005; Rohli & Rogge, 2012; Taylor et al., 2003).

Brower (2008) used the NSLLP database of living-learning programs to investigate the influence of LLPs on student drinking behavior. He compared non-LLP RH students with LLP RH students and found that LLP students were less likely to drink alcohol, less likely to have increased their drinking behavior after they came to college, and less likely to engage in heavy episodic drinking (five or more drinks in a row for men and four or more drinks in a row for women) than were non-LLP RH students. LLP students also suffered fewer negative consequences from their drinking than did their non-LLP peers. Brower suggests that LLPs create strong learning communities that exert a positive influence on the college binge culture. Similarly, McCabe et al. (2007) found that drinking behavior increased for first-year LLP students and non-LLP students but that the increase was stronger among the non-LLP students. In a follow-up study using the same student sample, Cranford et al. (2009) found that while LLP and non-LLP students both increased the numbers of drinks they had per drinking occasion from precollege to the first year, only the non-LLP students continued to increase their drinking through the second year of college. They also found that LLP students were less likely to be high-risk drinkers.

A more intellectual atmosphere, less heavy drinking, and a better social climate associated with LLCs helps explain lower attrition rates in some studies comparing LLC students with students in conventional RHs. Many studies (Johnson, 2001; Logan, Salisbury-Glennon, & Spence, 2000; Pike, Schroeder, & Berry, 1997; Stassen, 2003) show that LLC students are more likely to persist in college than students who live in conventional RHs. However, studies conducted at the University of Massachusetts–Amherst (Taylor et al., 2003), University of North Carolina–Greensboro (Goldman & Hood, 1995), and Colorado State University (Edwards & McKelfresh, 2002) found mixed results. Inkelas and Soldner's (2011) review of LLPs reached this same conclusion. They found that studies that imposed the most rigorous statistical controls tended to "show no (or diminished) direct relationship between LLP participation and persistence" (p. 27). Instead, they found that the relationship between LLP participation and persistence was likely to be indirect, influenced by faculty and student interaction, social and academic integration, and institutional commitment. This finding is consistent with Berger's (1997) path analysis of student departure, which showed the positive (indirect) influence of social involvement on persistence, and Pascarella and Terenzini's review of research, which showed that the influence of RHs was more likely to be indirect than direct.

Longerbeam and Sedlacek (2006) studied attitude change in students who participated in a civic type of LLP to determine if participation influenced students' attitudes about diversity. After three semesters in the program, results show no significant difference between LLP and non-LLP RH students. Yao and Wawrzynski (2013) found similar results when they compared the responses of men living in conventional RHs with those living in LLCs on instruments designed to access awareness and appreciation for diversity. Although pretest comparisons showed significant differences between the two groups, posttest comparisons showed no significant difference. The researchers attribute the change to students in conventional RHs increasing their awareness and appreciation for diversity and LLC students' awareness and appreciation scores for diversity declining because LLCs contained fewer students from underrepresented groups.

Inkelas et al. (2006) compared responses from students in LLCs and conventional RHs at University of Illinois, University of Maryland, University of Michigan, and University of Wisconsin on an instrument they developed to measure college environments and student outcomes associated with LLC program participation. The results of the study showed that LLC students reported greater learning on a range of intellectual outcomes including critical thinking, analytic reasoning, application of knowledge and abilities, and enjoyment of the challenges of intellectual pursuits. LLC students were also more likely to discuss academic, career, and cultural issues, and they reported more positive perceptions of the residential social climate and the campus racial climate than the comparison group. Among the demographic factors that contrasted LLC students from conventional students was that LLC students were more likely to be involved in liberal education pursuits and have a greater appreciation for art, music, and different cultures. The researchers did not find significant differences between LLC students and students in conventional halls on perceptions of personal growth and cognitive development or personal philosophy. In addition, the researchers found no significant difference in outcomes on dimensions of personalization and knowledge abilities, growth in cognitive complexity, growth in personal philosophy, and interpersonal self-confidence.

In 1998, I (Blimling, 1998) conducted a meta-analysis of studies published prior to 1997 that examined the effects of LLCs on academic performance, social climate, and retention. Results showed that students in LLCs had statistically significant but marginally better academic performance, better social climates, and increased rates of persistence into the next year compared with students in conventional RHs. In this same study, I also examined the effects of honors living units and homogeneous assignment by academic major (AAM) on academic performance and residential social climate. The meta-analyses showed that honors students assigned to live together had marginally better academic performance than honors students assigned at random. There were no statistically significant differences in academic performance between AAM students and students in conventional RHs. On social climate, I combined 16 of the studies in the meta-analyses that measured LLC social climate, AAM social climate, and LLC intellectual climate and conducted a diffuse test comparison to see if the studies were measuring the same underlying phenomenon. They were. The combined meta-analytic statistics show a significant influence of the programs on residential social climate.

Pascarella and Terenzini (2005) observed that studies conducted on LLC programs prior to the 1990s appeared to show more significant effects than those conducted more recently. Differences among these studies may be attributable to differences among the programs studied, instruments used to measure dependent variables, facilities, and degree of faculty/staff involvement. Ultimately, students form unique communities that have a greater or lesser impact based on the programmatic features of the LLC and the interpersonal environment.

Pointing to the work of Astin (1984) on involvement, Kuh et al. (1991) on engagement, and Pace (1984) on the quality of effort, Inkelas and Weisman (2003) observed that the effects of all special educational programs are most likely related to the amount of physical and emotional effort students put forth. The greater students' commitment, the more they learn. Time on task, increased faculty and peer interaction, and a higher degree of engagement translates into increased student learning in LLCs.

## Homogeneous Assignment Programs

Another way residence life professionals attempt to influence the academic performance, social climate, satisfaction, and overall success of students is by grouping individuals together on a common academic characteristic like class standing, academic discipline, honors program, or military affiliation. Examples of these programs include housing by academic discipline and housing for honors students, ROTC cadets, and student veterans. First-year student housing fits in this category; however, contemporary interest in the first-year experience and similar transition programs justifies a separate category, which is reviewed later in this chapter.

Although educators have tried many ways to organize the peer environment in RHs through homogeneous assignment programs, most of the research has concentrated on the effects of honors student housing and assignments by academic discipline.

## Honors Student Housing

Honors programs are common on college campuses, and independent of the residential component, they have a positive effect on critical thinking, mathematics, and composite cognitive development (Seifert et al., 2007). Many universities assign honors students to live together in the first year and sometimes in subsequent years.

Researchers have studied the homogeneous assignment of high-ability students to honors RHs (Inkelas & Weisman, 2003; Kohl, 2009). These studies generally show that high-ability students assigned to live together perform better academically and are more intellectually engaged in their RH environments than comparable high-ability students assigned to conventional RHs. The research also shows that honors students are more likely to engage in both social and career-related conversations with faculty than are other students (Inkelas & Weisman, 2003; Shushok, 2006). However, Wawrzynski and Jessup-Anger (2010) found that although honors students shared many of the benefits of creating intellectual environments, interacting with peers, collaborative studying, and increased faculty contact, these advantages were not unique to students in honors units. Students in other specially designed residential programs and LLCs shared most of the same benefits. The reasons for honors students' stronger academic performance are unclear but are possibly the result of increased competition for academic performance among high-ability students and the formation of informal study groups that emerged from common course enrollment.

Wawrzynski, Madden, and Jensen (2012) studied the effect of honors housing on three groups of honors students: (1) honors students on nonhonors floors in traditional RHs; (2) honors students on honors floors in traditional RHs; and (3) honors students on a floor that is part of an academic LLC. They compared the response of the three groups using an instrument that measured student–faculty interaction, sense of belonging, peer academic interactions, enriching educational environment, and peer intellectual conversations. Responses from the honors students in the three living situations were compared with one another and with a group of nonhonors students living in a conventional RH. Honors students living in the academic LLC had "increased levels of involvement, peer interaction, and sense of belonging that were statistically significant when compared to honors students living in the other two environments or with nonhonors participants" (p. 844). In addition, honors students living in LLCs reported significantly greater student–faculty interactions, sense of belonging, and peer intellectual conversations than nonhonors students who lived in conventional RHs. Despite these advantages, Humphreys (2010) was unable to find evidence that honors programs advance psychosocial development of first-year students any more than living in a conventional RH does.

### Assignment by Academic Discipline

This approach has been popular in preprofessional programs such as engineering for several decades. Frazier and Eighmy (2012) studied pharmacy, engineering, and architecture students assigned to living units based on their academic majors. Students on both the pharmacy floor and engineering/architecture floor reported better residential learning experiences than students with the same majors assigned randomly in the same buildings. Students in the homogeneously assigned units reported that faculty interaction improved their satisfaction and the quality of the learning experience. They also observed that having an RA enrolled in the same academic discipline benefited them more than if the RA was not in the same discipline. Frazier and Eighmy found that for a learning community to be successful, students, faculty, and staff all had to be personally invested and develop a sense of ownership in the program. Shushok and Sriram (2010) found similar results for social climate variables among students in a homogeneously assigned living unit for students in engineering and computer science.

Micomonaco (2011) investigated the effects of homogeneously assigning first-year engineering students to live together in an RH. Compared with other engineering students, he found that students in the homogeneously assigned engineering RH had stronger connections to their academic program and to their peers than did engineering students who were not in the engineering RH. Engineering students who lived in housing for engineering students remained in the program at slightly higher rates, but there were no reported differences in overall learning outcomes between the two groups.

Everett and Zobel (2012) studied the influence of a first-year residential engineering program designed to increase the retention of students from underrepresented and low-income families. They examined two cohorts of students using a combination of focus groups, survey instruments, and retention rates and found that the engineering students in the residential program had persistence rates that matched those of other engineering students, even though social and economic factors would have made it less likely for them to persist in engineering. They also found that the program students felt more connected to the university and reported a stronger connection with the engineering faculty than did other engineering students.

Szelenyi and Inkelas (2011) studied women in science, technology, engineering, and mathematics (STEM) homogeneously assigned to live together in an enriched residential experience. They found that students in the residential STEM programs were more likely to enter graduate programs in STEM fields than women in STEM programs who were not in a residential unit. In a subsequent study using the same database from the NSLLP longitudinal study, Szelenyi, Denson, and Inkelas (2012) found that participants in homogeneously assigned STEM living units had more internship experiences, reported that their RH environment was more socially supportive, and had higher fourth-year confidence levels than women in conventional RHs. In addition, women who lived in coeducational STEM living units reported that their RH environment was more academically supportive than women in conventional RHs.

Light (2001) discovered that science students at Harvard University were more likely to remain in the science curriculum when they studied together in groups. It is also possible that when students live together and are studying the same subject, the likelihood that they create informal study groups is increased. Parker (2012) tested this idea by studying the peer influence of students on academic performance in an introductory economic course at Reed College. He examined nine years of data from the course and compared them with data from students' RHs during their first year of college. After controlling for variables that could account for difference among students' academic performance (SAT, high school GPA, high school class rank, and reading rating of admissions application), Parker found that having economics classmates in students' RH had a positive effect on their academic performance in the class. However, living in the same RH with students who previously took the course had no significant effect on the academic performance of students taking the class. Parker concluded that first-year students draw a benefit from living in proximity to classmates and that this improvement is associated with the development of a classmate mentoring relationship. He also found that working on a difficult assignment with a classmate of the same or lesser academic talent is likely to force students to work harder and learn more than if one of the classmates was a much better student and simply helped the other student with the assignment.

First-year students planning to major in psychology at Loyola Marymount University can self-select to live together in the Psychology Early Awareness Program (PEAP). Grill et al. (2012) studied the effect of this program by comparing the first-year retention rates of PEAP students and other psychology students. They found that PEAP students persisted at higher rates and that this persistence continued through their junior year. Difference in academic performance was less clear. PEAP students did perform better in some classes than their psychology peers did, but there was no difference in academic performance in the introductory psychology course and no significant difference in overall GPA. Qualitative data and surveys from PEAP students showed that they felt a positive social climate of peer support in the program and thought the program helped them better connect to the field of psychology.

Louisiana State University offers academic-focused residential programs for first-year students in agriculture, science, business, engineering, and mass communication. Rohli and Rogge's (2012) investigation of these units found that students in the homogeneously assigned RH programs received slightly higher GPAs and were more likely to persist at the institution than were students in other RHs. Students in the academic-focused RHs also reported higher levels of satisfaction with their academic performance, comfort with academic progress, communication skills, and sense of community and social responsibility than did their peers in other RHs.

LaVine and Mitchell (2006) investigated the effects of assigning physical education majors together in an RH living unit. The program included a combination of linked courses and first-year interest group seminars designed to assist students with the transition to college, build a stronger community and connection with physical education program, and develop strong and positive interactions with faculty. The researchers compared the 12 first-year students in the homogeneously assigned living group to 13 first-year students in physical education who did not participate in the special program. On an instrument designed to assess the effectiveness of learning communities, the researchers found no statistically significant results. However, their qualitative analysis of students' open-ended comments on the questionnaire revealed that the students in the program developed a strong commitment to the academic program, had a very positive first-year experience, and believed that participation in the learning community helped them academically and socially. In a follow-up study, LaVine (2010) reported that the students in the program, over multiple years, had a retention rate of 82–85 percent compared with a university retention rate of 70–72 percent and that the program was instrumental "in maintaining student connection and involvement in the program and in the profession, as observed over eight years" (p. 34).

It is likely that academic-focused RH environments establish normative patterns of behavior that lead to increased studying, collaborative learning, better time management, and fewer distractions than conventional RHs, where students represent myriad fields of study and varied approaches to studying. Student–faculty interaction in these programs tends to be strong. Positive interactions with faculty outside the classroom environment facilitate students' academic self-concept and motivation for academic achievement (Komarraju, Musulkin, & Bhattacharya, 2010), which contributes directly to their academic success and retention.

## Theme Housing

*Theme housing* includes special housing programs through which students self-select into RHs based on themes or interests, such as specific cultures, social justice, lesbian, gay, bisexual, and transgender (LGBT), or service learning. Some institutions allow student groups to propose a theme living unit with appropriate faculty sponsorship or involvement.

Rowan-Keyon, Soldner, and Inkelas (2007) examined the outcomes associated with themed residential environments focused on civic engagement. Using the database of LLPs in the NSSLP, they found that students who participated in residential-based civic engagement programs developed higher mean scores for civic engagement than students in other types of LLPs or students in conventional RHs. However, they also learned that these students had significantly higher precollege perceptions of the importance of cocurricular involvement and community service.

Frazier and Eighmy (2012) studied the influence of a themed wellness living unit on students. They found no significant difference in level of satisfaction between students in the wellness unit and students in a control group living unit in the same building. However, students in the wellness unit reported more positive residential learning experiences than did students in the control group. Frazier and Eighmy also compared the students in the wellness unit with students in two academically themed living units (pharmacy and engineering/architecture). Students in the wellness unit reported fewer gains in learning than did students in the academically based programs. Students in the academically organized units reported higher quality and more frequent interaction with faculty and residence life professionals than did students in the wellness unit. The students credited this interaction to enhancing their residential learning environment. In contrast, students in the wellness unit reported that their peer interactions were primarily responsible for their positive residential experiences.

Purdie and Rosser (2011) compared retention rates and GPAs of first-year students who lived on academic theme floors (e.g., engineering, nursing) and FIGs (students taking four common course together including a seminar on a topic such as women in sciences) with students who took a first-year seminar course (seminar in a topic related to learning strategies, career exploration, money management). Academic theme floors and FIGs were residential programs; first-year seminar courses included students from RHs and off-campus. Only students in the FIGs had significantly better first-year GPAs and retention rates. Even though students in FIGs did better academically, the magnitude of the difference (.009) had no practical significance. This result is not surprising. Students in FIGs took multiple classes together and lived together. The FIG program in this study more closely resembles an LLC experience than traditional models of FIGs where students share a common interest in a particular topic, such as environmental preservation, and live together. Schussler and Fierros (2008) had similar results when they investigated the effects of residential learning communities on perceived academic experience, interactions with students and faculty, and sense of belonging. They compared four types of residential learning communities that varied in program intensity and found that students in the high-impact model (students lived and took two classes together) had significantly higher scores on measures of RH interaction than other groups in the study, but the difference was small. They found no significant differences among the groups on relationships with faculty, sense of belonging, or level of competitiveness. The researchers also performed a qualitative analysis of focus group responses with students in the learning communities. Results supported the positive benefit of the residential experience in developing social and academic networks and in developing a stronger sense of belonging with the university.

Gender-neutral housing (also referenced as gender-inclusive housing) is a lifestyle theme program available on some campuses. Willoughby, Larsen, and Carroll (2012) located 148 universities with gender-neutral housing policies. Approximately half of these institutions were located in the northeastern United States, and about two-thirds were private. Some institutions on the West Coast and in the Midwest also offered this option but none in the South that the researchers could locate. Through a survey administered to 48 of the institutions, the researchers found that gender-neutral housing policies usually restricted access for first-year students, had a strong relationship with the LGBT and gender-nonconforming community of students, and discouraged couples who had a romantic relationship.

Krum, Davis, and Galupo (2013) surveyed 103 transgender and gender-nonconforming students about their student housing preferences. They found that these students preferred living in apartments (34%) or in a self-contained single room (28.2%) over other housing options, including gender-neutral housing (19.4%). Students in the study believed that gender-neutral housing should be on an opt-in basis, that they should sign a values agreement to ensure a prejudice-free environment, and that they should select their own roommates.

Themed living units are a good method of engaging students in a common interest that is likely to improve their knowledge of and commitment to the issue around which the living unit is organized. Themed lifestyle units such as LGBT and gender-neutral living units offer students a safe environment where they enjoy the same freedoms other students have without the fear of being unfairly judged or discriminated against. Beyond those educational outcomes, students also are likely to increase their satisfaction with the residential experience and develop stronger interpersonal relationships with other students in the program. Both of these factors have indirect effects on other important learning objectives of the university, such as retention.

## Cooperative Housing

*Cooperative housing* is a type of self-governing living arrangement with limited residence life supervision and shared responsibility among students for the routine maintenance and cleaning of the facility. Examples include cooperative housing programs (co-ops) developed for agricultural programs in the 1930s, some of which continue to exist today, and co-ops developed in the 1960s and 1970s as communal living arrangements.

It was a common form of student housing at land grant colleges as far back as the late 1800s. Universities often employed students to assist with livestock and related agricultural functions as part of the academic program and to assist some students with extra funds. In 1938, the National Association of Deans and Advisers of Men (Nowotny, Julian, & Beaty, 1938) discussed cooperative student housing at great length, including in the discussions the development of new cooperative housing programs at Texas A&M University, the University of South Dakota, and programs under development at the University of Arkansas, University of

Kentucky, and the University of Florida. During the U.S. economic depression of the 1930s, many students struggled to pay for college. Students formed cooperative student housing as one way to save money. This housing was less expensive because students provided the labor to maintain the facility and often did their own cooking. Cooperative student housing programs started at a number of universities, including University of California Berkeley, University of Texas–Austin, and University of Oregon. Prior to World War II, about 150 cooperative student housing associations existed and collectively had around 10,000 student housing members (NASCO, 2008).

After the war, student housing co-ops declined, in small part because of the decrease in the number of students attending college but more perniciously because of McCarthyism (NASCO, 2008). Student housing cooperatives were identified with collectivism, which was akin to communism and socialism. Various forms of student housing cooperatives remerged in the 1960s and 1970s on campuses such as Rutgers University, University of Connecticut, and Reed College. Some of these programs focused on promoting communal and independent living, while others focused on reducing students' housing costs. Today cooperative student housing exists in two general forms. Some student housing cooperatives, such as Helyar House at Rutgers University, are owned and operated by the university. Students perform basic housekeeping chores, cook together, and govern the house democratically within university guidelines. Others are private student housing cooperatives owned and operated by the members of the cooperative, such as those at University of Michigan–Ann Arbor and University of California–Berkeley (NASCO, 2014).

The rising cost of higher education has increased interest in student housing cooperatives as a way for students to save money. In 2007, there were an estimated 240 student housing cooperatives near at least 51 U.S. campuses, with more under development (Kim, 2007).

Three general principles guide the development of cooperatives: the user benefits principle; the user participation principle; and the user control principle. The *user benefits principle* holds that students who live in cooperatives benefit by significantly reduced housing rates and also board rates in units with cooking facilities. The *user participation principle* holds that the students are collectively and individually responsible for the maintenance, cleaning, cooking, and enforcement of the rules that govern the living unit. As such, everyone must participate in the activities necessary to maintain the cooperative. The *user control principle* holds that the cooperative is a self-governing democratic unit in which students control the activities of the living unit through a democratic process—subject to institutional policies for university-operated cooperatives. The students are essentially the owners of the cooperative and normally have a membership fee or buy-in to join.

Research on the educational benefits of cooperatives is lacking. Altus (1996) describes some of the benefits from living in a cooperative as lower costs, learning to set and work toward goals, group decision making, learning to reach compromise, and learning how to get along with other people. She believes these are transferable skills for life after college. Not all of the reports about private cooperatives are positive. Some news reports suggest that behavior in some private cooperatives is at times a ruckus and disruptive to neighbors (Martinez, 2005).

The only published research on university-owned cooperative housing I found concerned the Intentional Democratic Community (IDC), which functioned at the University of Connecticut between 1975 and 1984 (Crookston, 1973, 1974; Fried, 2010). The IDC operated through a democratic process with limited institutional oversight. Students shared responsibility for housekeeping and maintenance and voted on activities and some group living policies. A number of educational benefits were associated with the IDC, including the development of interpersonal skills, negotiating skills, group-processing skills, and increased responsibility for self-care

(Crookston, 1973, 1974). Despite its success, the IDC closed as students became less interested in this type of participatory lifestyle. Crookston observed that there were clear educational benefits associated with the cooperative but that it required considerable skill in medication and conflict resolution and a high degree of tolerance for obstinacy, ambiguity, and the democratic process.

## Independent Living

The two most common forms of *independent living* are apartments owned and operated by the university and apartments owned and operated by a private student housing developer, sometimes on university property or on property close to the campus in some form of agreement with the university. Both of these housing options offer residence life services, but the services are often different. A partner of one large privately owned student housing corporation described managing off-campus student apartments as "analogous to managing for the hospitality industry" (Feldman & Feldman, 2005, p. 32), which is an uncommon operating philosophy for residence life professionals. Instead, residence life professionals work with on-campus apartment residents to organize programs for community development that allow students to meet more people and develop a greater sense of group attachment. They provide counseling, advising, and other support services to assist students with roommate conflicts and to help students accomplish their educational goals.

Ong, Petrova, and Spieler (2013) collected information from a sample of 1,267 college and universities in the United States to investigate factors such as cost of living off-campus, campus life, school characteristics, and crime rate that might influence where students lived. They found a strong positive relationship between on-campus living and campus activities, campus setting, size, campus security, and the cost of off-campus apartments.

Other forms of independent housing include houses owned or controlled by a university and leased to individual students or to student groups, boarding houses operated under contract with the university, and a small number of apartments or rooms located in student centers, religious centers, recreation centers, and other college facilities.

Research on the educational value of apartment living is sparse. A few early studies (Hawkins, 1980; May, 1974; Selby & Weston, 1978) compared the academic performance of students in conventional RHs with students in off-campus apartments. However, results are mixed, and significant methodological differences among the studies make any conclusion speculative. Because these studies looked at academic performance and off-campus apartments, it is not clear how residence life services and programmatic support for on-campus apartments may influence students in university-affiliated independent living situations.

Regardless of the study outcomes, the purpose of apartments is not to increase students' academic performance, nor is it to structure the peer environment to enhance other educationally meaningful objectives. As students mature, they gain greater self-confidence and independence. The community experience of conventional RHs that is so important to their psychosocial development and to their integration into the university community as first- and second-year students becomes less critical as they mature and seek increased independence. Apartment living provides this independence. However, apartments also require students to develop a different set of skills to negotiate issues of privacy and housing with roommates.

Although exceptions need to be available for students with special needs, apartment-style living is not a good fit for most traditional-age first-year students (Pica, Jones, & Caplinger, 2006). Residence life professionals recognize the importance of having first-year students live in conventional RHs where they are encouraged to interact with a large number of students and adapt to the student culture. Research on the greater or lesser value of apartment-style living for second-year students is limited, and it is difficult to draw any conclusions about the educational merit of moving to an apartment or remaining in a conventional RH as a second-year student.

## Special Housing Programs

Some universities use *special housing programs* to create atmospheres targeted at addressing specific challenges some students face on their campuses. In the ESSENCE (Entering Students at South Engaging in New College Experience) program at the University of South Alabama, student affairs administrators implemented the program to "increase academic achievement and retention among incoming first year students" (Noble et al., 2007, p. 41). Components of the program included students living in an RH together, orientation, structured group activities, relationship building, peer advising, and tutoring. Program results show that after controlling for variables that influence academic performance, ESSENCE students had higher first-year GPAs and were more likely to persist than either nonparticipating on-campus students or off-campus students. Over five years, ESSENCE students graduated at higher rates than did other students. Noble et al. found that the ESSENCE students are "50 to 60% more likely than other students to obtain their degrees, even when controlling for ACT score and GPA" (p. 55). They attribute the program's success in part to the social ties students developed through their RH experience and the effect this had on students' academic performance.

Recovery house programs are another type of special housing program. They were created to help students with alcohol and drug dependence issues. These residential units normally operate as a partnership between residence life and the university counseling center or alcohol and drug education and treatment program. In 2012, 15 such programs were operating in the United States at universities such as Brown, Rutgers, Texas Tech, and Case Western Reserve (Laitman & Stewart, 2012). The common elements of these programs include a dedicated substance-free residential facility, involvement of a counselor trained in substance abuse recovery, connection to a self-help recovery network, student participation in a 12-step group, and student participation in the residential support group. In addition, students may receive special counseling and support to address emotional health, financial, and academic needs. Recovery house programs are successful in helping students to remain substance free and to graduate. As one example, the recovery house program at Texas Tech has a relapse rate of only 8 percent, a graduation rate of 70 percent, and an average student GPA of 3.18 (scale of 4) (Laitman & Stewart).

## Transitional Housing

*Transitional housing* includes first-year students in conventional RHs, FIGs, specialized housing for transfer students, sophomore transition housing, and specialized housing for seniors. The basic goals of these programs are to assist students with the transition to the college experience, to integrate them fully into the college environment, or to assist them with the transition to life after college.

Housing first-year students together allows an institution to apply different policies to first-year halls than to those for upper division students. These differences usually concern alcohol usage in RH rooms but may also include policies regarding coed halls, visitation, and a limitation on single-room options.

Placing first-year students together can promote stronger bonds and can make it easier for institutions to provide special transitional advising and support services. Historically, many private universities and some small public colleges housed first-year students together because their students progressed through the institution in cohorts grouped by graduating class.

### First-Year RHs

Findings from studies about the effects of first-year RHs compared with random assignment of first-year students are mixed. Kanoy and

Bruhn (1996) found better academic performance for first-year students assigned to live together, while Chafin (2006) found no significant difference. When compared with random assignment, students in first-year living units do not show a statistically significant increase in retention after one year (Kanoy & Bruhn, 1996), adaptation to the college environment (Westbrook, Danielson, & Price, 1996), or increased self-esteem or self-efficacy (Rice & Lightsey, 2001).

The perception of some residence life professionals is that housing all first-year students together increases the likelihood that the intellectual atmosphere in these living units will be more raucous and less academic than housing first-year students with upper-division students. Little empirical research is available to support or contradict this perception. However, the homogeneous assignment of first-year students tends to create more secure environments for new students and may open students to more friendships in the first year (Westbrook et al., 1996). These environments may also provide increased opportunities for informal tutoring among students because core course requirements in the first year are similar and students are likely to take some of these courses together (Parker, 2012).

### First-Year Interest Groups

The idea behind FIGs is straightforward. Instead of housing only first-year students together, FIGs add an organizing component based on a common interest or experience, which provides another dimension for how the community develops in the residential unit and allows students to interact and learn as a community. FIG topics frequently include academic themes, extended orientation programs, or social issues such as social justice, community service, world hunger, or the environment.

A number of studies (Inkelas & Weisman, 2003; Pike, 1999; Rice & Lightsey, 2001; Pike, Schroeder, & Berry, 1997) have examined the educational impact of FIGs and reveal that students living in FIGs have higher levels of involvement, peer and faculty interaction, and greater gains in learning than do students in conventional RHs. Purdie (2007) found that students living in FIGs earned higher grades and had increased probability (approximately 18%) of remaining in college compared with students living in an academic learning community or students who enrolled in a first-year experience course that was not part of a FIG. Kanoy and Bruhn (1996) found that first-year students in a residential program similar to a FIG had higher grades than students who did not live in FIGs but did not find that the program increased retention.

However, Pike (1999) found that the influence of FIGs on academic performance was only indirect, mediated by greater involvement and faculty interaction, and that students in FIGs did not have a statistically significant advantage over students in conventional RHs on measures of academic or personal integration. Program interventions in FIGs, such as academic advising, contribute to student learning and appear to help students more fully engage the college experience (Arms, Cabrera, & Brower, 2008). Students who live in FIGs also appear to develop greater self-confidence about their academic abilities and their generalized learning in college than do students in conventional RHs (Inkelas et al., 2006; Yan et al., 2005).

**Sophomore and Senior Housing**

Sophomore students sometimes experience college transition issues because the excitement of the first year of college is behind them and the demands of the next three or more years of college lie ahead. To assist students with the transition, some institutions have experimented with transitional housing for sophomores. Finning-Kwoka (2009) found that students who lived together on campus and enrolled in a sophomore-year experience program increased their sense of purpose, academic self-efficacy, and certainty about their academic majors.

Seniors also have need of transition programs. The senior year is a stressful time for many students as they seek employment, wait to hear from graduate school, and wrestle with completing courses they need to graduate (Gardner, Van der Veer, & Associates, 1998). Family expectations, financial aid debt, the job market, intimate personal relationships, and the demands of completing a degree culminate in this final year of college and can challenge students' self-esteem, autonomy, and emotional stability. On-campus apartments have been one answer to the needs of seniors. They offer greater independence while providing them with the programs and services they have come to expect from residence life professionals.

### Transfer Student Housing

Woosley and Johnson (2006) gathered data for four years on sophomore transfer and nontransfer RH students. They compared responses of 2,142 students on an instrument that accessed student satisfaction, amount of time spent studying, and student involvement. No significant differences existed between transfer and nontransfer RH students on the amount of time spent studying or on satisfaction with the overall academic experience. However, transfer students reported significantly less campus involvement, time spent in student activities, and satisfaction with student activities. Self-reported personal progress (writing, speaking, reading, problem-solving, personal and academic growth, career preparation) scores of nontransfer RH students were significantly greater than those of transfer students. Woosley and Johnson suggest that the lack of involvement reflects a lack of integration into the university community and, together with lower perceptions of personal growth, may reflect a belief by transfer students that transferring delayed their academic progress.

Campus housing officials frequently assign first-year and returning students to RHs before transfer students. Some institutions put transfer students on waiting lists and use them to fill in vacancies that occur during the summer. Transfer students have the same needs as other new students. Although they are usually older than first-year students and have prior exposure to the demands of the college curriculum, they are strangers to the campus peer culture and want to be accepted as members of the community. Special residential programs are needed to help transfer students make the transition to college in much the same way as first-year RH programs. Transfer students do not want to be lumped with first-year students; rather, they desire recognition that they are partway through their college educations and have greater experience and maturity. However, university administrators should not assume that transfer students, including community college students, are unfamiliar with living in a college residence hall. Townsend (2007) estimates that approximately 20 percent of public two-year community colleges offer on-campus housing.

## What Influence Do Residence Halls Have?

Different types of housing programs have more or less influence on students depending on the degree of student involvement in the program. Figure 4.1 depicts the Housing Program Intensity Scale, which uses the eight types of RH programs discussed in this chapter, plus off-campus apartments, to illustrate the relative degrees of involvement among these different housing types. The involvement scale is plotted along three dimensions: engagement (the degree of commitment and time on tasks associated with the program); structure (the organizational structure of relevant program components); and connectivity (the degree to which the program is likely to develop stronger peer, faculty, and staff relationships).

The Housing Program Intensity Scale is a theoretical scale based on the conceptual models of each type of housing program. Thus, it is possible that a program might fall outside of a category and be more or less involving than the category to which it is assigned in the diagram. Special housing programs, themed programs, transitional programs, and homogeneous assignment programs share some

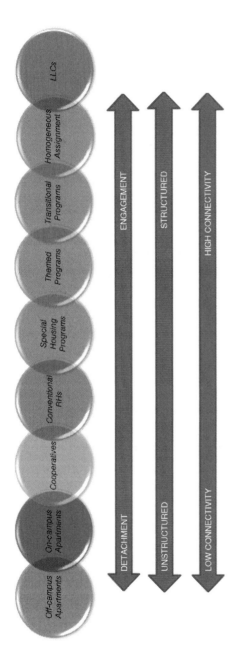

Figure 4.1    Housing Program Intensity Scale

Note: (1) Off-campus apartments, apartment-style living off-campus. (2) On-campus apartments, apartment-style living on campus. (3) Cooperatives, type of self-governing living arrangement with limited residence life supervision where students often assume some housekeeping responsibilities. (4) Conventional RHs, enriched residential program in which students experience traditional residence life support. (5) Special assignment programs, programs designed to assist students with a particular skill, to remediate difficulties, or to accommodate a lifestyle need under policies different from those in other housing facilities. (6) Theme programs, RH assignment based on interest in a topic or issue, such as social justice. (7) Transitional programs, housing designed to address the needs of students in transition, such as first-year students and seniors. (8) Homogeneous assignment, RH assignment based on a common academic characteristic, such as academic discipline or honors program. (9) Living and learning centers (LLCs), academic communities in RHs with faculty involvement, academic courses, and a distinctive mission.

Note: Intensity of living experience for special assignment programs, theme programs, transition programs, and homogeneous assignment programs is program dependent based on level of engagement and structure.

of the same features, and the structure and intensity of those programs is highly idiosyncratic. Generally, the more engaging the RH program and the more involved faculty and residence life professionals are in the program, the more engaged the students are and the more students learn.

The Housing Program Intensity Scale is somewhat analogous to the relationship people have to their local gyms. Some people never join the gym and either exercise on their own or avoid it all together. These are like the students who choose not to live on campus. Many people join a gym and develop their own exercise routines. The degree of involvement they have with the gym might vary from going once a week and doing very little exercise to going seven days a week and spending a lot of time at the gym each day. These people are like the students who enter conventional residence halls and have various levels of engagement in organized activities and peer interaction. There are also people who go to the gym regularly and hire trainers to help them with their exercise routines, monitor their progress, and design new workouts for them. These people are like the students who enter various types of live–learn programs based on their interests and the degree of engagement they desire. Like those who put in the most effort at the gym, students who engage in the most intense educational experience in the RHs under the guidance of faculty and residence life professionals are most likely to get intellectually, socially, and emotionally stronger and be the most satisfied with their experiences. Quality and quantity of effort are likely to be the best predictors of student learning outcomes.

What is not obvious from this diagram is that students need different types of housing at different stages of their psychosocial development. While conventional RHs might be the right learning environments for 18-year-old first-year students, they might be the wrong learning environments for 22-year-old seniors ready to graduate who desire more privacy and independence.

Most of the influence of RHs on college students focuses on eight outcomes: (1) academic performance; (2) social climate; (3) satisfaction; (4) retention; (5) personal growth and development; (6) peer relationships; (7) participation in cocurricular activities; and (8) faculty interaction. The following sections summarize what I believe the research shows about each of these outcomes. I based my observations on a close reading of the available research cited earlier and elsewhere in this book. In summarizing these findings, I offer my observations about the benefits RH students are likely to receive.

### Academic Performance

Many studies have attempted to demonstrate that living in a conventional RH compared with living at home and commuting to campus increases the academic performance of students; however, little evidence supports this conclusion. Once past academic performance and socioeconomic factors are controlled, there is little difference in actual performance (Blimling, 1993, 1998; Pascarella & Terenzini 1991, 2005; Pascarella, Terenzini, & Blimling, 1994, 1996).

This should not be terribly surprising. A student does not get smarter simply by living in a college residence hall. Some type of academic intervention or program that helps students do better academically needs to be part of the experience. Precollege enrollment characteristics such as socioeconomic status, past academic performance, and first-generation college student status can explain most of the differences in academic performance between RH students and students who live off-campus. Add that most studies have focused on first-year GPA and it's easy to see that a range of other life experience factors could explain differences.

Although conventional RHs do not appear to exhibit a significant independent effect on students' academic performance, special educational programs in RHs appear to have a positive effect on measures of academic success. LLCs, honors living units, FIGs, assignment by academic discipline, and other similarly structured academic programs often have small but measurable positive effects on academic performance, critical thinking, and perceptions of the academic atmosphere when compared with students living in conventional RHs.

### Retention and Graduation

A large body of research supports the conclusion that living in a college RH for at least one year increases the chance of a student remaining in college and graduating (Astin, 1993; Kuh, Kinzie, Bridges, et al., 2006; Pascarella & Terenzini, 1991, 2005; Schudde, 2011). Because the peer group is so important in the first two years of college, the close relationships students develop in RHs can have significant influence on students remaining committed to an institution. Opportunities RH students have to become involved increase the chance that they will connect with a program, student organization, faculty member, or other learning experience that engages them meaningfully in their own learning.

Closely related to the influence of the peer group is the focus of an academic community on scholarship. The common student experiences of studying, preparing for exams, faculty interaction, social life, sporting events, and the daily rhythm of classes and the academic calendar draws students into membership as part of the academic community. In many ways, students' living group can become a surrogate family that helps them define aspects of their own personal development and academic and career aspirations. All of these experiences contribute to a student's commitment to remain at an institution and graduate.

### Student Satisfaction and Perception of the Campus Social Climate

Students living in RHs are generally more satisfied with their college experiences and with their living situations than students who live off-campus and commute (Astin, 1993; Blimling, 1993, 1998; Pascarella & Terenzini, 1991, 2005). RH students perceive the campus environment as friendlier, more involving, and more abundant with opportunities to interact with peers. When compared with commuter students, RH students are more satisfied with the campus interpersonal environment and their college experiences. Special programs, such as LLCs and FIGs, further enhance student satisfaction. Students in these special living–learning programs usually perceive their living environments as more academic, friendlier, and more socially engaging than students who live in conventional RHs.

Students living in RHs view the campus social climate more positively than students who live off-campus. Students who live in LLCs, FIGs, units assigned by academic discipline, and various themed housing generally report a more positive social climate in their RHs and on campus than students who live off-campus or in conventional RHs (Arminio, 1994; Blimling, 1998; Kuh et al., 2005; Inkelas & Soldner, 2011; Schein & Bowers, 1992). In addition, students who live in academic-focused RHs, such as LLCs or honors programs, tend to view the residential atmosphere as more academic and usually report greater faculty contacts.

Closely related to the perception of residential social climate is student satisfaction with the residential experience. Students who live in RHs associate satisfaction with college and their living situations. There is no conclusive evidence that student satisfaction is enhanced further by special academic programs offered in RHs, and it is not lessened by the more focused residential program experience.

## Involvement in Cocurricular Activities

Students who live in RHs are more likely to be involved in cocurricular activities such as clubs, organizations, intramural sports teams, and student government than students who live off-campus (Gellin, 2003; Grayson, 1997; Kuh, Kinzie, Bridges, et al., 2006; Pascarella & Terenzini, 2005; Pascarella, Terenzini, & Blimling, 1994). These results are consistent even after controlling for past academic performance, expectations for academics success, and other factors that might influence level of involvement.

The simplest reason that RH students are more involved than commuter students is proximity. Living on campus allows students to easily navigate the campus and become involved without having to commute from their off-campus locations. Also, peer environments in RHs support and contribute to involvement. Playing intramural sports, attending on-campus events, and participating in student organizations are easier when a student lives on campus and is in close association with peers who are engaged in the same types of activities. Each of these experiences increases the likelihood of time spent with peers, faculty, and staff in informal situations that allow for both academic and personal exchanges that, in turn, provide students with feedback and depth in their self-knowledge. These associations also help students navigate the bureaucratic labyrinth of academic policies that can overwhelm less tenacious students.

## Personal Growth and Development

Some of the greatest differences between RH students and commuter students are revealed in studies that compared aspects of students' personal growth and development (Blimling, 1993; Goetz, 1983; Pascarella, 1984; Pascarella & Terrenzini, 1991). Students in RHs report greater gains in personal growth and development than do commuter students. Psychosocial and cognitive developmental theories suggest that the transitional experience of living in an RH creates adaptive responses that facilitate students' development (Chickering & Reisser, 1993). The challenges presented to students in adjusting to the heterogeneous social environment of RHs support a greater rate of personal growth and development than living at home with parents because it requires students to adapt to demands of a new environment and in doing so forces them to alter perceptions and learn new ways of interacting in that environment. The need to identify with the peer culture in the RHs sets the expectation for greater maturity and should result in students adapting to this environment by developing greater self-knowledge and maturity.

The intensity of the residential experience can support certain behaviors that are potentially disruptive to students' academic performance and persistence, such as excessive alcohol consumption, experimentation with drugs, sexual adventurism, and other high-risk behaviors, particularly during the first two years of college. Even though developmentally many of the hedonistic excesses of adolescent experimentation diminish over time, these behaviors can have long-term consequences for students.

### Peer Relationships

The residential experience helps students develop friends. In situations in which students are from diverse racial, ethnic, and cultural backgrounds, it decreases cultural stereotypes and increases friendships among diverse groups of students (Crisp & Turner, 2011; Laar et al., 2005; Pascarella, 1996). Although participation in an LLC or a similarly structured program can strengthen peer relationships, there is no consistent evidence that the peer relationships are stronger in these programs than they are in conventional RHs.

### Faculty Interaction

In most LLCs and special housing programs, students have more faculty interaction and have stronger relationships with faculty than students have in conventional RHs (Blimling, 1993; Pascarella & Terenzini, 1991). However, this is not true in all programs; the degree of faculty interaction is program specific.

Table 4.1 summarizes the influence of different types of student housing on educational outcomes. The body of research on the effects of various types of student housing contains mixed results. Therefore, the yes, no, or maybe contained in each cell is a judgment I made based on the weight of the research evidence and my knowledge of developmental experiences associated with

**Table 4.1  Influence of Place Residence on Students**

| Outcomes | Living at Home | Off-Campus Apartments | On-Campus Apartments Independent Living | Cooperatives | Conventional Residence Halls | Special Assignment Programs | Themed Housing | Transitional Programs | Homogeneous Assignment | Living and Learning Centers |
|---|---|---|---|---|---|---|---|---|---|---|
| Academic Performance | No | No | No | No | No | Maybe | No | Yes | Yes | Yes |
| Intellectual Development | No | Yes | No | No | No | Maybe | Yes | Yes | Yes | Yes |
| Psychosocial Development | No | Yes | Yes | Yes | Yes | Yes | Yes | Yes | Yes | Yes |
| Moral Development | No | No | No | No | No | No | Maybe | No | No | No |
| Academic Engagement | No | No | No | No | Yes | Yes | Yes | Yes | Yes | Yes |
| Intellectual Atmosphere | No | No | No | No | No | No | Yes | Yes | Yes | Yes |
| College Transition | No | No | No | Maybe | Yes | Yes | Yes | Yes | Yes | Yes |
| Persistence | No | No | No | Yes | Yes | Yes | Yes | Yes | Yes | Yes |
| Degree Attainment | No | No | No | Maybe | Yes | Yes | Yes | Yes | Yes | Yes |

(*continued*)

Table 4.1 (Continued)

| Outcomes | Living at Home | Off-Campus Apartments | On-Campus Apartments | | Conventional Residence Halls | Special Assignment Programs | Themed Housing | Transitional Programs | Homogeneous Assignment | Living and Learning Centers |
| --- | --- | --- | --- | --- | --- | --- | --- | --- | --- | --- |
| | | | Independent Living | Cooperatives | | | | | | |
| Faculty Interaction | No | No | No | No | Yes | Maybe | Yes | Yes | Yes | Yes |
| Peer Interaction | No | No | Yes | Yes | Yes | Yes | Yes | Yes | Yes | Yes |
| Cocurricular Involvement | No | No | Yes | Yes | Yes | Yes | Yes | Yes | Yes | Yes |
| Campus Involvement | No | No | Yes | Yes | Yes | Yes | Yes | Yes | Yes | Yes |
| Satisfaction | No | Yes | Yes | Yes | Yes | Yes | Yes | Yes | Yes | Yes |

*Note:* The body of research on the effects of various types of student housing contains mixed results. Therefore, the yes, no, or maybe contained in each cell is a judgment based on the weight of the research evidence presented in this book. Some of the determinations are based on how various aspects of the living environment facilitate students' development and learning.

the various types of housing. Judgments were also made based on research reviewed in Chapter 3 on how students learn in RHs.

## What Works, What Doesn't, and Why: Policy Implications from the RH Research

The extensive amount of research on RHs has policy implications for strengthening housing and residence life programs. However, policy decisions cannot be guided by research alone. The practical implications of implementing policies and the financial implications of creating expensive programs used by only a few students are part of the analysis. Several financially practical policies emerge from the research and contribute positively to students' education: (1) requiring first-year students to live in RHs for at least one year; (2) encouraging students to live in RHs for a second year; (3) placing first-year students in conventional RHs with roommates; (4) providing multiple housing options; (5) providing multiple special program options; (6) requiring traditional-aged transfer students to live in RHs for at least one year; (7) regular assessment of special housing programs; and (8) abolishing programs that have outlived student interest.

### First-Year Students Should Be Required to Live in Campus Housing

The educational benefits students receive from living in an RH for at least one year are evident from the research reviewed in this chapter. These benefits accrue to traditional-aged first-year students and have a significant influence on advancing their psychosocial growth, improving their chances of graduating, and securing their places as members of the university community. Although such a policy benefits students, universities need to make practical exceptions for students who cannot afford the cost of living in an RH, older students who do not benefit in the same way as traditional-aged first-year students, and students whose life circumstances (single parent, religious exception, or health circumstance) prevent them from living in RHs.

## Students Should Be Encouraged to Live in RHs in Their Second Year

Much of the RH research focuses on the effects of residential programs on first-year students. Less research exists on the impact RHs have on second-year students. Available information suggests that second-year RH students extend some of the benefits they gained in the first year and continue the advantage of proximity to campus events, increased contact with a wide variety of students, and expanded opportunity for campus involvement (Blimling, 1993; Finning-Kwoka, 2009). Although there are good educational reasons to have first-year students live in RHs with roommates, there is no educational reason that second-year students cannot move into a living situation that affords them more privacy and greater independence, such as suite-style or apartment-style housing. These latter forms of housing meet the need for proximity and involvement but provide the privacy students usually seek by the end of the first year.

## First-Year Students Should Live in Traditional RHs with Roommates (When Possible)

The benefits of group living and the influence of peers are enhanced when students live in conventional RH settings with roommates. These environments systematically force students to interact with peers and limit the potential for isolation. Living in this type of environment helps students make multiple connections with other students and helps them to feel part of the community. Although such environments lack privacy and can be interpersonally stressful for some students, the overall benefits outweigh these disadvantages in the first year. Roommates can either add to or detract from the quality of living environment, but generally having a roommate redefines students' rooms as shared spaces and requires roommates to negotiate common housing agreements around room use, cleanliness, and guests. Because the room is not theirs alone, first-year students cannot retreat into private space and ignore contact with other students.

By eliminating the option for single rooms and establishing a policy of roommates, institutions systematically increase the likelihood that first-year students will join the community of other students in their living units. The first-year residential experience should be structured to invite students to make connections with other students both in the living unit and through involvement in programs and activities on campus. The stronger the relationships students form with faculty, staff, and peers, the greater the likelihood that they will be able to draw on these personal resources for emotional support and advice throughout their college experiences. Conventional RH arrangements—where two students share a room and students in the living unit share a floor lounge and a common bathroom—increases opportunities for students to assimilate into normative peer environments.

Of course, there are exceptions to such a policy. First-year students with special needs who want to live on campus may require single rooms, private baths, or apartment-style living.

### Multiple Housing Options Should Be Available to Students

One type of housing does not meet the needs of all students at all stages of their growth and development in college. While conventional RHs where two students share a room are most appropriate for most first-year students, they may be least appropriate for seniors. To the extent possible, universities should provide a variety of different residential living arrangements. The four most common types are conventional RHs, junior suites, suites, and apartments. Apartments have full kitchens, and junior suites have a common bathroom between two rooms that four students share and are in other ways most like a conventional residence hall. This variety allows students to move from a conventional RH or junior suite in the first year to a suite in the second year and into an apartment for the last two years of college.

To the extent possible, institutions should also provide both coeducational and single-sex RH options. Although coeducational RHs are the most common form of contemporary student housing, living units being assigned exclusively for women and men permits students to have choices, which may be particularly important for individuals with cultural or religious backgrounds that prohibit communal living arrangements with members of the opposite sex.

### Multiple Educational Program Options Should Be Available to Students

A strong housing and residence life program should provide students with opportunities to participate in honors programs, programs assigned by academic discipline, and FIGs. To the extent practical, other housing options such as LLCs, themed housing, cooperatives, and special housing programs like gen-der-neutral housing are worthwhile educational opportunities for students. LLCs offer students important educational oppor-tunities and can help them connect their educational experi-ences and interests with their living environments. However, students' participation in any special housing program should be optional. Students forced into a living unit who have no real interest in the program can interfere with the learning expe-rience of other students who are interested in what the program has to offer.

Conventional RHs without specialized housing programs may be the best option for some students. Housing and residence life programs should provide students with choices in the same way they are given options about which classes to take to meet degree requirements. One way to think about the special educational programs offered in RHs is to see them as academic experiences or learning seminars. Some students want to engage in these specialized experiences and others do not; the choice should belong to the students and not to the institutions. The one exception to this general policy of choice is living in RHs during the first year. In the same way that many universities require students to take a set of foundational courses, the RH experience in the first year helps students build a foundation for success throughout college.

### Traditional-Age Transfer Students Should Live in RHs for at Least One Year When Possible

Many transfer students struggle with finding ways to connect with the student community and feel that they missed part of the college experience. One way to integrate them more fully into the campus community is to connect them with other students through the peer environment of the RHs. The experience aids in making connections to other students and helps them acquire some of the knowledge other students have gained about navigating the institutional environment. Financial and age-related considerations should be used to make exceptions when merited by students' individual circumstances.

### Special Educational Housing Programs Should Be Regularly Assessed and Abolished When They Have Fulfilled Their Purpose

Specialized educational housing programs often attract small numbers of students unless students are required to participate as extensions of broader educational experiences, such as a first-year seminar, engineering, or honors programs. The programs are often expensive to operate, are time-consuming, and may not be worth the time and effort to maintain. Programs of this type have lifespans. Too many innovative programs continue beyond their useful lives because they are not assessed or because the political price of abolishing them is too onerous. Clearly articulated criterion and discussions with the programs' stakeholders should guide yearly reviews.

**Institutions Need Criteria to Establish Programs, Abolish Programs, and Create New Living Environments**

The logistics of trying to run dozens of educational housing programs with a finite amount of RH rooms while trying to meet student demand for housing is difficult. Offering dozens of special housing programs is a nice option, but only if they do not force institutions to hold vacancies in the hope that students will fill them. Regardless of the criteria established, the process should be clearly articulated and be part of an overall plan for how the institution intends to balance special programs, conventional RHs, apartment-style living, and other kinds of living arrangements as housing options for students.

## Concluding Thoughts

What residence life educators should take away from this discussion is that special housing programs have a beneficial influence on students. The effect of a particular program depends on the interpersonal environment created among students, the level of commitment and involvement of faculty and staff, the quality of facilities, the amount of student engagement, and the quality of students' effort. All of these factors open doorways for students. The next chapter addresses how to select and develop residence life educators and student staff who can help students open these doors.

# 5

# Selecting and Developing Residence Life Staff to Advance Student Learning

Ask any university president what makes a university great, and the president is likely to tell you that it is the quality of the faculty. Institutional reputations are built on the reputations of faculty. However, what keeps students at a university is the quality of student life, which includes classroom and out-of-classroom experiences (Braxton, Hirschy, & McClendon, 2004; Kuh et al., 2007; Weber, Krylow, & Zhang, 2013). Students experience college as a whole, and all parts of it have roles to play in the success of an institution.

A college campus without faculty is little more than a set of buildings. The same is true of residence halls (RHs). Without residence life staff, RHs are little more than buildings that house students. What differentiates high-quality housing and residence life (HRL) programs from poor-quality programs is the quality of the HRL staff. They are HRL departments' most valuable resources.

RHs can be operated in a way that helps students become successful, make friends, feel connected to the institution, and improve their chances of graduating from college. Alternatively, RHs can be operated in a way that isolates students, frustrates them with institutional overregulation, and makes them eager to leave the RHs and perhaps the institution. What distinguishes these experiences from each other is the quality of the HRL staff and their knowledge, experience, skills, and attitudes.

This chapter is about how to select and develop residence life professional staff and resident assistant (RA) student staff. Although this chapter is about the work of residence life professionals, one should not assume that residence life professionals are more important to the success of HRL programs than are housing and operations professionals. The foundations of successful HRL programs are the effective and efficient management of residence hall facilities and finances. Without well-managed housing resources, residence hall programs could not exist, students would not want to live in the RHs, and institutions would be loath to support them.

## Residence Life Professionals and Other Educators

### Resident Directors

No position in student affairs is more immersed in the daily lives of students than entry-level residence life professionals employed to direct college residence halls (RHs) as resident directors (RDs). The RD position is one of the best ways for student affairs professionals to learn about students and enhance their skills and experience. The RD position is also one of the most challenging positions in student affairs. These residence life professionals live, work, and socialize in the same building 24 hours a day, 7 days a week. They are on call at all times of the day and night for emergencies in their buildings, share call duty for other buildings, and respond to a multitude of high-stress situations such as suicides, drug overdoses, sexual assaults, involuntary psychological commitments, and racial strife. All of that is in addition to helping students with the normal developmental issues undergraduates experience as they grow into adulthood. No matter how well new residence life professionals plan their weeks, any number of student crises can consume their time.

RDs also perform a number of administrative tasks, supervise undergraduate staff, develop staff training programs, advise RH student government, and provide educational programs for students. If that were not enough, most RDs also participate on various housing and residence life (HRL) committees, including resident assistant (RA) selection, RA training, professional staff selection, and orientation.

The live-in responsibilities of the RD position come with a degree of intrusion into the personal lives of these new professionals. For many years, it was common practice to prohibit RDs from sharing their apartments with others unless they were married. Many HRL programs expected RDs to live by the same general policies applied to RH residents. The rationale was that RDs were role models and that their lives in the RHs were on display to students. Some institutions have retained these policies; others have modified them. Living and working in the same location under whatever protocols and policies that institutions deem reasonable for undergraduates place unique lifestyle restrictions on RDs' personal lives that are not expected of other student affairs professionals. Add to this the feeling that many RDs have of never getting away from their jobs and that many RDs have lived in RHs for most of their adult lives, and it is little wonder that the live-in experience is one that many new residence life professionals wish to leave within three to five years.

Not everyone belongs in a residence life position. Some candidates do not have the temperament, patience, or disposition. Part of the challenge of finding the right people for residence life roles is to assess both the intangible qualities necessary to do this work and the objective criteria based on education, experience, skills, and knowledge.

The most common profile for an entry-level HRL professional in 2007 was a person who completed a bachelor's (57.6 percent), lived in an RH with responsibility for the building (83.2 percent), and held the position for two to three years (St. Onge, Ellett, & Nestor,

2008). Approximately 31 percent of the entry-level professionals in 2007 had master's degrees, and 11 percent were pursuing them (St. Onge et al.). Most residence life professionals come to their positions through their work experience as RAs and graduate assistants in the RHs. Belch and Mueller (2003) found that 71 percent of the college student affairs graduate students who intended to pursue careers in HRL had been both RAs and graduate assistants in HRL programs.

Staffing models for HRL programs vary considerably. A common model for large HRL programs is to use some combination of full-time master's-level student affairs professionals as area coordinators and graduate students as RDs. At institutions with smaller HRL programs, a number of staffing models exist, including live-in student affairs professionals with master's degrees who serve as RDs and often perform other duties at the institution. Often HRL programs add area coordinators as experienced professionals who provide supervision and support for graduate RDs or entry-level professionals.

### Faculty

RDs may be the mainstay of successful HRL programs, but they are not the only educators who work to advance student learning in RHs. Faculty are often involved in living and learning centers (LLCs), living units assigned by academic major, and first-year interest groups (FIGs). They also serve on advisory boards, provide occasional programs, and sometimes even live in RHs as faculty in residence.

Student–faculty interaction can have many benefits for students including improving students' academic engagement, persistence, and psychosocial development (Pascarella & Terenzini, 1991, 2005; Tinto, 1993). Kretovics and Nobles (2005) found in a study of first-year RH students that students who perceived faculty members as approachable, respectful, and available for frequent interactions outside the classroom were more likely to report confidence in their academic skills and motivation. Students who were comfortable talking informally with faculty found the student learning process to be more enjoyable and stimulating. Similarly, students who believed that faculty members were uninterested in them and what they learned reported feeling discouraged and apathetic about learning. These findings are consistent with a Gallup (2014) national survey of college graduates that found those whose faculty members took an interest them and their education were more engaged in their work after college and had a greater sense of personal well-being and greater loyalty to their alma mater.

However, finding faculty to spend time with undergraduates in RHs can present a challenge. Einarson and Clarkberg (2004) studied the reasons for faculty participation and nonparticipation in out-of-class interaction with undergraduates. They surveyed faculty at a selective research university and found little support for the explanations that faculty were too busy to interact with undergraduates outside of class or that the institution failed to provide adequate rewards for out-of-class interaction with students. Instead, they found that faculty lacked personal knowledge about opportunities for out-of-class interaction with students and that they had concerns about social skill differences beyond small talk between themselves and undergraduates. Little difference in the amount of undergraduate out-of-class interaction was found among assistant, associate, and full professors; however, nontenure-track faculty were more likely to be engaged in nonresearch-based out-of-class interactions with students. Faculty who taught in the biological sciences were more likely to have out-of-class interaction with undergraduates around research projects, but faculty in humanities and fine and applied arts were more likely to engage in nonresearch-based out-of-class interactions with students.

To better understand the role that academic culture plays in faculty members' decision to participate in out-of-class interactions with undergraduates in RHs, Golde and Pribbenow (2000) interviewed 15 faculty members who participated in residential learning communities for multiple years. Their interviews with the faculty identified a faculty culture that rewarded research productivity, graduate education, and teaching over out-of-class interactions with students. Although these interactions were not dismissed, the academic culture did not encourage them. Faculty that did participate in the residential learning communities did so because of their interest in knowing students better, a belief in the value of interdisciplinary and innovative education, and their personal commitment to the idea of a residential learning community.

Cox and Orehovec (2007) used a multimethod qualitative design that included participant observation, interviews, and focus groups to study student–faculty interaction in an LLC. Analysis of the information they developed led them to a typology that described the level and type of student–faculty interactions. They found that faculty interaction with students was not all or nothing. The interactions could be arranged in a hierarchy of five fluid types of interactions based on the content of the interaction, its importance to students, and the frequency of interaction, which are as follows: (1) disengagement; (2) incidental contact; (3) functional interaction; (4) personal interaction; and (5) mentoring. Unlike Einarson and Clarkberg (2004), who found little support for the notion that faculty out-of-class interactions were limited by intensity of competing time demands and institutional commitments, Cox and Orehovec observed both of these in their qualitative study.

Students are not the only ones who gain from out-of-class student–faculty interaction. Faculty members also benefit. Sriram, Shushok, Perkins, and Scales (2011) interviewed faculty members who lived in RHs as part of a faculty-in-residence program. They found that faculty members had a number of positive experiences with students that produced three learning outcomes for them as faculty members. As a result of living on campus and interacting with students, faculty members reported that they developed as educators, advanced their understanding of teaching and learning, and created a deeper commitment to connecting the in-class and out-of-class learning experience. Golde and Pribbenow (2000) report similar faculty learning in their study, noting that it helped faculty create a sense of place within the campus community and a deeper sense of meaning for their professional work.

### Other Professionals in Residence Halls

Housing professionals who manage the daily operations, assignments, and finances of RHs are essential to the success of education in RHs. Without their work, RHs could not function efficiently and students would be dissatisfied with the quality of the RH experience.

HRL programs frequently include educators and other professionals with special skills to assist students in learning. Among these educators and other professionals are academic advisors, tutors, librarians, information technology professionals, learning specialists, recreation professionals, public health educators, and leadership educators. Sometimes these professionals work across many RHs, and at other times they serve only special populations of students such as students in first-year RHs or LLCs. Often they are supported in their work by students who work with them as peer advisors, tutors, intramural sports coordinators, outdoor trip advisors, peer mentors, and leadership program facilitators. All of these people share the common goal of advancing learning in students, but they approach this goal in different ways.

## The Selection of Housing and Residence Life Professional Staff

When a search begins for a tenure-track assistant professor in any field, universities mount a national search to find the very best person available for that position. They advertise widely, contact graduate programs in the field, interview the best candidates, and select the person who the departmental faculty and the college dean believe can make the greatest contribution to the education of students and the advancement of knowledge in the field. The institution hopes to find a person who is a great educator, researcher, and colleague and is likely to earn tenure.

Hiring a new residence life professional involves no less effort to find the best person available, but usually there is no long-term commitment for employment. Most HRL programs want RDs to live in and operate a RH for three to five years. Where an academic department might conduct one employment search every three or four years, the turnover in residence life positions at large HRL programs usually requires conducting multiple searches every year.

Senior housing officers (SHOs) frequently express concerns about finding adequate numbers of qualified entry-level professionals to meet the continuing demand for RDs as they leave entry-level positions after three to five years (Belch & Mueller, 2003; Jones, 2002; Scheuermann & Ellett, 2007). Belch and Mueller surveyed SHOs and found that they believed there were fewer entry-level applicants and fewer qualified applicants among them. Between 2004 and 2007, the Association for College and University Housing Officers–International (ACUHO-I) conducted several member surveys (Ellett et al., 2008) to learn more about the recruitment and retention of entry-level professionals in the field. Their findings confirmed the perception that there were fewer qualified applicants. However, further analysis showed that the perception of the problem differed by the size of the HRL program. St. Onge, Ellett, and Nestor (2008) found that 28 percent of SHOs at small HRL programs (housing 1,000 or fewer students) and 45 percent of SHOs at large HRL programs (housing more than 1,000 students) agreed or strongly agreed that recruitment of entry-level professionals was a concern on their campuses. While SHOs at smaller programs reported less of a problem recruiting entry-level residence life staff, they reported a greater problem retaining those staff; 38 percent of SHOs at small programs reported that retention was difficult or very difficult on their campuses versus 18 percent of SHOs at large programs. St. Onge et al. (2008) estimated the annual turnover rate for entry-level HRL professionals to be approximately 14 percent, leading them to conclude that the concern about retention of HRL professionals may be overstated.

SHOs also were asked to identify the most important factors in recruiting entry-level staff. In order of importance, they responded that (1) salary and benefits, (2) location, (3) availability of professional development funds, and (4) job responsibilities were the most important factors (St. Onge et al., 2008). When these same respondents were asked to identify the most important factors in successfully retaining entry-level staff, they cited (1) professional development opportunities, (2) salary and benefits, (3) supervisor support, and (4) opportunities for advancement. The SHOs thought that if they could improve these features, they would improve their overall recruitment and retention of entry-level staff.

Belch and Mueller (2003) asked a sample of college student affairs graduate students why they thought new professionals might be reluctant to apply for HRL positions. Of their sample of graduate students, 28 percent intended to enter HRL work, and 72 percent indicated that they were not interested in working in HRL. Graduate students who were *not* interested in HRL work indicated that the quality of life, salary, and the type of work were among the reasons they did not intend to pursue HRL positions. Graduate students who *did* intend to pursue HRL work put salary near the bottom of the reasons for interest in HRL careers. Instead, they were interested in HRL because of the student contact, their past experiences in HRL, their qualifications, and the chance for employment.

To learn what it was about HRL work that differentiated it from other student affairs areas, Collins and Hirt (2006) asked a sample of HRL professionals and other student affairs professionals at four-year institutions to respond to a survey about professional life. Their analysis of the differences between these two groups showed that HRL professionals divided their work lives into institutional and professional lives. Entry-level HRL professionals described their institutional lives in terms of isolation, workloads, and extensive evening and weekend commitments. Compared with other student affairs professionals Collins and Hirt surveyed, HRL professionals were less involved in institutional committees, less connected with faculty, and in less contact with academic administrators. However, HRL professionals were more likely than other student affairs professionals to be involved in professional associations and to participate in professional development workshops, seminars, and conferences. Collins and Hirt observed that their isolation on campus and the greater involvement in professional associations made many HRL professionals tied more closely to HRL colleagues at other institutions than to their institutional student affairs colleagues.

Unlike other new student affairs professionals, many RDs spend much of their workdays alone in RHs, some distance from the center of campus. In contrast, other student affairs professionals usually work as members of teams in traditional office environments. Isolation can create feelings of abandonment, disconnection from peers, and feelings of not being appreciated. When isolation is added to the other stresses of the live-in experience, it seems reasonable that new professionals limit the number of years they work in traditional entry-level RD positions.

## Selection Criteria and Competences

No matter how much training new HRL professionals received or what degrees they hold, there is nothing more important to their success than the personal qualities, judgments, demeanors, human understanding, dedication, and work ethics they bring to their positions. Education can improve individual performance, but it cannot replace personal qualities.

Griffith and Segar (2006) tried to identify the personal qualities of new residence life professionals that make them successful by isolating a set of competencies needed to perform entry-level HRL positions. They began by developing a series of informational surveys to determine what competencies residence life professionals thought were important and followed those surveys with an instrument that asked participants to rate the importance of each of these competencies. Through this process they determined the following competency categories: (1) interpersonal awareness; (2) commitment to profession; (3) social justice awareness; (4) social justice advocacy; (5) serving students; (6) professionalism; and (7) interpersonal awareness. Within each of these categories, they were able to isolate attributes associated with each competency. For example, under the competency "serving students," the associated characteristics included the desire to work with students, ability to connect with students, understanding student development needs, ethical behavior toward students, and critical consciousness. Of these characteristics, study participants rated "ethical behavior toward students" as the most important attribute in this category.

Dunkel and Schelber (1992) also studied competencies associated with successful residence life professionals. To identify the most important competencies, they asked SHOs throughout the United States to rank a set of 49 competencies they identified as critical for entry- and mid-level HRL professionals. The competencies that SHOs ranked as most important were interpersonal communication skills, working cooperatively and effectively with a wide range of individuals, supervising staff, engaging in effective decision making, training staff, crisis management, and selecting staff.

Kretovics and Nobles (2005) surveyed HRL employers at an American College Personnel Association (ACPA) national conference about the qualities they were looking for when hiring entry-level residence life professionals. After the conference, they mailed a questionnaire to the people they surveyed to determine if the qualities they sought in candidates were the same ones they used to hire new professionals; there was a high degree of consistency. Employers hired new residence life professionals based on their relevant assistantship experience while they were graduate students, completion of master's degrees in student affairs, demonstrated helping skills, personal commitment to diversity, and other student affairs-related work while in graduate school. Other criteria rated to be of importance were reputation of the student affairs divisions where candidates worked previously, the academic reputation of the graduate schools where they received their master's degrees, and computer skills. While this study mixed qualification types (e.g., graduate degrees, practicum experiences) with personal qualities (e.g., demonstrated helping skills, personal commitments to diversity), it showed that experienced HRL professionals recognize the value of these attributes in new employees and include them among the criteria they use to hire.

Komives (1991) took a somewhat different approach to studying successful entry-level residence life professionals. She looked at their leadership styles while employed as RDs. She asked both the RDs and their RAs to complete questionnaires about leadership qualities. After comparing responses, she found that the RD leadership qualities most important to RAs were the ability of RDs to clarify objectives, exchange rewards for performance, build confidence and trust, determine individual needs, increase performance to higher levels by setting expectations, and take corrective action when mistakes occurred.

ACPA and NASPA (2010) jointly agreed on 10 competences student affairs professionals should have, and many college student affairs graduate programs use them to guide course learning objectives: (1) advising and helping; (2) assessment, evaluation, and research; (3) equity, diversity, and inclusion; (4) ethical professional practice; (5) history, philosophy, and values; (6) human and organizational resources; (7) law, policy, and governance; (8) leadership; (9) personal foundations; and (10) student learning and development. Under each competency is a set of specific knowledge and skills student affairs professionals should have mastered at basic, intermediate, and advanced levels.

From these studies, reports, and my personal experience, it is possible to group the most desirable selection criteria for new residence life professionals into five categories:

1. *Educational qualifications* based primarily on the completion of graduate degrees in student affairs or closely related fields completed at universities with strong academic reputations.

2. *Practical experience* in HRL, such as graduate RDs or graduate programming advisors at institutions with good HRL reputations.

3. *Skills* that include the ability to select, train, and supervise staff, manage crises, make decisions, work cooperatively with others, and lead others. Also included are interpersonal skills, helping skills, communication skills, and computer skills.

4. *Personal qualities* of successful HRL professionals, such as empathy, trust, self-knowledge, the ethic of caring about students, and the ability to contextualize student needs.

5. *Character traits*, such as professionalism, commitment to doing what is right, commitment to the welfare of others, personal integrity, and commitment to social justice.

Some selection criteria, such as academic qualifications and experience, can be determined objectively, but others, such as interpersonal skills, personal qualities, and attributes, must be inferred from interviews with candidates. This is where HRL experience and knowledge combine to develop professional judgment in interviewing candidates and deciding who to hire. Intangible qualities—sometimes referred to as personality traits or human relations skills—are the sense experiences or impressions HRL professionals discern from their interactions with candidates. Ultimately, successful candidates for entry-level HRL positions are the persons with the most knowledge and experience and who are the best fit with the personality of the hiring institutions.

## Deciding Who to Hire

Because of the turnover in entry-level HRL positions, senior HRL professionals with responsibility for hiring new employees become highly skilled at conducting searches and interviewing candidates. Add to this experience the fact that most of these professionals at one time in their careers also served in less senior HRL roles in which they hired and interviewed dozens of RAs, HRL professionals are usually among the most experienced and insightful interviewers in student affairs.

Gladwell (2005) discussed the adaptive unconscious through which persons are able to rapidly process large amounts of information to develop a sense impression based on their expert knowledge of a particular subject. As an example, he used the ability of professional musicians to sort exceptionally good musicians from good musicians after hearing them play for only one or two minutes. Gladwell referred to this ability as *thin slicing*—the ability to sort out the important attributes from the less important attributes based on extensive experience. This depth of experience manifests itself as a first impression on intuition. What Gladwell discovered is that even when experts cannot immediately articulate why they have the impression they do, their first impressions are more often right than wrong.

Many senior HRL professionals with extensive interviewer experience report that they have a feeling about candidates who would be good fits for their campuses. This judgment is normally based on candidates' attitudes, demeanors, personalities, and levels of openness. It is also based on how candidates answer questions, their approaches to problem-solving, how they talk about their residence life experiences, and why they want to enter the field. All of this information contributes to an impression that helps senior HRL professionals reach judgments about candidates.

In the case of hiring RDs, the challenge is to find the right persons for particular RHs. RHs have personalities just like people do. An RH that is known on campus for the avant-garde character and bohemian lifestyle of its residents would probably be a poor match for an RD who is highly structured and conservative. Therefore, part of the job of senior HRL professionals is not only to find the strongest professionals who care about students but also to match the right person to the right RH. No matter how strong the HRL program, there is no substitute for hiring the right person for the right job.

## Retention of HRL Professionals

Once good people are hired, the next challenge is to keep them. Dissatisfied employees whose talents are underutilized or unappreciated move to find other employment. Turnover among new HRL professionals is common, and probably necessary for the health of the HRL program, but HRL programs do not want to lose good employees too soon. Professional staff recruitment, training, development, orientation, and supervision are expensive and time-consuming. Frequent turnover among professional staff and the lack of continuity that results affect RAs and students and make it difficult for HRL programs to move beyond basic management of the RHs to something more.

Scheuermann and Ellett (2007) reported on the results of a survey that looked at why entry-level HRL professionals left their positions. The reasons included leaving the housing profession, advancement at the institution, quality of life in the position, and the position responsibilities. When the survey participants were asked about quality-of-life issues, they indicated that lack of privacy, burnout, domestic partnership restrictions, apartment sizes, and living where you work were disadvantages. Other studies have shown that feelings of isolation (Collins & Hirt, 2006), role ambiguity (Ward, 1995), and lack of promotion opportunities and salary levels (Davidson, 2012) also contribute to dissatisfaction among entry-level HRL professionals.

Burnout, described by Palmer et al. (2001) as the "depletion of personal motivation, concentration, physical and emotional energy, and other internal resources required for effective performance" (p. 36), has been cited as a reason that new HRL professionals leave their positions. Palmer and colleagues studied RD burnout using an international sample of RDs from the United States, Canada, Australia, New Zealand, and Belgium. They found that RDs in the United States were more likely to experience emotional exhaustion than RDs in other countries, and women were more likely than men to report that feeling. RDs in countries outside of the United States also tended to be older, got more sleep, left their RHs more evenings per week to pursue activities unrelated to their jobs, and were more likely to be male. Palmer et al. discovered that emotional exhaustion was not significantly related to the number of years a person was employed as an RD, whether the RD responsibilities were full-time or part-time, or whether the RD was a student or nonstudent. The number of students in the RH, the size of the HRL program, hours worked, or the public or private affiliation of institutions were not significantly related to burnout. Although this study did not show cause-and-effect relationships, it suggested that individual lifestyle choices, such as getting enough sleep and spending time away from the RH in activities not related to the RD role, may help moderate some of the inherent stress factors in the position.

Kraft (2006) observed that the best employees—those with the most enthusiasm for their jobs—are most likely to burn out. As a response to the workload of their jobs, they work longer hours, reduce sleep, limit recreation time, skip meals, and cancel family commitments. Kraft found that a contributing factor to burnout is the degree of control people have over their jobs. Under normal circumstances, HRL professionals have about as much control over their work lives as other student affairs professionals, but life in RHs is not always normal. Student suicide attempts, drug overdoses, sexual assaults, alcohol intoxication, disruptive student behavior, roommate conflicts, pranks, and RA conflicts with residents are common. Although any one event may be stressful, it is the accumulation of these stressful situations over time that causes emotional exhaustion and disengagement characteristic of burnout.

Freudenberger and North (1985) identified 12 phases in the cycle leading to burnout: a compulsion to prove oneself; working harder; neglecting personal needs; displacement of conflicts; revision of values; denial of emerging problems; withdrawal; obvious behavioral changes; depersonalization; inner emptiness; depression; and burnout syndrome. These phases are not invariant, and some people skip phases while others linger in a phase.

Unlike most entry-level student affairs positions, HRL programs often hire entry-level residence life professionals under a limited term employment contract, usually lasting three to five years. The limitation on years of employment recognizes the quality-of-life issues inherent in the RD position and that RDs fully committed to the position often burn out during that time because of the intensity of the work environment.

The limited term contract for entry-level positions means that new professionals start their positions knowing that they will need to find other employment in a few years. If they intend to stay in the field of student affairs, their options are promotion at their current institutions, employment at other institutions, or possibly graduate school. Opportunities at any particular institution are idiosyncratic to the circumstances on campus at the time a professional is ready to leave. The most reliable opportunities are likely to be student affairs positions at other institutions or possibly advanced graduate work. New professionals are aware that the organizational pyramid narrows quickly after the entry-level experience and that there will be far more applicants than positions available when they are ready to move from their entry-level positions. Lorden (1998) found that as many as 60 percent of all new student affairs professionals leave the field within the first five years after completion of the master's degree. Because HRL professionals account for the largest percentage of new student affairs professionals, it is reasonable to conclude that the rate of attrition from HRL positions is comparable.

Certain best practices may reduce the turnover rate among entry-level HRL professionals. Among those identified in the research (Ellett et al., 2008; St. Onge et al., 2008) are allowing RDs to have pets and domestic partners in the RHs, more collaborative assignments with other student affairs departments, increased professional development opportunities and funding, 12-month contracts (versus 9- or 10-month contracts), and greater flexibility in work schedules. Process issues related to greater involvement in decision making, greater clarity of their roles as entry-level professionals, and stronger mentoring and collegial relationships also contribute to greater satisfaction and retention of entry-level HRL professionals (Davidson, 2012).

However important these factors are, the overriding need is for new residence life professionals to feel supported. Boehman (2006) studied the level of commitment student affairs professionals have to the field at various stages of their careers. He found that among new professionals, organizational support, overall job satisfaction, and minimal organizational politics were strongly associated with commitment to staying at an institution. New professionals who do not feel supported in their positions are more likely to be dissatisfied with their employment situations and leave.

## Professional Staff Development

What most entry-level HRL professionals bring with them to their first full-time professional positions is experience as RAs or as graduate student RDs or both. They usually have completed various forms of training at their previous institutions, and some have attended conferences and workshops about residence life. Although these experiences are good sources of knowledge, what new HRL professionals know varies widely. Often new professionals have no grounding in the basic historical, philosophical, and educational foundations of HRL as a professional field. Without this foundational understanding of the field, new HRL professionals are left to surmise the broader context of their positions, their place within the student affairs division, the context of their roles as educators, and connections to the HRL department and institutional missions. This absence contributes to a sense of role ambiguity and a search for direction.

The way to address the need for additional education, role clarity, and direction is through professional staff development. Ideally, all new entry-level HRL professionals would have individual professional development plans that they developed with a supervisor. The plan should span more than one year and should recognize that at some point within three to five years they will leave. Although all HRL programs have a responsibility for the professional development of their staff members, HRL programs with limited term contracts for new professionals have a special duty to see that new HRL professionals have the knowledge, background, and experiences necessary for them to move to the next level of responsibility in the profession.

Professional staff development programs are built on four pillars. Table 5.1 outlines the goals of these four pillars. The first pillar is the initial orientation and training that usually occurs in the summer before RAs arrive on campus and the academic year begins. This period allows new residence life professionals to settle into their RH apartments, become familiar with professional colleagues, prepare for the arrival of RAs, and learn HRL and institutional procedures and policies as required in their new responsibilities. A number of state and federal laws (see Chapter 10) require universities to maintain records, follow detailed procedures, and report certain types of conduct. To ensure compliance, institutions need to train new personnel. Because residence life professionals work so closely with students, they must have a clear understanding of what laws

**Table 5.1 Professional Staff Development Model**

| Pillar I<br>Orientation and Team<br>Building | Pillar II<br>Opportunities for<br>Development of<br>Tradecraft Skills | Pillar III<br>Support for<br>Continuing Education | Pillar IV<br>Support for Teaching<br>and Scholarship |
|---|---|---|---|
| Goals: | Goals: | Goals: | Goals: |
| 1. Develop collegial relationships with peers and supervisors | 1. Acquire tradecraft skills through experience | 1. Increase and broaden HRL knowledge | 1. Develop expert knowledge in a subject |
| 2. Master institutional HRL policies and procedures for compliance with federal, state laws and policies | 2. Learn from colleagues | 2. Increase and broaden student affairs knowledge | 2. Improve communication skills |
| 3. Master other HRL policies and procedures | 3. Connect with other student affairs professionals at the institution | 3. Learn informal HRL and student affairs knowledge through networking | 3. Contribute to the professional development of others |
| 4. Complete institutional supervisor training and related institutional policies | 4. Develop knowledge of another student affairs department that may be of future career interest | 4. Apply relevant theories and practices in current work | 4. Create knowledge about a subject that contributes to scholarship in the field |
| | 5. Learn how to apply student learning theory to practice | 5. Acquire expertise in a particular subject matter or specialized skill | 5. Create knowledge that informs institutional decision making |
| | 6. Learn how to forge partnerships with faculty | | |

5. Prepare for RA training
6. Prepare for arrival and orientation of students

Examples:
Team-building exercises, policy review sessions, move-in programs for students and parents, RA welcoming activities, policy compliance training

and other academic colleagues

Examples:
RA selection, RA training, professional staff selection, representative to student affairs committee, assessment team, supervisor training, temporary or part-time work in other student affairs offices

6. Acquire specific knowledge about federal and state regulations or laws necessary for work in student affairs

Examples:
Workshops, programs hosted by professional associations, in-service education programs, online courses, academic courses at institution, serving as an officer in a professional association

Examples:
Teaching RA course, teaching first-year seminar, writing for publication, conducting institutional research for use in HRL decision making, writing and implementing a proposal for a new HRL lifestyle program

apply to them and the procedures and policies they need to follow when working with students or supervising others.

New residence life professionals may join an HRL program and be expected to supervise any number of people including under-graduate RAs, graduate assistants, fulltime RDs, clerical and house-keeping staffs, and other educators and professionals that work with students in RHs. Supervision is a skill that is learned through experience, feedback, coaching, and study. Although new profes-sionals may have developed good supervisory skills, universities usually have specific policies concerning ethics, nondiscrimination, harassment, grievances, confidentiality, public records, and personal conduct. Institutions with employee unions may have additional policies about supervision, employee feedback, and record keeping.

The second pillar of professional development is opportunities for development of tradecraft skills in residence life and student affairs. Residence life professionals acquire these skills through experiential learning and coaching from more experienced profes-sionals. Experiences that contribute to tradecraft skills are working as a member of a team to design and run RA selection, RA training, and professional staff recruitment and selection. Participation in policy committees, judicial hearing boards, and committee assign-ments outside of RHs also contributes to these skills because it allows new professionals to learn through their involvement and observe the work of experienced professionals. Some HRL programs allow new professionals to spend a portion of their time working in other student affairs departments, such as student conduct or orientation offices. These experiences help new professionals strengthen skills in other student affairs areas and provide them with exposure to areas that may be of future career interest.

The tradecraft skills learned through these experiences might include how to run a meeting, set an agenda, manage a budget, deal with conflict in a professional setting, give a professional presenta-tion, negotiate an agreement, persuade others, organize a major project, navigate bureaucratic obstacles, organize a team, and learn how to follow as well as how to lead. For example, a second-year RD who assists with recruitment and selection of new professional staff has the opportunity to see hundreds of applicants' resumes, participate in discussions with colleagues about the strengths and weaknesses of candidates, ask employment questions of fellow professionals, and evaluate different types of information. The experience provides opportunities to learn the skills and attributes that are most valued by other HRL professionals.

New RDs also need guidance on how to forge partnerships with faculty and other academic colleagues. Developing these relationships is important to students and their learning. Making an RH a community of learners is not an independent process; it is a collaborative process that requires residence life professionals to connect with other educators and invite them to be partners in helping students learn. Campus cultures are different, and new RDs need direction and skills in how to develop these relationships.

Despite the academic work that most RDs complete before joining HRL programs as residence life professionals, new RDs often need assistance in translating theories about student learning and development into practice. Student learning cannot remain as an abstract concept. Translating student learning concepts into concrete action can be learned not only through professional development programs but also by observing colleagues who have developed this skill and by receiving coaching and guidance from supervisors and other professionals. Regardless of the source, putting student learning concepts into practice is an indispensable skill for an educator in residence life.

The third pillar of professional development is support for continuing education. Law, medicine, psychology, accounting, and many other fields require professionals to maintain current knowledge by accumulating continuing education credits. Although student affairs professionals have no such requirement, as educators they should have a commitment to continuing education. SHOs invest in the education of their residence life professional because they know that it increases opportunities to improve the quality of student learning in RHs.

Multiple learning opportunities exist for residence life professionals. Among these are workshops, professional meetings, academic courses, in-service education, and online educational programs. Attendance at professional association meetings fulfills the goals of providing information and enhancing skills in student affairs areas, but it also serves other important functions. Networking is first among these because it serves as a forum for sharing informal knowledge and experience within the field. As an applied field, much of the knowledge about student affairs work is contained in the stories colleagues tell one another. These professional life experiences are like small case studies. Information sharing among colleagues not only enriches the listener's knowledge base but also allows the person telling the story to review and analyze the situation or event when telling of the story.

Taking advantage of professional development opportunities usually requires financial support. Every new HRL professional should have a professional development budget sufficient to attend at least one national meeting per year. In the same way that SHOs budget for new professionals' salaries and benefits, SHOs should budget for individual employees' continuing education and professional development. A popular way to do this has been to allow HRL staff to request funds based on programs they will present at professional meetings or by the volunteer positions they hold with regional or national professional associations. Such an approach makes support for professional development a reward for those who have the time and interest to develop programs and the good fortune to have their programs accepted at conferences. However, professional development should not be a reward; it should be an expectation. HRL professionals should be able to plan their continuing education and professional development activities knowing that absent unplanned budgetary restrictions, they will have the travel and registration money they need.

The fourth pillar of professional development is support for teaching and scholarship. Two of the best ways to learn a subject in-depth are to teach it and write about it. These experiences require professionals to organize their own thinking about subjects of interest and what they want to tell others about it. Many institutions provide HRL professionals with opportunities to teach RA training courses for academic credit or first-year seminar courses. They are also frequently asked to teach in-service education programs or RA training modules. Another forum for teaching is presentations given at state, regional, and national professional meetings. HRL professionals should be supported in their scholarly efforts because it helps them grow as professionals, increases their knowledge of a subject, provides useful information to other professionals, and also enhances the reputation of the HRL program among other professionals, which can be important when recruiting new professional staff.

Professional development also results from research and assessment projects used for HRL decision making. These research projects offer HRL professionals opportunities to conduct research, analyze results, and present their findings in a technical report written to answer questions of importance. Some of what is learned from these studies may be worthy of publication. SHOs can financially support research efforts by staff members, allow time for preparation of technical reports, and provide forums for staff members to share the results of their research. All of these experiences contribute to the education of new HRL professionals and make them stronger and more informed educators.

## Leadership and Supervision

RDs manage RHs in large part by working with student staff composed of RAs, graduate assistants, and student workers. An RH of 500 students might have 20 RAs, 1 graduate assistant, and more than 20 student workers to operate the main desk and provide night security. On some campuses, RDs have oversight for house-keeping and RH clerical personnel.

Effective supervision of staff in RHs is based on conceptual models of how RH organizations function. Bolman and Deal (2013) studied hundreds of organizations and found four common patterns or frames to describe how organizations function: structural, political, human resource, and symbolic. Organizations that function primarily in the structural frame have highly defined rules and processes. The metaphors Bolman and Deal use for the structural frame are factories and machines. The political frame is organized around advocacy and negotiation and is characterized by competition for power and resources. The metaphor Bolman and Deal use for the political frame is a jungle with shifting power dynamics and competing interests. Neither of these frames offers a good organizational model for RHs.

Some RHs could operate under Bolman and Deal's (2013) symbolic frame, which places emphasis on the roles people play and the mission served by student affairs work in RHs. The metaphors they use to describe the symbolic frame are carnival, temple, or theater. In this organizational frame, people have roles to play and share a commitment or sense of faith that binds the organization through inspiration. A deep commitment to helping students in need could serve as the focus for this unified commitment under an inspirational and a charismatic RD. To the extent that the organization is inspired by passion in what they do, the symbolic frame could operate within a RH.

The best organizational model Bolman and Deal (2013) presents for thinking about managing RHs is the human resource frame, in which organizations exist to serve human needs. Individuals find meaning in the organization and satisfaction in working together. The organization uses the talents and energy of the people to fulfill its mission. The metaphor they use to describe the human resource frame is family. Organizations functioning within this frame exhibit an ethic of caring, value individual contributions, and place an emphasis on team approaches to problem-solving. Collegiality and good fit improve the efficiency and effectiveness of the organization under this frame. Empowerment and servant leadership are commonly associated management styles.

Bolman and Deal's (2013) human resource frame makes the most sense for understanding the organization of an RH. RDs and RAs frequently see their responsibility for the RH as a collective effort with an emphasis on a team approach to addressing student needs. The relationship between RDs and RAs is often one of mentorship and coaching. It is common to find RDs and RAs close in age with similar generational interests. Because RDs spend so much of their time in the RHs away from other student affairs professionals, they frequently develop close relationships with RAs. However, one note of caution is appropriate for Bolman and Deal's frames: it is possible for an individual RH to operate within the human resource frame but to be part of a larger HRL system that uses one of the other frames, such as the structural frame, to manage the RH system as a whole.

RDs are responsible for making sure that RAs fulfill their duties and also succeed as students. Some RAs may enter student affairs work, but most will not. RDs' first responsibility to RAs is to help ensure that their academic work comes before their RA responsibilities. One exception to this is a student crisis that requires the RA to respond for the welfare of a resident. Balancing the RA and student responsibility can be a problem for some students because the RA role is engaging and, at times, all-consuming. Even though this type of RA dedication is admirable, it may undermine the best interests of the RA as a student.

RDs are likely to have different relationships with other student staff members than they have with RAs, perhaps best characterized as employer and employee. Although the relationships may be cordial, other student employees are likely compensated with hourly wages and may or may not live in the RHs in which they are employed.

Sometimes RDs are assisted by graduate students who are preparing to enter the field of student affairs. Although RDs may supervise graduate students who help them manage RHs, this relationship is best described as an apprenticeship in which experienced RDs provide training and guidance to less experienced graduate students.

## The Resident Assistant (RA)

No matter how dedicated the SHO and RD are in making RHs positive educational environments for students, they cannot succeed without the support and dedication of RAs. Good intentions are just that until they are implemented by RAs, who do the frontline work with students in their living units. For most students, RAs are the faces of HRL programs. From the time students check into the RH at the start of the term to the time they check out for summer break, the HRL staff members they are most likely to see most and know best are their RAs.

RAs serve as the eyes and ears of the university, making sure RH students are given the support they need to succeed. RAs are there when students are depressed, when their anxiety levels are high, when loved ones die, and when romantic relationships end. They are asked to be informal counselors, friends, confidants, role models, programmers, administrators, rule enforcers, and conflict mediators. They are the first RH students to arrive in the fall and the last to leave in the spring. RAs learn to balance their academic work with the demands of service as student leaders who could be called upon at any hour of the day or night to respond to the needs of students. Their student experiences are altered by the jobs they do. Some residents will avoid them, and others may harass them with juvenile pranks (Ketchum, 1988; Schuh & Shipton, 1983). They sacrifice their social and recreational time for duty nights, in-service education, RH programs, staff meetings, student crises, documenting student misconduct, and a host of small administrative responsibilities that frequently consume more time than anticipated. Why would any student want this job?

Deluga and Winters (1991) asked 144 RAs employed at eight different universities why they served in the role. Their answers could be grouped into six reasons: desire to counsel and help other students (helping behaviors); interest in building their own resumes to improve future employment or graduate school opportunities (career development); desire to control others (desire for power); desire for self-improvement in areas such as assertiveness (personal growth); need to pay college expenses (financial obligations); and desire to connect with other RAs and make friends (RA cohesiveness).

Deluga and Winters (1991) also explored how the reasons RAs wanted the job related to their satisfaction and interpersonal stress after they became RAs. They found that students who became RAs because of the desire for power, financial obligations, career development goals, or for personal growth were significantly less satisfied with the RA job and had higher levels of interpersonal stress than students who became RAs to engage in helping behaviors or for RA cohesiveness. The students who became RAs out of a desire to control others experienced more stress and were less satisfied, likely because of interpersonal conflict they experienced with RH residents and the lack of support they found among supervisors. Frustrated that their efforts to control others met resistance, dissatisfaction and interpersonal stress seemed likely. Similarly, RAs who became RAs to pay for college were likely to find that the demands on their time outweighed the monetary rewards. However, students who became RAs to help others or to make friends and work as team members found their intentions fulfilled and were happy with their positions.

## RA Selection

The most satisfied RAs are those who are interested in helping others and want to be team members. This is consistent with other leadership research (Grant, 2013) showing that leaders who focus on giving to others without expectations of receiving something in return perform better than those who focus on taking something for themselves. Also, leaders who matched giving with taking quid pro quo fell between leaders who give without expectation and leaders who seek personal gain in terms of effectiveness.

Posner and Brodsky (1993) studied RA effectiveness with a modified version of the Kouzes-Posner Leadership Practices Inventory to assess RAs' leadership characteristics. The researchers asked the RAs' supervisors and residents to rate the RAs' effectiveness and then had the RAs rate their own effectiveness. A comparison of the results showed that the frequent use of the following five leadership practices resulted in the highest RA effectiveness ratings by the RAs of their own performance and by their residents: challenging the process; inspiring a shared vision; enabling others to act; modeling the way; and encouraging the heart. Supervisors' evaluations of RAs' effectiveness were similar, but the RAs they rated as most effective were those who most frequently engaged in enabling, modeling, and encouraging—all of which are helping behaviors. Posner and Brodsky believed that these three leadership qualities might distinguish the most effective RAs.

Wetzel (1991) used the Tennessee Self-concept Scale—a standardized assessment of self-concept—to determine the relationship between RAs' positive self-concept and effectiveness. He found that RAs rated as most effective reported more positive feelings about their own self-worth, abilities to be open and honest about their feelings, personal adequacy, and understandings of themselves than RAs who were rated as ineffective.

Similarly, Fedorovich, Boyle, and Hare (1994) discovered that students who scored higher on assessments of emotional awareness and acceptance were more likely to be selected as RAs than students with lower scores. The characteristics associated with effective RAs that emerged from Fedorovich et al.'s research included emotional maturity, positive self-concept, motivation to help others, preference to be a giver rather than a taker, maintenance of open and honest relationships, and desire to be a team member. The researchers also found strong correlations between RA selection and participation in physical exercise, good nutrition habits, better physical self-care, overall healthy lifestyles, and higher grade point averages. Although not necessarily related to effectiveness or success as an RA, this suggests that physical fitness, overall wellness, and intelligence may enter into the decision to hire one student over another as an RA. These behaviors may be highly correlated with physical attractiveness, a factor known to influence hiring decisions (Hosoda, Stone-Romero, & Coats, 2003). However, there is no evidence that these criteria have anything to do with being a successful RA other than perhaps to indicate self-discipline and could be correlated with positive self-concept.

The RA selection process varies among campuses. The most successful of these processes begins with a strong recruitment effort that includes approaching students who current RAs and HRL professionals believe have the qualities necessary to become successful RAs. This referral process is an important way to recruit RAs, but staff referrals should be used to augment the applicant pool and not to replace an open system based on how students perform in interviews and others forms of applicant evaluation.

The selection process is an opportunity to teach and should be conducted in a way that fosters learning. Both the students selected to become RAs and those who are not selected should leave the process feeling like they learned something through the selection process and that the process was fair. The RA selection process usually includes individual and group interviews, small group discussion or decision-making exercises, and assessment of objective criteria, such as grade point averages, review of past conduct violations, involvement in student leadership activities, and personal statements. Some institutions also include recommendations and construct role-playing scenarios to assess human relations skills.

# RA Training

Selecting great students to become RAs goes a long way to ensuring a successful program, but RAs still need to acquire the knowledge and skills necessary to do their jobs effectively. RA training programs are about sharing information students need to perform RA duties, helping them turn knowledge into skills, and building on the talents and personal qualities they bring to their positions. Training needs to help RAs build confidence in their abilities, work as team members, develop skills, and improve their judgment and decision making. RA training is also about bringing RAs into the HRL community as partners in the educational process and building a sense of teamwork between RDs and RAs. Interaction with professional staff should connect RAs to the core mission of the HRL program and convey institutional commitment to advancing the success of students through the experience of living in RHs.

RA education programs frequently have four phases. The first phase consists of orientation and initial training for first-year RAs that usually begins in the spring, shortly after they are selected for the position. The second phase of training starts in the summer, a week or two before the start of the fall term. This phase extends training started in the spring semester for first-year RAs and is focused on team building among RH staffs, reviewing procedures and processes, setting schedules, introducing RAs to people in offices that support students, and preparing RHs for the arrival of students. The third phase of training is an RA class offered in the spring term after selection or during the fall term, or sometimes the course is divided between the spring and fall terms. The training is frequently offered as a course for academic credit (Bowman & Bowman, 1995a) and is usually taught by HRL professionals. Instruction in the course provides the knowledge base for under-standing the student experience and serves as a vehicle to develop the skills and knowledge for RAs to address the needs and interests of students with whom they work.

The fourth phase of RA training is in-service education that occurs throughout the academic year and includes RAs at all levels of experience. This training extends the basic information RAs receive in the RA class and provides the institution with the opportunity to familiarize RAs with policy changes and improve RA knowledge and skills. In-service education also includes workshops and conferences frequently offered to RAs through membership associations and by universities that hold RA conferences. These activities also build community among RAs across an institution.

One way to approach RA training is to consider the types of issues RAs are most likely to encounter in their roles and to design training to address those issues. This was the approach that Shipton and Schuh (1982) considered when they studied the types of counseling problems RAs encountered. They found that the most common problems included roommate conflicts, physical confrontations, sexual harassment, rape, alcohol abuse, normal developmental issues, racial issues, abortions, academic problems, health-related crises, and homesickness. They later confirmed these findings (Schuh, Shipton, & Edman, 1986) and grouped the problems into three categories: remedial, preventive, and developmental. They found that male RAs with male residents encountered more remedial problems, such as alcohol abuse, while female RAs with female residents encountered more preventive issues, such as homesickness. Bowman and Bowman (1995b) studied the frequency of these same counseling issues among RAs at eight universities and found similar results.

Student affairs professionals with experience in HRL have considered student concerns, the needs of RAs, and the educational mission of HRL programs to develop areas of training for RAs. Winston, Ullom, and Werring's (1984) recommendation was for training to ensure that RAs understand the RA position as a peer helper and other roles and responsibilities, goals and philosophy of the housing program, the concept of role modeling, student development theory with an emphasis on how it applies to the RA, interpersonal and human relations skills, active listener skills, values clarification concerning attitudes toward underrepresented groups, needs assessment techniques and goal-setting strategies, basic study skills, knowledge of campus and community agencies, and referral techniques and other strategies. I (Blimling, 2010) identified 23 training areas, including peer counseling; race, culture, and sexual orientation; student behavior problems; mediation; suicide intervention; alcohol abuse; sexuality; educational programming; and community development. Other educators have suggested similar areas for RA training (Ender & Newton, 2000; Ender, Newton, & Caple, 1996).

Bowman and Bowman (1995a) surveyed ACUHO-I members about what they taught in RA training courses. The top four content areas were racism/diversity, peer helping/counseling skills, community development strategies, and student development theory. The authors also found that the three primary goals of these courses were skill development, knowledge of RA roles and responsibilities, and knowledge of subject-specific content (such as suicide prevention).

Institutions use a variety of ways to teach RAs. In addition to lectures and discussion, RA training frequently includes case studies, role playing, group problem-solving, and team-building exercises. Some institutions incorporate overnight camping or field trips or use team-building courses, such as a high ropes course, to strengthen relationships among RH staffs. Research on the effectiveness of RA training programs shows that training increases both knowledge and skills in RAs (Murray, Snider, & Midkiff, 1999; St. Onge et al., 2003; Twale & Muse, 1996).

Some universities have considered competency-based RA training programs. Part of the interest in this approach is driven by institutional accountability measures focused on what students know rather than on what they have been taught. Regardless of the reasons, competency-based RA education programs operationalize skills by establishing specific measurable criteria. The practical implication of this approach is that well-trained RAs should be able to help more students, therefore freeing time for residence life professionals to devote to students with the greatest needs.

Table 5.2 shows a competency-based RA education model built on the previously cited material and my knowledge of the training needs of RAs. The focus of the model is on developing RAs' skills, knowledge, and abilities to promote student learning, to ensure student welfare, and to help students advance their personal and academic interests. RAs need helping, crisis management, conflict resolution, multicultural, administrative, resource, problem-solving, leadership, educational, relationship, technology, and student skills to perform their responsibilities.

**Table 5.2  Skill-Based Educational Competencies for RAs**

**Helping Skills**

Description:   RAs must have helping skills sufficient to recognize students in need of assistance and connect those students to professionals who can help them. They also need helping skills sufficient to provide emotional support to students with less severe emotional challenges and those struggling with the routine stresses of college life.

Knowledge of basic helping skills
Ability to listening effectively
Ability to establish rapport with other students and gain their confidence
Ability to refer students for additional help
Ability to empathize
Ability to maintain confidentiality
Intervention skills
Ability to recognize students in need of professional counseling services
Ability to recognize the signs in students who may be contemplating suicide and know how to intervene to get them help

(*continued*)

**Table 5.2**  (*Continued*)

Ability to recognize the signs of students with substance abuse problems and know how to intervene to get them to help

Ability to recognize the signs of students with destructive eating disorders and know how to intervene to get them help

Ability to recognize the signs of students with emotional distress, depression, or traumatic stress and know how to intervene to get them help

Ability to recognize the signs of students in relationship violence and sexual assault and know how to get them help

**Crisis Management Skills**

Description:  Although most RAs never experience a major crisis, they must have the knowledge and training to respond appropriately when a student is in crisis or there is a threat to the safety of residents.

Knowledge of correct emergency procedures to ensure student safety

Ability to follow established emergency procedures

Ability to seek assistance and not act autonomously

Ability to maintain calm during crises

Ability to take control in crises

Ability to compel compliance of peers during a crisis

Ability to be assertive

Knowledge of how to respond to incidents of relationship violence, sexual assault, suicidal ideation, criminal behavior, and other acts of violence or dangerous behavior

**Conflict Resolution Skills**

Description:  Through discussion, patience, and time, the RA can resolve most conflict between students. Some conflicts require the intervention of student affairs professionals with more training and skills. Conflicts resulting from students' refusal to follow institutional policies require an educational intervention that can sometimes be addressed by the RA but at other times require the educational intervention of student affairs professionals who can ensure uniform application of policy, fair treatment, appropriate record keeping, and the opportunity to change the behavior in question.

Knowledge of roommate conflict resolution and room change policies

Conflict mediation skills

Knowledge of student conduct policies

Ability to articulate institutional policies and the reasons for them

Ability to confront peers about their behaviors

Ability to refer a peer to the resident director or other student affairs professional for a violation of institutional policies when necessary

**Multicultural Skills**

Description:  RAs have responsibility for diverse groups of students, and students have the right to be free of mistreatment or negative bias based on race, gender, sexual orientation, ethnicity, religion, culture, age, or physical ability. RAs have a responsibility to treat all students fairly and show every student the same courtesy and friendship. When RAs observe behavior of residents that is disrespectful, it is their responsibility to address it.

Knowledge of race, gender, ethnicity, sexual orientation, religious, and cultural issues of diversity and identity among college students

Understanding of cultural, religious, gender, sexual orientation, racial, physical ability, and social class differences and how those difference may influence the life experiences of college students

Understanding of how gender, race, culture, sexual orientation, and related factors influence identity development in traditional-aged college students

Understanding of one's own perceptions and misperceptions about people whose backgrounds are different from one's own

*(continued)*

**Table 5.2**  (*Continued*)

        Ability to engage other students as peers, form friendships, and gain trust regardless of differences.

        Ability and skill in confronting other students' statements or behaviors based on ignorance or prejudice.

        Ability to talk openly about race, gender, sexual orientation, cultural differences, and related areas without offending others

        Ability to engage students from different multicultural backgrounds fairly by not showing favoritism or bias

**Administrative Skills**

Description:  RAs help manage the administrative tasks necessary to operate a residence hall. These duties require RAs to have good administrative skills.

        Ability to manage and follow through on administrative duties

        Ability to meet deadlines

        Knowledge of how to write reports and document student behavior difficulties

        Ability to maintain accurate records

        Ability to explain administrative procedures and process to students and gain their compliance

**Resource Skills**

Description:  RAs help students navigate institutional offices, policies, and procedures. They are among the first people students seek out to answer questions about the institution, to get help in using an institutional database system, or to discuss where and how to get assistance at the institution.

        Knowledge of institutional support services (e.g., financial aid, counseling services, emergency loans, writing labs, tutoring services, health services)

        Knowledge of academic calendar and dates for various processes (e.g., drop/add dates, last date to withdraw from class without a grade)

        Knowledge of institutional refund policies and procedures

Knowledge of HRL policies and the reason for those
    policies
Knowledge of institutional student conduct code and
    procedures under that code
Knowledge of institutional policy on confidentiality of
    student records and parental notification
Knowledge of institutional grievance procedures (e.g.,
    sexual harassment, grade appeal)
Knowledge of how to use online registration system
Knowledge about recreation programs and starting
    intramural teams
Knowledge about how to join student clubs and
    organizations
Knowledge of basic dining services policies
Student knowledge (e.g., how to navigate campus bus
    system, setting up class schedule to have enough time
    between classes)
Knowledge of where to go on campus to get questions
    answered

**Problem Solving Skills**

Description:  RAs are one of several sources students use when trying to
    resolve personal, financial, academic, or family problems.
    Students benefit from the perspective of the RA who has
    knowledge of institutional resources and a systematic
    way to analyze the problem.

Knowledge of problem-solving techniques
Ability to engage students in thinking about problems from
    multiple perspectives
Ability to help generate strategies to resolve problems
Willingness to engage with students
Willingness to include others in helping to advocate for
    students when appropriate
Ability to help students not overreact to problems
Ability to recognize when a student's problem needs the
    assistance of the resident director or another student
    affairs professional

*(continued)*

**Table 5.2** (*Continued*)

**Leadership Skills**

Description:  RAs should exhibit the leadership qualities and skills that inspire students and put the interests of residents and the HRL program ahead of their own self-interests.

Understanding of mission of HRL program and the role of RAs

Understanding of the duties, responsibilities, and limitations of RA authority

Ability to lead a team

Ability to take charge when circumstances require it

Ability to inspire a shared vision

Ability to build commitment to community through consensus

Ability to empower others to act

Ability to express passion about interests and ideas

Ability to engage others through modeling behavior

Ability to give without expecting to receive

Ability to put the needs of others before self-interests

**Educational Skills**

Description:  RAs educate other students by leading programs, organizing group activities, developing community in their living units, connecting students with other educational activities, stimulating discussions among students about academic and nonacademic topics, and helping to create opportunities for students to interact and learn from one another.

Knowledge of programming resources of interest to students

Knowledge about the purposes of programming

Skill in implementing a programming model

Ability to involve and motivate others

Ability to create a sense of community among residents

Ability to work as a member of a team on a project

Ability to organize and take responsibility for a program

Teaching skills

Ability to follow-through on projects and attend to details

Ability to role model positive behavior in compliance with institutional policies

## Relationship Skills

Description:   RAs need to have good people skills, enjoy personal interaction, and convey a sense of warmth and approachability.

Understanding of self in relationship to others

Emotional maturity

Ability to interact with students from many backgrounds

Personal warmth, friendliness, and approachability

Ethic of caring

Ability to interact in a mature, friendly, and engaging manner with parents and families

Ability to role model positive behaviors for other students

Knowledge about relationships, including motivation, sexuality, and issues of stages of physical and psychological maturity

Understanding of common adjustment issues in college students

## Technology Skills

Description:   RAs need to be able to communicate with other students using contemporary electronic forms of communication and be sufficiently knowledgeable about current technology in order to provide basic help to students or know how to get them the help they need.

Ability to use multiple forms of social media (e.g., Facebook, Twitter)

Ability to use basic computer word processing and presentation software

Ability to navigate institutional online programs (e.g., housing assignment systems, library access, preregistration, student portals, academic advising systems, course management systems) and demonstrate these programs to other students

Knowledge of how to solve basic internet connection problems, knowledge about institutional technology

(*continued*)

**Table 5.2** (*Continued*)

support systems, and knowledge of students in the
residence hall who are known to be good at technology

Knowledge of what information is contained on the HRL
website and how to navigate it

Reliability in reading and responding to email messages and
other forms of electronic communication

Knowledge of appropriate etiquette in electronic
communication and the appropriateness of certain types
of communication

**Student Skills**

Description:  The RA's first responsibility is to be a student. HRL
programs have an ethical responsibility to make sure that
the responsibilities of the RA position do not hinder
students from completing academic work and graduating.

Knowledge and skill in how to study and take tests

Time management skills and ability to set limits on
commitments

Commitment to academic integrity

Skill in setting realistic class schedules

Ability to balance RA and academic responsibilities with
recreational and social interests

Ability to model positive study habits for other students

Other competency-based models exist. Baker (2004) suggested the following six competences for RAs serving in residential colleges and LLCs: (1) links hall/community programs and activities to the learning community's mission, materials, curriculum, theme, and classes; (2) establishes a sense of community among students; (3) provides students with opportunities to interact with faculty; (4) actively motivates and encourages students' academic success; (5) connects students with academic resources on campus; and (6) communicates and collaborates with learning center faculty and staff.

## What Works, What Doesn't, and Why

SHOs have three levels of responsibility. The first is the effective and efficient management of the HRL operation. Without this, an HRL program cannot succeed. RHs are capital assets that generate revenue. Without attractive, well-maintained, and safe buildings, students will not want to live on campus and students who are required to live in RHs will not want to return. More importantly, students' dissatisfaction with the quality of their living environments affects their overall satisfaction with their RH, the campus environment, and their student learning.

The second major responsibility of SHOs is to select personnel who help students navigate the inevitable mishaps and normal developmental issues of late adolescence. Just like institutions invest in selecting the best faculty and supporting them as they develop professionally, SHOs must do the same with HRL staff members. The quality of student learning in RHs is better when there are qualified and committed educators working with students. A highly skilled professional HRL staff is also pragmatic. Qualified people with good judgment and clear understandings of how to respond to students can make the difference between minor roommate squabbles and major conflicts in RHs. The RDs who have the skills and experience to understand when students need help, know how to intervene at the right times for the right reasons, can spot students with problems before they become crises, and can respond appropriately to emergencies can save an institution thousands of hours of administrative time and possibly avert tragedies. The presence of great HRL staff members does not prevent crises, but having experienced and knowledgeable people respond almost always makes situations better rather than worse.

However good the professional HRL staff members are, they cannot do their jobs without the support of well-trained RAs. These students are the backbone of any HRL program. The selection and training of these students are no less important than finding the right residence life professionals to lead student learning in the RHs. Both entry-level residence life professionals and RAs require training. New professionals usually have academic backgrounds in college student affairs and experience working in residence halls. However, few have taken courses in housing and residence life, and most have never held full-time professional positions. They need continued professional development to remain connected to the profession and the work of other HRL professionals. Teaching RAs is part of the educational mission of HRL programs because it advances the welfare and learning of residents and also, just as important, helps the RAs as individuals.

The third responsibility of SHOs is as educators. Most SHOs have limited contact with students. They influence student learning by working through others. Their abilities to guide, mentor, and supervise other HRL professionals affect the retention and recruitment of professional staff, which in turn influence the selection and supervision of RAs. Educational leadership of HRL programs advances student learning by giving students what they need to succeed, supporting students in their growth toward maturity, and empowering others to act benevolently for the welfare of students.

# 6

# How Residential Environments Influence Student Learning

One of the most powerful influences on student behavior in college is the residence hall (RH) experience. Although students do not usually select colleges based on the RHs, the experiences they have in RHs contribute significantly to what they learn, the friends they meet, their identities, their likelihood of graduating, and their overall satisfaction with college. A variety of RH features—including educational programs, architectural design, administrative policies, campus location, staffing, and social climates—play a role in creating these experiences. These factors have both direct and indirect effects on student satisfaction with the collegiate experience, the development of a sense of community in RHs, the intensity and frequency of interaction among students in RHs, comfort with the physical settings in which they live, and feelings of crowding and territoriality. RHs are places where students make friends, connect with the larger university community, and create memories that become the foundation for meaningful college experiences. Alternatively, RHs can isolate students, diminish their self-esteem, cause unnecessary stress, negatively influence their academic performance, and contribute to decisions to leave an institution.

In this chapter, I discuss how physical and organizational variables in RHs influence students' perceptions and behaviors. Also, I address the organizational/structural climates of RHs, including how staffing patterns and policies influence student behavior. Later I use systemic change theory to explain how to create positive peer cultures and address disruptive student behavior. The chapter concludes with my thoughts about the environmental conditions that work best in maximizing the educational benefits of RHs.

## Influence of the Physical Environment of RHs on Students

Students' satisfaction with RHs is influenced by the physical environment of the building in which they live. Foubert, Tepper, and Morrison (1998) found that students' perceptions of the physical facilities of RHs accounted for 30 percent of the variance in predicting overall resident satisfaction, which was greater than any of the other 100 variables they studied. This finding is consistent with earlier findings by Strange (1991) and Blimling (1993). The importance of the physical design features of a building creates or limits opportunities for student interaction and can offer students a warm homelike atmosphere or one that is cold and alienating.

The importance of the RH physical environment captured the interest of social psychologists in the 1970s and 1980s. They were interested in how the social and physical environments of RHs influenced student behavior and constructed new social science theories about how such environments affected students. The timing was ideal given the uptick in construction of new RHs to accommodate enrollment from the baby boom generation. In addition, restrictive RH policies, such as visitation and curfews for female students, were the subject of heated debate on many college campuses.

Interest in how the physical environments of RHs influence student behavior generated a number of studies during the 1970s and 1980s, but not much research has been published since that time. Although this body of research was conducted with earlier generations of students, many of the RHs on which the research was based are still in use, and there is no reason to believe that the feelings students experienced in those buildings would be different today. Features commonly explored in this early research on the environmental influences of RHs include the effects of social density, environmental arrangement, environmental stimulation, environmental control, environmental coherence, and environmental aesthetic.

## Social Density

Social density is the number of people in a space and the feeling that people have about that number relative to the size of the space. People can feel loneliness in a large space with few people or crowded in a small space with many people. Both of these social density situations can create stress for an individual. The question environmental psychologists wanted to answer about RHs was how building size and the height of the building influenced students' perceptions. Researchers compared high-rise and low-rise RHs and large RHs with smaller RHs and found that students were more dissatisfied in high-rise RHs and large RHs because the size of the building created a perception of greater social density and crowding (Holahan & Wilcox, 1978; Sommer, 1987; Wilcox & Holahan 1976). They also found that social privacy in high-rise RHs was greater on the highest floors compared with the middle or lowest floors (Holahan, Wilcox, & Culler, 1978).

RH configuration can influence students' patterns of interaction in a building, their opportunity to meet other students, and their feeling of isolation and community. To explore the influence of building configuration, a number of early studies focused on corridor length. They all found essentially the same result: students living in RHs with long corridors were less satisfied, expressed greater feelings of crowding, felt more isolated, reported fewer relationships, and had fewer social mechanisms for coping with complex social environments (Baum & Gatchel, 1981; Baum, Mapp, & Davis, 1978; Huang, 1982; Sommer, 1987; Zuckerman, Schmitz, & Yosha,

1977). Long corridors created social climates that were less engaging than those fostered by short corridors and created feelings of isolation and anomie in students. The size and layout of the corridor were alienating and make it more difficult for students to define socially manageable group boundaries. As a result, the physical environment appears too large and students retreat from it rather than engage it.

Another approach to studying the influence of social density in RHs investigated the relationship between it and vandalism. Brown and Devlin (2003) found that after controlling for the number of residents in the building a greater amount of vandalism occurred in large buildings than in smaller ones. They also found that the level of student involvement was less in larger buildings, suggesting a link between level of student disengagement and vandalism.

### Environmental Arrangement

Evans and McCoy (1998) observe that different types of building configuration influence a sense of environmental coherence and control. Both of these functions influence stress and behavior in those environments. Devlin et al. (2008) wanted to understand how different RH configurations influenced students' sense of community and relationships. They compared students who lived in conventional RHs with students who lived in suites and found that those in suites were more satisfied with their living arrangement but had less feeling of community than students in conventional RHs. However, Rodger and Johnson (2005) discovered that students in suite-style housing felt a greater sense of belonging and were more involved than students in conventional RHs.

Brandon, Hirt, and Cameron (2008) compared students living in suite-style RHs with students living in conventional RHs and learned that students in the conventional RHs had significantly more interaction with fellow students than students in the suite-style RHs, suggesting that students in the conventional halls had an easier time meeting other people than did students living in suites. They also found differences in the physical locations in which students interacted with other students. In the conventional RHs, students interacted with other students in their rooms and in public areas of the building. However, almost all of the interactions for suite-style residents occurred within the suites.

Cross, Zimmerman, and O'Grady (2009) were interested in learning if RH building design influenced students' drinking behaviors. They found that students in suite-style halls drank alcohol more often and consumed more alcohol in heavy drinking episodes than do students in conventional RHs. The researchers suggested that part of the reason for the increased rates of drinking in suite-style halls was their design, which provided more privacy and greater opportunities for social interaction in which the situational ethos dictated consuming alcohol as a normal part of routine socializing.

## Environmental Stimulation

Environments contain different amounts and intensity of information that both define how to behave in that environment and influence emotions. People need a balance of stimulation in the environment. Too much stimulation creates stress, and too little creates boredom. Noise, light, bright colors, crowding, visual exposure, and proximity to circulation are environmental stimulants that influence environmental stress (Evans & McCoy, 1998).

Vandewalle et al. (2010) demonstrated that the spectral qualities of light influence emotional brain processing. Light quality can influence work productivity and feelings of stress and anger (Knez, 2000). Students in later adolescence tend to prefer more illumination and more natural lighting (Knez; Wheeler, 1985).

Noise is another environmental stimulant given frequently by students as a source of distraction in RHs (Rogers, 1990; Strange, 1991). Many RHs have enforced quiet hours under the premise that noise impairs cognitive performance. There is ample evidence to suggest that noise is disruptive to certain cognitive tasks (Hiller & Beversdorf, 2006). However, some research (Metha, Shu, &

Cheema, 2012) suggests that certain ambient noise at moderate levels, such as the sounds of a coffee shop, may increase focus and creativity, particularly in people with strong creative abilities. For some students, low ambient noise levels may actually aid them in studying.

Arboleda et al. (2003) found that both students who lived in quiet RHs, which prohibited noise outside of students' rooms, and students who believed that their living unit was too noisy were less involved in their living units. What the researchers learned from this study is that environments that operate at the extremes—too quite or too noisy—discourage student engagement. A residential environment that has some level of noise indicates student interaction and is likely to invite other students to engage the social environment.

### Environmental Control

People have a need to control their environment in a way that addresses their physical and emotional needs. They need to master the spatial syntax, defensible space, privacy, flexibility, and responsiveness of their environment (Evans & McCoy, 1998). Altman (1975, 1976) proposed that, like other animals, humans are predisposed to mark, control, and defend a territory. Territories have both physical and social boundaries that distinguish members who belong from those who do not belong and allows for private behavior in what would otherwise be public space. In two-person RH rooms, students frequently arrange furniture or hang decorations to mark territory and define separate space.

Benfield (2008) studied territorial formation in RHs for honors students. He tracked the development of territorial components, such as perceptions of space and privacy, and the amount of room personalization over an 11-week period in the fall semester. Within the first three weeks of the semester, he found some territorial group bonding, but the greatest gains in territorial cognition took place after prolonged exposure. Once the territorial bonding was established among the group, it became strongly associated with student satisfaction and other social climate variables.

Environmental control also concerns optimum balance in the amount of private time and social time. Altman (1975) described privacy as part of a continuum, ranging from solitude at one end of the continuum to high levels of social interaction at the other end. People's needs for being alone or being with others are based on cultural variables, individual preferences, and other factors. Altman believed that people adjust their levels of engagement with others to achieve their own optimal levels of privacy. Too much solitude can lead to feelings of loneliness, and too much social engagement can lead to feelings of crowding and stress.

Being socially engaged with multiple people for prolonged periods of time causes feeling of crowding that can overwhelm emotional senses and working memory. Although people have varying needs for social and private time, both are needed for psychological health. Periods of private time give people a break from the demands of social encounters and allow them to process their experiences. The negative effects of chronic overcrowding cause psychological distress that manifests itself as stress, microaggression, and depression (Lepore, Evans, & Palsane, 1991). When coupled with other stressors, such as financial concerns and academic pressure, the psychological impact of overcrowding may be underestimated (Lepore et al.).

In conventional RHs where two students share a room on a floor with many other students, the opportunity for social engagement is easy. The challenge is finding privacy, particularly when many students come from homes where they had their own bedrooms and were accustomed to private space to regroup and reenergize. Single rooms might seem like the obvious answer for students seeking privacy, but they do not work well for most first-year students because new students need to engage with other students and become part of the campus peer culture (Pica, Jones, & Caplinger, 2006). Part of the value of conventional RHs is that the building design leads students into frequent contact, which over time helps them form friendships and integrate into the university community.

Some research suggests that American students need more privacy than students from other countries. Kaya and Weber (2003) compared first-year students who lived in two-person RH rooms at Oklahoma State University with students who lived in similar RHs at Bilkent University in Ankara, Turkey. They found that the American students desired more privacy in their rooms than Turkish students, and in both cultures male students had higher needs for privacy than female students.

Results of studies on the effects of overcrowding in RHs are mixed. Early studies found that tripling students in RHs designed for two students had negative repercussions for the students in triples. Compared with students in rooms that were not overassigned, students in triples had lower first-semester academic performance (Glassman et al., 1978; Karlin, Rosen, & Epstein, 1979; Parsons, 1982), were not as happy (Glassman et al.; Karlin et al.), had more mood and adjustment problems (Hughey, 1983; Zuckerman et al., 1977), were more stressed (Aiello, Baum, & Gromley, 1981), and expressed greater feelings of crowding (Hughey, 1983; Ronchi & Sparacino, 1982). However, more recent studies found no significant differences between students in two-person rooms and over-assigned three-person rooms on residential retention (Long & Kujawa, 2012) or mood and stress levels (Clark, Jackson, & Everhart, 2012).

## Environmental Coherences

Not all buildings are easy to navigate. When they lack a sense of coherence and predictability, buildings create user stress. Buildings organized in ways that make it easy to move between spaces create a sense of user competence and certainty. People can feel lost or not in control in a complex environment that is incoherently designed with misaligned pathways, unique room numbering schemes, and undefined spaces. Environmental complexity and the density of space require greater cognitive processing because processing specific features of the space requires more rule-bound forms of cognition (Harvey, 2010). Less complex and smaller spaces are easier to remember and process. When this happens, it creates dissatisfaction and frustration. RHs that lack spatial congruence to include features such as circulation patterns that align with building facades are the types of incongruence in buildings that cause user stress (Evans & McCoy, 1998).

### Environmental Aesthetic

The architectural design of buildings creates a sense of what the building is like. Age, class, race, gender, and even college major can influence how people perceive an architectural style and the cognitive framework they use to process it (Harvey, 2010; Purcell, Peron, & Sanchez, 1998; Simpson, 1996). People often attach adjectives to the way buildings look, such as *stately*, *modern*, or *contemporary*. A building constructed of large open spaces with large expanses of glass and stone floors conveys a different feeling than a building constructed of brick with interior wood-paneled walls, heavy drapes, wood floors, and area rugs. Both may have an appeal but convey different aesthetics. Bennett and Benton (2001) used attribution theory to understand how students perceived architectural style (such as modern or collegiate Gothic). Students were shown photographs of various types of buildings on college campuses and asked to attribute various characteristics to those buildings using a standardized instrument. The results of the study showed that students assigned greater individual success, a superior education, and more stimulating environments to campuses with modern architecture. Students associated modern architecture with public institutions and traditional architecture with private institutions. In general, students perceived buildings that looked new as better and buildings that looked old as not as good.

Another architectural design feature that has appeal for students is enclosed spaces or courtyards. Buildings with common green areas or quadrangles that define closed areas convey senses of protected space, privacy, and group territory that reinforce a sense of community (Proctor, 2008). Spaces that buttress nature have positive effects on increasing feelings of self-worth and attention capacity and reducing stress in students (Hartig, Mang, & Evans, 1991; Harvey, 2010).

In RHs, students are interested in both the aesthetics and functionality. No matter how attractive a building is, students want RHs to have certain features that make them convenient and livable. Argon (2009) found that students wanted new RHs to have air conditioning (99 percent), carpeting (71 percent), classrooms (29 percent), computer access to the library (46 percent), electronic access to buildings (67 percent), electronic access to rooms (25 percent), elevators (67 percent), fitness centers (21 percent), wired internet access (79 percent), wireless internet access (75 percent), kitchens (63 percent), laundries (79 percent), and TV rooms/lounges (79 percent).

Building aesthetics include how well the building is maintained. An attractive RH that is poorly maintained will be viewed by students as less desirable than a well-maintained building. Li et al. (2007) examined the influence of custodial and maintenance services on student satisfaction. Their study revealed that landscape maintenance was associated with student satisfaction but that custodial service was not a significant predictor of overall student satisfaction. The most important factors influencing satisfaction were students' feelings of comfort within their living units, their abilities to know each other within their living units, satisfaction with resident assistants (RAs), and the effectiveness and inclusivity of house governing associations. The fact that the interpersonal environment was more predictive of student satisfaction than custodial and maintenance services is not surprising, particularly when considering that the maintenance on buildings featured in the study was good. Had custodial and maintenance been substandard, students' perceptions of the importance of these services may have been very different.

## Organizational Structure and Function: Staffing and Policies

Both the organizational structure and the policies used to manage RHs have effects on the quality of student life. Policies governing RHs are organized in six categories: (1) health and safety; (2) landlord–tenant; (3) state and federal laws; (4) housing assignments; (5) small-group living; and (6) RH staffing and training. Each of these policy areas influences the social dynamics of RHs. Housing and residence life (HRL) professionals create and implement these policies and relevant organizational structures, including staffing, which in turn influence student life. Together, RH policies and organizational structures help to shape RH environments and students' learning experiences.

### Health and Safety Policies

Today's RHs have highly mechanized technical systems that help ensure fire safety, building security, energy efficiency, Internet access, emergency response, video surveillance, efficient water management, climate control, and access for students with disabilities. These buildings are mechanically sophisticated and need qualified engineers and technicians to maintain them. Even older buildings have been retrofitted with additional fire safety equipment and upgraded to allow access for students with disabilities.

Policies in this category are usually imposed by state building codes and include fire safety equipment (sprinklers, smoke alarms) and rules concerning open candles in rooms, extension cords, automatic door-closing devices, flame-retardant furnishings, fire evacuation procedures, required exits, trash disposal regulations, and elevator use restrictions. These regulations are such routine parts of operating RHs that few administrators consider how they influence students' social interactions.

These policies affect RH social climates in subtle ways. For example, many states have adopted fire code regulations that require room doors leading to hallways to have automatic closing devices, similar to doors in hotels. Prior to the imposition of this regulation, students were encouraged to keep their room doors open when in their rooms so that other students in their units would feel welcome to enter. The open and friendly atmosphere created by open doors helps build community in living units. Although this fire code regulation is unlikely to have an appreciable influence on fire safety in buildings equipped with smoke detectors, sprinklers, fire extinguishers, addressable alarm systems, and flame-retardant carpet, curtains, and furniture, requiring students to keep their room doors closed at all times makes it much more difficult for them to develop open and friendly environments within their living units.

### Landlord–Tenant Policies

Institutions create landlord–tenant policies to ensure the efficient management of RHs. State regulations governing leasing and eviction influence some of these policies, but most are created by institutions. Examples include room rental rates, what students are allowed to have in their rooms (weapons, animals), dates that RHs are closed (vacations, holidays), and other terms specified in housing contracts. Although institutions may have implemented these landlord–tenant policies for good reasons, such as no pets and no guns, state and federal laws may void enforcement of the regulations because of changes in state gun laws or interpretations by federal agencies on use of comfort animals in public housing (National Conference of State Legislatures, 2014b; U.S. Department of Health & Human Services, 2013).

### State and Federal Laws

Institutions enforce state and federal laws in different ways. Some institutions have no-tolerance policies about student misbehavior and actively pursue violators. Administrators report violations to law enforcement agencies, refer violators to institutions' conduct offices, and inform parents and guardians of alcohol or drug violations. Other institutions treat these violations within the context of learning opportunities rather than as issues of accountability. The social climates and staff relationships created under these two sets of enforcement approaches are very different. In the environment characterized by a high level of enforcement and police involvement, students are likely to view residence life staff as rule enforcers and authority figures. Students may feel that social environments of RHs are rigid, harsh, nonsupportive, and alienating. In contrast, RH policies that completely ignore even the most egregious student behavior can lead to an equally dysfunctional social climate for students. Creating the right balance requires professional judgment, experience, and clear educational objectives for administrators who want students to learn through the residential experience.

## Housing Assignment Policies

Universities have adopted many different ways to assign students to RHs. Some involve offering special academic programs and others restrict students from living off-campus or in on-campus apartments for at least the first year. Other housing assignment policies that influence the social dynamics of RHs are roommate matching rules or the housing of nontraditional older students with traditional-age undergraduates.

Housing assignment policies affect RH social climates by controlling students' options to return to the same rooms or apartments for second or third years and by policies that influence which students receive their most and least desired options. Rolling housing assignments that provide students who apply earliest with the most desirable housing usually leave transfer students and other students who apply late with the least desirable housing. To the extent that students admitted last to the university are students whose predicted academic performance is less competitive, housing assignment policies could unintentionally assign the weakest academic students to live in the least desirable RHs. A similar issue exists in differentially priced RHs. If the costs of the housing options vary too widely, students from the lowest income groups could opt for the least expensive housing, the result of which would be to have a high percentage of low-income students housed together in the least expensive RHs and students from the highest income groups housed together in the most expensive RHs. From a social justice perspective, neither of these housing situations is desirable.

Housing assignment policies control where students live in RHs and set in motion the initial elements of RH social climates. Housing assignment policies that regulate how many students are assigned to each room, who can be assigned to a single room, and whether to assign three students to a two-person room have significant effects on students' perceptions of social density, community, crowding, privacy, and satisfaction.

### Small-Group Living Policies

RH policies help students learn to live as a member of a small group. Examples of policies that fall into this category include RH hallway lighting, recycling, kitchen use, frequency of overnight guests, and group use of common space. At one time, policies concerning visitation, curfews, dress codes, and sign-out procedures would have been included, but these rules have all but disappeared from campuses.

Also, some living units schedule study hours or quiet hours as well as community time when students are encouraged to participate in sanctioned floor activities, such as corridor Nerf soccer, Nerf basketball, or similar group interaction games.

### RH Staffing and Training

The education, training, knowledge, and experience of residence life staff guided by the expectations and philosophy of the institution influence the social climate of RHs and the opportunities afforded students to learn through their RH experiences. Just as classroom instructors can teach the same subject in different ways and obtain different results, residence life educators can create very different learning environments in identical RHs. The differences usually reflect teaching styles, experiences, professional judgments, and the personalities and characteristics of the residents.

Different staffing models work for different types of institutions, different-size buildings, and different types of student housing. The general rule of staffing is that the most experienced residence life staff members should direct the most challenging RHs. A 500-bed conventional RH housing for first-year students typically requires a residence life professional with a higher level of knowledge and experience than a 150-bed apartment building housing junior and senior students. Both offer challenges, but the first-year conventional RH will usually present more.

## Systemic Thinking

Systemic thinking is based on general systems theory, which considers behavior within the context of interrelated social, physical, and behavioral systems. Problems are viewed as disruptions in a holistic context, and solutions are approached by analyzing how the system functions as a whole. RHs create social systems defined by features such as the physical design of buildings, organizational cultures, peer cultures, and social climates. Too often, administrators think about student life in RHs by focusing on part of the student experience, such as students' stages of psychosocial development or the need for educational programming, without considering how the environments and social systems influence students as a whole. The compartmentalization of universities contributes to this piecemeal approach.

At one level, RHs have a clear educational purpose, but at another level, they function as a place of disengagement for students from the academic rigors of the classroom, laboratory, and library. RHs are where students go to retreat from the academic demands of college. Although the demarcation between RH living and the formal academic experience has blurred, for most students there remains a distinction between the roles that RHs and academics play in their lives.

Creating a new learning environment starts with students and their expectations, personalities, interests, likes, and dislikes. The challenge for residence life educators is to take these student characteristics and talents and employ the right combination of educational programming, organizational structure, person–environmental interaction theory, and staff resources to build a learning environment. Building this positive social system is not a linear process; it is a systems process. Each part of the social system is connected to other parts of the system. Systemic thinking focuses on the interrelationship of the systems elements to engage students (Bausch, 2001).

Systemic thinking also includes how to use and maintain the physical environment to shape behavior. Consider the ways the physical condition of a building influences how students behave in that environment. A broken window left unattended, in theory, will encourage people to break other windows. Kelling and Wilson (1982) used this example to explain how environments influence criminal behavior. They reasoned that an "unrepaired broken window is a signal that no one cares, and so breaking more windows costs nothing" (pp. 2–3). The broken window theory has two elements: the first is the repair and maintenance of the physical environment, and the second is enforcement. Although the environmental elements of this urban policing theory, namely, a well-maintained physical environment, may translate well into providing a positive educational environment for students, the enforcement part of the theory needs to be adapted to the RH environment. The goals of maintaining order in an urban neighborhood and of providing supportive educational environments in RHs that nurture learning are very different. Unless policing student behavior is the goal of the RH system, the broken windows theory of no-tolerance enforcement is not well adapted to the lives of students in RHs.

Changing or altering a social system is another use of systemic thinking in RHs. Sometimes parts of the residential social system go awry. Individual personalities of residents, the needs of some students to rebel against authority, and mistakes made by RAs and other residence life staff occasionally create social systems that need to be changed.

The best way to change behavior in a social system is to change the system that supports the behavior (Bausch, 2001). A common problem in older RHs is residents who exit the building by the most convenient door and prop it open so that they can return through that door instead of the main entrance. Routine use of these fire exits is a potential safety hazard for building residents because it allows uninvited persons to enter the building. A systemic approach to this problem would be first to install an alarm on the door with a large sign that warns that an alarm will sound when opened. If that does not stop casual use of the exit, the next step would be to install a video camera outside of the door to record anyone using the door and to place a large sign informing people of its use. The next step is to use the video to identify people that violate the policy and to talk with them about their conduct. The use of the door alarm and the video monitor change the physical environment that supports the undesirable behavior by increasing the risk of detection.

Other examples of this systemic approach include installing breakable glass shields to cover fire alarm pull stations to discourage students from pulling alarms as a practical joke; using fire alarm pull stations that spray dye on the hand of the person who pulls the station; adding comfortable chairs to student rooms to stop them from taking lounge furniture into their rooms; increasing outdoor lighting and trimming shrubbery to eliminate hiding places to make outdoor areas appear more active and safer; changing room décor colors to decrease noise levels and activity; dimming RH corridor lights in the evening to discourage rowdy corridor behavior when residents are studying or sleeping; placing restrictors on RH room windows limiting how far a window can be opened to discourage students from throwing objects outdoors and limiting their ability to accidentally or intentionally exit through windows; and adding electronic key access to building entrances, elevators, and room doors to increase building security and students' perceptions of safety. All of these changes use passive modifications to the physical environment in a way that alters behavior in that environment.

Changing the physical environment does not always solve a problem; some problems require a different systemic approach. To change the social dynamics of a group, the group needs to change. Increasing the number of single rooms in a living unit is likely to change the social climate of the unit by reducing the social density. If a small group of students becomes disruptive and has not responded to adult conversations about the group's behavior, finding a way to exert peer pressure on the disruptive student group might work. If that fails to stop the offending behavior, changing the group dynamic by reassigning some or all of the students to other buildings should resolve the problem. Without peer support for the behavior, it usually stops.

Some institutions use group billing for damages as a way to exert peer pressure on students who vandalize public spaces in RHs. However, this approach is usually unsuccessful and results in other problems (Richmond, 1989). Vandalism is expensive, creates a poor behavioral environment, and deprives other students of the use of property. Generally, satisfied students who feel a sense of community and attachment to their living units are less likely to vandalize buildings (Brown & Devlin, 2003; Devlin, 2007). Therefore, one systemic approach to vandalism is to consider various methods of increasing community in RHs. Other systemic approaches might include increasing the number of women residents in a building because women are less likely to damage property and more likely to discourage males from vandalism (Brown & Devlin; DeMore, Fisher, & Baron, 1988; Devlin). Using furniture and other building materials that are less susceptible to damage might also alleviate the problem.

## What Works, What Doesn't, and Why

What students want in an RH is not difficult to discern. They want small manageable environments where they can easily make friends and feel part of a group. They want flexible room furnishings, neutral room colors, and rooms that feel spacious and open. They want large windows overlooking green space and plenty of sunlight. They like new modern buildings in locations convenient to their classes, places to retreat for privacy, clean well-maintained buildings, places to find other students for casual spontaneous interaction, fast wireless Internet access, environmentally friendly buildings, and amenities that make their lives easier.

Similarly, students want housing and residence life policies that are student centered and designed to work for them rather than for the convenience of administrators. They want RH staff who are friendly, trustworthy, and put the interests of residents ahead of their own personal interests. Students would rather live in an RH where the staff exhibit an ethic of caring, helpfulness, and nurturing than in one in which the staff are aloof and are busy worrying about holding students accountable and making sure no rules are broken.

Consider an RH in which the hall director spends most evenings walking through the building late into the night getting to know students; residents are encouraged to keep their room doors open; RAs know each of their residents well; students on each floor have an intramural team, a name for the unit, and a floor mural; policy enforcement is done only when necessary and within the context of helping students understand the rights of others and to learn from their own mistakes; students in living units routinely participate in RH-sponsored activities, such as weekend hiking and camping trips, potluck dinners, and homecoming activities; students know each other well, spend social time with each other, help each other study, and can identify 8–10 close friends in the RH; and students know the names of the housekeeping and maintenance staff and treat them with respect.

Contrast that social environment with an RH in which the hall director only appears to solve problems; students keep their room doors closed at all times; RAs are available to help students only when asked; RAs are frequently away from the RH except when they have duty; students know only a few people in their living units and spend most of their social time away from the RH; programming consists of a series of speakers selected to meet departmental programming requirements with no thought to what students might want to learn; students ignore the housekeeping and maintenance staff; and the building is operated under a no-tolerance policy and all behavioral infractions are referred to the campus police and/or the student conduct office.

One of these two social systems is likely to create a positive educational experience for students. The other one has less of a chance to do so.

HRL professionals seldom have the luxury of starting over with all new RHs and abandoning those buildings from earlier generations. Renovation can solve many design problems with older RHs by creating spaces that help students connect with each other. RHs built in the 1960s and 1970s seem to present the most design challenges. Many of the designs centered around providing the highest number of rooms at the lowest overall cost without much consideration of the influence of social or physical environmental features. Eight-foot ceilings, nonmoveable furniture, long double-loaded corridors, concrete block walls, community bathrooms with gang showers, single-pane window glass, buildings without air conditioning, limited power outlets and electrical systems, no fire suppression equipment, high-rise towers, crowded rooms, bunk beds, small windows, asbestos insulation, steam radiators, linoleum floor tiles, limited public space, and poor lighting were the results. Expectations for privacy, community, and educational programs were not as well understood as they are today, and students' expectations and technology needs were different.

Although some older buildings have utility, they do not always aid in advancing students' educational experiences. Renovating these older buildings with the intention of changing the physical environment is one systemic approach to changing the social dynamics of RHs.

Some design features are easy to implement at little cost, such as painting, lighting, carpet, tile, window treatments, artwork, and furniture. These visual changes make significant differences in the feel of buildings and should result in increased student satisfaction. At a little more cost, lounges can be added or expanded; kitchens added or remodeled; TV monitors installed near elevators for use as digital display of RH and campus events; long corridors partitioned into shorter corridors; drop ceilings replaced where possible with finished sheetrock ceilings; bathrooms renovated to improve privacy and efficient water use; niches and alcoves developed to increase private spaces; central desks can be made to appear open; and outdoor space improved with better landscaping, lighting, patios, recreation areas, green space, and seating areas. At more cost, main lobbies can be renovated to increase circulation; mailrooms relocated or replaced with a key coded locker system to free space for other uses; programming space expanded; coffee shops, exercise areas, student and classroom space, and recycling rooms added; laundry rooms improved; elevators upgraded; air conditioning installed; closets redesigned and improved; and technology, electricity, and related systems upgraded. All of these renovations increase student satisfaction, and some improve community and student engagement.

Of course, at some point renovation costs exceed the cost of new construction. Buildings can outlive their usefulness, and when they do, it is economically more beneficial to replace them rather than renovate them. Indeed, for much of the past decade new RH construction has focused on providing more single student rooms, suites, and apartments (Argon, 2009; Balogh, Grimm, & Hardy, 2005; Eligon, 2013; Jacob, McCall, & Stange, 2013; Martin, 2012). However, information from the 2008 ACHUO-I construction survey (Balogh et al., 2010) shows that there may be a transition away from single rooms and apartments to more traditional double-occupancy rooms in modified traditional halls. Balogh and her colleagues suggest that this shift in the type of housing being constructed may indicate an "interest in building community (double-occupancy rooms and fewer apartments) while at the same time increasing privacy (bathrooms shared by fewer students)" (p. 89).

It is much easier to operate RHs as hotels than as educational facilities. Running them as hotels is mostly about administration and management; running them as RHs is mostly about education and student learning. Students and learning should be at the center of creating social systems in RHs. If they are not, students will still grow, develop, and learn, but not as much as they would otherwise; what they learn may not be what educators want them to learn.

State law or institutional regulations may mandate some policies, but many exist to make the lives of administrators easier even when it makes students' lives more difficult. Writing a policy is a common response to a problem that once occurred or a problem that occurred at another institution. Over time, policies accumulate and become burdens for both students and staff. Every year, HRL professionals should examine their policies and find ways to eliminate those that make students' lives more difficult.

As important as the physical, organizational, and structural environments are to student learning in RHs, they influence only a portion of the social climate in RHs. By far, the most important element is the social environment created by students. How peer groups form and influence students and how students come together to create a sense of community in RHs have a significant influence on the success of the RH experience. This is the subject of the next chapter.

# 7

# How to Shape the Peer Environment in Residence Halls to Advance Student Learning

Much of the conversation among student affairs professionals focuses on student development from a psychological perspective. As important as psychology is to understanding students, it represents only one perspective. An equally important perspective is to understand students as members of social groups. In many ways, the management of college residence halls (RHs) is about working with students as members of peer groups.

The story of helping RH students engage with the college environment is a story about how students make friends, how peer groups are formed, and how networks of peer groups connect within an RH to create a sense of community. "The student's peer group is the single most potent source of influence on growth and development during the undergraduate years" (Astin, 1993, p. 398). It is through the peer environment that new students come to understand the university and engage in campus life outside the classroom.

The first part of this chapter examines the development and influence of peer groups during college for students 18 to 24 years old. The second part of the chapter draws on this information to identify the key elements that form a psychological sense of community in RHs. In the final part of the chapter, I make suggestions about how to create community in RHs.

## College Peer Groups

College is a transition time that invites students to make new friends. It is a time when the influence of parents is declining and before long-term emotional partnerships and career issues occupy individuals' lives. Many students have left their closest high school friends behind and are predisposed to developing new friendships and fitting in with their social environments (Chickering & Reisser, 1993; Way, 2013). RHs provide an ideal place to meet new people and sufficient opportunity to become acquainted. Because students are in the midst of self-discovery and identity development, college friendships take on added meaning and can be among the most memorable and influential relationships people develop in their lives. Students turn to their peers for affirmation and feedback about themselves. Shared experiences and self-disclosure come to form bonds of trust and friendships that have significant influence on students' attitudes, behaviors, sense of belonging, self-worth, and self-knowledge (Chickering & Reisser; Erikson, 1968; Jones & Abes, 2013).

Friendships are the bases of all peer groups, and the formation of these groups in RHs starts when new students arrive for the fall term. However, new relationships can be sustained only if there is frequent contact and meaningful interaction. Social media has made it easier to maintain contact, but having hundreds of friends on Facebook is not the same as face-to-face interaction. Barkhus and Tashiro (2010) looked at electronic socializing through online social networks and the interpersonal social lives of students. The majority of students they studied participated in an online social network, such as Facebook, but they used it primarily to inform friends of their whereabouts and activities and to maintain relationships with student clubs and organizations. Students did not use the online social network to manage relationships with faculty or as a substitute for more meaningful, in-depth communication with their closest friends. They saved those interactions for face-to-face communication—the type of experiences in RHs where students have long periods of uncommitted time to socialize.

College peer groups serve a critical role in how undergraduates experience college in that they affect students' success and influence what they learn about themselves. Although the influence of peer groups diminishes as students mature and become more trusting of their own internal decision making skills, peer groups are near their peak of influence during the first few years of college, when students are most likely to live in RHs. Astin (1993, p. 402) recognized the importance of peer groups during the college years and offered six observations about their importance and functioning:

1. Students tend to become more like their peers.

2. The peer groups having the greatest impact will be those with whom the individual most strongly identifies.

3. The impact of the peer group will be proportional to the extent to which the individual seeks acceptance and approval from that group.

4. The magnitude of any peer group effect will be proportional to the individual's frequency and intensity of affiliation or interaction with that group.

5. Individual members of the peer group who exhibit beliefs and behaviors that are at variance with the peer group norm will be more likely to leave that peer group than will students whose beliefs and behaviors are consistent with peer group norms.

6. Individual peer group members with deviant beliefs or behaviors will be less likely to leave the peer group if they change their beliefs or behaviors in the direction of group norms.

## Peer Groups Formation

Although the foundation of all peer groups is friendship, friendship alone does not define a peer group. For peer groups to form and have power to influence students, several conditions must exist, including frequent contact, homogeneity, peer group size, shared experiences, and similarity of values and beliefs (Newcomb, 1962).

### Frequency of Contact

By assigning students to live together, RHs create peer environments that provide significant periods of unscheduled time during which students engage each other in unstructured interactions based on events most meaningful to them. The design of many conventional RHs facilitates this interaction by minimizing private space and inviting students into public spaces where interaction with others is most likely to occur. Research reviewed in the previous chapter (Baum & Gatchel, 1981; Brown & Devlin, 2003; Cross, Zimmerman, & O'Grady, 2009; Rodger & Johnson, 2005; Sommer, 1987) shows that physical features of a building's design, such as corridor length, room type, room size, number of students in an RH, and building height, influence student behavior.

Research on student room location and friendship formation shows that students who live close to one another are more likely to form friendships and to become roommates in subsequent years than students who live farther apart (Brandon, Hirt, & Cameron, 2008; Cullum & Harton, 2007; Stinebrickner & Stinebrickner, 2006). An ongoing debate in social psychology concerns whether people pick friends based on demographic traits (race, religion, political beliefs) or whether their friendships are based on opportunity for contact (proximity or propinquity). Godley (2008) investigated this question with college students at a small college in the northeastern United States. She found that while demographic traits predict friendship patterns in the first year, propinquity was the strongest determinant of friendship choices over the four years of college.

## Homogeneity

People gravitate to social groups that are most likely to accept them (Harris, 1998; Wright, 1994). Age, race, gender, social status, and religious affiliation are among the characteristics that form the bases for initial interactions and possible friendships. It is not uncommon to find students of the same race or national origin sitting together in a college dining hall at mealtime. This eating arrangement is usually not a sign of racial or ethnic segregation (Tatum, 2003). Instead, students sit together because they share a common bond, including similarities in language, musical interests, religious observance, and social experiences. Although homogeneity is instrumental in the identification of social groups in which students believe they will be accepted, the experience of living in RHs breaks down stereotypes among students from different racial, ethnic, and socioeconomic backgrounds and opens opportunities to form friendships based on common interests (Cullum & Harton, 2007). In many ways, students learn best from students who are different from them (Pascarella & Terenzini, 2005).

Several researchers (Robinson, 1987; Shook & Clay, 2012; Shook & Fazio, 2008; Van Laar et al., 2005) examined the role proximity plays in forming friendships among students who come from different ethnic and cultural backgrounds. This research shows that when students of different racial, ethnic, and cultural backgrounds live together in RHs, the experience breaks down stereotypes and increases the number of friends from diverse backgrounds.

Mark and Harris (2012) investigated interracial roommate relationships from data collected from 195 white first-year students at Stanford University. They found that students assigned a different-race roommate of a given race have more friends of their roommate's race than do students assigned same-race white roommates; however, the students did not develop more different-race friends that were not of their roommate's race.

Tyson (2005) studied roommate racial composition and its effect on the development of interracial friendships among first-year students at Duke University. He found that students from under-represented groups placed in residence halls with fewer students of their own races/ethnicities developed more interracial friendships. Also, students who had interracial roommates developed more interracial friends than students who were assigned roommates of the same race. Students' previous experiences with race also played roles in their abilities to develop interracial friendships. White students who had friends with different racial and ethnic back-grounds before they entered college had higher proportions of interracial friends during the first year of college than students who had few non-white friends.

Antonio (2004) studied interracial friendships at the University of California–Los Angles, a highly diverse campus. He found that the interpersonal environment of peer friendships served as micro-environments in college socialization and mediated the impact of the college environment but that it also isolated students from the general milieu of the campus peer environment. Students from underrepresented groups who had diverse sets of friends benefited through this association by increasing their intellectual self-confidence, educational aspirations, and personal self-confidence (Antonio, 2001, 2004). Although the white students he studied did not show significant changes in these areas, their interaction with students from underrepresented groups helped them by increasing their understanding of these groups. Studies also show that white students who have diverse ethnic, racial, and cultural interactions are likely to increase their overall psychological functioning (Crisp & Turner, 2011).

Bresnahan et al. (2009) conducted two studies in different regions of the United States to investigate how race influenced the resolution of roommate conflicts in mediation processes. They found that white students were more likely to seek intervention from third parties when their roommates were of different races than they were, and they did this more often than students from other racial groups. The race of the RH advisor did not affect the decision to seek third-party intervention in resolving roommate conflicts.

In a three-year longitudinal study at 23 colleges and universities, Pascarella and the other members of the National Study on Student Learning found that diversity experiences in the first year of college had a significant positive effect on critical thinking and appeared to have a greater impact on white students than students from under-represented groups (Pascarella, 2001). Pascarella concluded that "diversity experiences at the beginning of college may positively affect a student's cognitive growth throughout his or her entire college career" (p. 25). He also observed that students benefit from exposure to many forms of diversity including racial, ethnic, cultural, religious, and political diversity.

During late adolescence, group acceptance is particularly important because of the power peer groups hold to affirm, reward, and punish nonconforming behavior. The development of group affiliation and attachment among students during this period has some unique features. For example, emerging adult males can be more competitive with other males as they try to establish dominance or group social position (Ellis et al., 2012; Harris, 1998; Kimmel, 2008; Wright, 1994). Although physical intimidation is involved occasionally, most of the power in group relationships is defined through cleverness, humor, athletic ability, and social skills with females. In recent years, technological adeptness is a way to gain social status within male peer groups (Nasser, 2012; Westcott, 2012).

Although women sometimes exhibit some of these same characteristics, such as competitiveness, they tend to be more supportive of each other and more emotionally invested in each other's success, and their social statuses within groups are based on being cooperative and popular (Santrock, 1987). Intelligence, empathy, verbal skills, self-confidence, social intelligence, personal style, and being a reliable friend are among the more valued traits in female student groups (Casey, Jones, & Hare, 2008; Harris, 1998).

## Peer Group Size

Peer groups come in different sizes and have different levels of influence on students. Degree of influence is inversely proportional to the size of the group with which students identify (Astin, 1993; Newcomb, 1962). Figure 7.1 illustrates five levels of peer influence, ranging from close friends, who have the most influence on students, to the national peer group, which has the least direct influence.

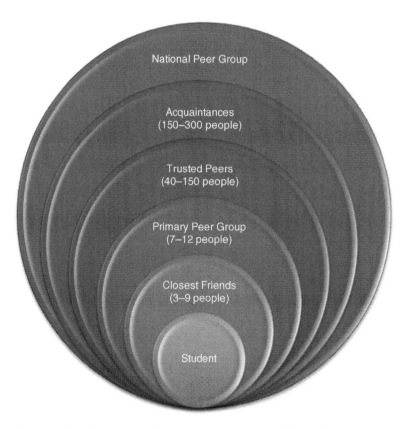

**Figure 7.1**  **Number of Peers and the Level of Their Influence on Students**

## Closest Friends

At the center of influence are students' closest friends. These are students with whom they are likely to have intimate disclosure and to share private thoughts and personal knowledge. Among these trusted peers may be long-term romantic partners and childhood friends. These relationships often extend over long periods, and the history they share serves to deepen the relationships and emotional trust. The number of people in this circle varies, but it is estimated to be between three and five people (Brugha et al., 2005).

Research findings indicate that adolescent males have fewer intimate friendships than adolescent females (Santrock, 1987; Way, 2013). Although the reasons are not clear, the more collaborative interpersonal environments fostered by adolescent women and the more competitive interpersonal environments fostered by adolescent men may explain the difference. Other factors that may discourage greater male intimacy include male adolescent fears around homosexuality, lack of expressed intimacy by male role models, lack of experience with expressing feelings, and substitution of female companionship that provides emotional intimacy not available from male peers (Santrock, 1987; Way, 2013).

## Primary Peer Group

Many studies of group behavior assert that the ideal size for groups of all kinds is between 8 and 12 (Hall, 1976; Karotkin & Paroush, 2003; Miller, 1956). This includes business working groups, committees, athletic teams, military squads, and therapy groups. Students' primary peer groups represent the individuals they see most often, trust with confidential information, and go to for advice and support. There is a reciprocal level of trust, genuine friendship, and comfort with these peers. The primary peer group changes as students mature, leave college, or develop deeper and more intimate relationships with other individuals.

## Trusted Peers

Evolutionary biologist Robin Dunbar (2004, 2010) studied social group formation. Based on extensive anthropological and primate research, Dunbar discovered that the neo-cortex region of the brain (part of the cerebral cortex that controls language, sensory perception, spatial reasoning, and conscious thought) defines the maximum number of relationships a person can manage at one time. He estimated that an individual can manage a maximum of 150 personalized reciprocal relationships. These are relationships with shared histories of trust, respect, and friendship.

## Acquaintances

A much larger group of peers that influence behavior is people students have met, recognize on campus, or with whom they have social media connections. Social media makes it possible for people to have many friends with whom they have casual relationships, but not all of them are trusted peers. These people could be friends of friends or simply people they met at social gatherings. Acquaintances may also be part of reference groups, such as fraternities, sororities, or academic honor societies, with which students identify. The influence of acquaintances is limited to their ability to communicate with a student and others. The effect this has on students' behavior is limited to the importance assigned to the person communicating the opinion.

## National Peer Group

The national peer group influences college students' choices of music, dress, hairstyle, language, and humor. Part of this influence is a function of marketing, which promotes style popularity, and a function of the media promotion of entertainment personalities, including athletes, musical groups, comedians, and movie stars. The national peer group creates a normative environment for college behavior that has its strongest influence in areas such as dress and music. Its influence diminishes as students mature and become more internally directed about their personal choices. Also, college students are a target market for many companies that want to influence their lifelong preferences for name-brand products.

Peers are not the only people with influence on students. Parents and other family members still have influence during college (Doumas et al., 2013; Wetherill & Fromme, 2007). Faculty members also are important in students' decision-making, but their sphere of influence tends to be limited to their areas of scholarly expertise. Milem (1998) found that the effects of faculty on student attitudes were mediated by students' interactions with their peers and confined to behaviors in which faculty and students have the most direct contact. In their review of published research in this area, Pascarella and Terenzini (1991) reached a similar conclusion: they found that student peer groups were at least as influential as—and frequently more influential than—faculty, confirming earlier observations by Newcomb (1962) and Feldman and Newcomb (1969). While most students would not think to seek faculty members' opinions about their clothes, hair length, or taste in music, they rely on faculty to help guide their academic pursuits and frequently process that advice with their peers.

**Shared Experiences**

Students must invest in a peer group through participation to identify with it. The frequency and quality of participation binds a group together; common experiences reinforce bonds and distinguish group members from individuals outside of the group. These shared experiences act as psychological boundaries for inclusion. When the shared experiences contain private information about students' behaviors, it further strengthens peer relationships by adding a layer of confidentiality that reinforces the bonds of trust.

### Similarity of Values and Beliefs

Although age, gender, race, and ethnicity are important aspects of homogeneity, the most powerful peer relationships are those in which students share common values, attitudes, and interests (Newcomb, 1962; Weidman, 1989, 2006). These factors promote consensus rather than conflict in relationships and offer a mutually rewarding and supportive interaction. Peer relationships in which students share the same values and beliefs provide another level of interpersonal intimacy that affirms commonality and closeness. A good example of this is found among students with strongly held religious beliefs who form relationships through their deeply held commitments to a common faith (Magolda & Gross, 2009).

## How Peer Groups Influence Behavior

Peer groups have particularly strong influence during the first two years of college when students focus on external validation, social acceptance, and greater autonomy (Astin, 1993; Milem, 1998). As discussed in Chapter 2, evolutionary psychologists (Ellis et al., 2012; Harris, 1998; Way, 2013; Wright, 1994) believe that adolescent peer groups are important vehicles for learning social skills, testing social status, developing group hierarchy, and supporting greater risk-taking than older members of a community would condone. The three primary ways that peer groups influence behavior are through conformity, socialization, and social status.

### Conformity

People assume that they are more likely to be accepted by a group if they look, act, talk, and behave like other members of that group (Wright, 1994). People find ways to reduce difference by adopting appearance, language, and mannerisms of the dominant group. This happens at many ages and in many environments, whether it is wearing a suit to work because everyone else wears suits or wearing a T-shirt to class because that is what most students wear. Through their interaction with other students and their connections with the adolescent peer environment, students learn the behavioral norms of being in college.

In RHs, the process of conforming to the peer environment starts with new student orientation. One can easily notice differences in appearance among students during this time. The contrast among students from urban, rural, and suburban environments in their dress, language, and hairstyles can be dramatic. However, most of these differences begin to disappear early in the fall term as students conform to the dominant campus culture.

Students are most likely to conform in matters of appearance, music, social opinions, and social/recreational pursuits. They are least likely to conform in areas in which they have deeply held religious or moral beliefs, when meaningful life experiences have taught them differently, or regarding behaviors that put them at personal risk (Brown, 1990; Steinberg, 2009). The areas of conformity represent students' efforts to minimize the differences between themselves and the dominant peer culture so that they blend in with other students and become indistinguishable from their peers. During this phase of their lives, students do not want to stand out or appear different. Most seek social acceptance, not alienation.

Of course, not all students conform; some rebel against adolescent conformity. They fight it by adopting nonconformist behavior evidenced in their outward appearance, such as hairstyle, body piercings, dress, and neck or facial tattoos. These personal appearance statements may indicate any number of choices or interests, including conformity to a particular type of nonconformist lifestyle (which in itself is conformity), struggles with resolving personal identity issues, or rebellion against parents. Or these signs may represent nothing at all and simply reflect having tried something different. Because college campuses usually support more than one peer culture, students may conform to the normative standards of one of these subculture groups and change to another later in their development. Students describe these subcultural groups with names like *hipster, goth, geek, nerd, jock, preppy, farmer, cowboy, tree-hugger, freak, druggie,* and *Greek.* Most of these groups distinguish themselves by outward symbols like clothing, eyewear, hair fashion, Greek letters, tattoos, and musical interests. The desire to conform diminishes as students become less focused on external sources of validation and more trusting of their own judgments.

The situation, person, and topic of discourse influence the social register or language code used by speakers who have access to more than one language code, register, or dialect (Bernstein, 1972; Littlejohn & Smith, 2005). Use of languages or dialects is a way for identity-based groups to affirm their membership, in part by excluding others without access to the same language or dialectic. Peer group relationships can define both the style of speech and the conditions under which it is used. Students might use slang terms to discuss popular music with close friends but use entirely different vocabulary to describe that same music to a college professor. Or a male first-year student might use profanity within his peer group to demonstrate some form of masculine toughness but refrain from using that language when he is with his parents. This process of alternating language codes is known as *code switching* (Bernstein, 1972) and can be conscious or subconscious depending on how the speaker reads social situations, topics, and relationships with others.

## Socialization

Normative behavior in RHs establishes itself through the interplay between individual students' behaviors and expectations established by the intermediate peer environment, with closest friends having the most intense influence. The residential peer group sets the normative environment in RHs through a socialization process that rewards students with positive social reinforcement (e.g., admiration, supportive comments, popularity) and negative feedback (e.g., ridicule, teasing, bullying, confrontation, ostracism, and diminished group social status). Peer approval or disapproval may be transmitted in any number of ways from nonverbal cues, text messages, bullying, social media comments, or verbal communication.

Developmentally, first-year and second-year students are emerging from middle adolescence and place a high degree of value on external sources of validation (Chickering & Reisser, 1993; Erikson, 1968; Jones & Abes, 2013). The more students value external validation, the more likely they are to conform to the normative peer environment. As students come to develop greater autonomy and self-knowledge, they become less reliant on what others think and are more inclined to act independently.

Gender and race also influence the socialization process. Although gender roles are defined during childhood, much of adolescence is devoted to learning the expectations of socially defined adult gender roles and merging those expectations into personal identity (Cobb, 2010; Eliot, 2009; Jones & Abes, 2013; Way, 2013). Gender conformity places pressure on students to adapt to the prevailing normative male or female gender stereotypes. Although there has been greater acceptance of students whose gender identities or sexual orientations deviate from the prevailing adolescent stereotype of masculine or feminine in recent years, students who do not identify as heterosexual and gender specific are frequently alienated from their peers (Kimmel, 2008).

Race and ethnicity play a role in the socialization process because of the expectations defined within those communities (Antonio, 2001). Membership in peer groups defined by race, ethnicity, or cultural background gives students a point of common experience and a reason for interaction. Initial peer interaction within these groups places an emphasis on the commonality that defines the group (Tatum, 2003). Religious traditions may further exert peer pressure on students to conform to certain prescribed behaviors or traditions, such as wearing a hijab (head covering used mostly by Muslim women). Although there is increasing evidence that student peer groups are multiracial and are ethnically diverse, students often perceive much more balkanized campus racial climates, based in part on cultural stereotypes and occasional conflicts (Antonio, 2001).

Figure 7.2 draws from previous research on peer socialization (Astin, 1993; Lacy, 1978; Pascarella, 1984; Weidman, 1989, 2006)

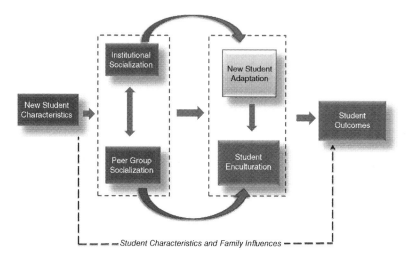

**Figure 7.2    College Socialization Model**

*Notes:* New student characteristics: personality, maturity, past experience, socioeconomic status, career interests, demographic variables, college expectations. Institutional socialization: orientation, first-year programs, residence hall experience, academic advising, faculty/classroom experience, institutional history/traditions. Peer group socialization: residence hall peers, trusted friends, clubs/organizations, classmates, romantic interests, identity group affiliations, reference groups, roommate, social life. New student adaptation: information seeking, relationship building, joining behavior, surveying environment. Student enculturation: adjustment/adaptation, routine, friendships, role clarification, identity development, institutional knowledge, community engagement, social knowledge, collegiate experiences. Student outcomes: identity as a student, values clarification, acceptance, satisfaction, career choices, self-knowledge, self-efficacy, knowledge. Student characteristics and family influences: family expectations, student interests and talents, family financial support, family relationships, student expectations for achievement.

and the author's experience to depict factors that influence socialization of college students. The primary factors begin with students' precollege characteristics that shape their expectations about college. The primary institutional agents of socialization include faculty, student affairs staff, college work environment, and peer group.

Adaptation to the college environment is similar to what people experience when starting a new job: individuals want to learn about the environment, seek information, build relationships, and try to establish their place in the organization. College students go through this same process, but the environment is different, the degree of involvement is greater, and the experience and maturity level of traditional-age students is less than occupational adaptation in the adult years.

Adaptation to the normative peer and institutional environments, identified in Figure 7.2 as *student enculturation*, is the process by which students adjust to the college culture by modifying their behaviors. Changes in routine, new friendships, clarification of institutional and peer expectations, identification with the peer and institutional environments, and an increase in institutional knowledge facilitate the enculturation process. Interactions with peers, parents, faculty, and staff exert what Weidman (1989) described as normative pressure on students to conform to the collegiate environment.

The outcomes associated with the socialization process are complex and vary with individual students' experiences and the particularities of institutional environments (Weidman, 2006). The socialization process facilitates changes in students' attitudes and beliefs and helps students develop senses of identification with their institutions by adopting the identity of *college student*.

The process of socialization also results in greater self-knowledge, clarified career choices, and a sense of self-efficacy about how to operate within the institutional culture. The more students are involved in the college environment, the more influence the environment has on them (Astin, 1984). Students who successfully connect with the college environment tend to be more satisfied with their experiences. Students who do not successfully adapt to the normative institutional environment are more likely to leave the institution (Tinto, 1993).

## Social Status

Social status operates in two spheres. One involves the immediate peer groups with which students most closely identify, and the second is the statuses assigned to social groups, such as fraternities and sororities, which may serve as reference groups for students. Wiseman (2013) studied precollege adolescent male peer culture and identified seven male adolescent archetypes: mastermind (leader); entertainer (social/funny); associate (social point person); conscience (worrier); bouncer (takes the fall for the group); punching bag (mistreated individual); and fly (hovers outside the group). Social status within these groups is part of the high school adolescent peer culture, but some of the associated behaviors follow students into the college environment as first-year students. Kimmel's (2008) study of undergraduate males shows many of these same status-related issues operating within male college groups. College women exhibit fewer status-seeking behaviors, but they are more evident as women seek careers in competitive fields (Kindlon, 2007). Other studies of the college culture (Moffatt, 1989; Nathan, 2005; Seaman, 2005) and research by evolutionary psychologists (Ellis et al., 2012; Harris, 1998; Hawley, 2011; Wright, 1994) lend support for social status differences operating within peer groups.

Some peer groups enjoy higher social statuses and levels of prestige than others. These groups are sometimes referred to as reference groups because they define standards of comparison for students who aspire to gain status through their association and acceptance by the group. Students use reference groups to guide their own behaviors and as baselines against which to judge how they compare. Reference groups might be student athletes, sorority women, resident assistants (RAs) in a building, or outspoken social activists.

Astin (1993) drew a link between students' desires to be accepted by groups and their identification with the idealized concept of those groups. For example, for some students part of the attraction of joining a fraternity or sorority could be social status, popularity, or perceived power.

## Peer Groups and the Social Environment

College peer groups influence students' behaviors and help create social environments that encourage and reward student engagement in college or, conversely, lead students into less productive pursuits. Congruence, environmental press, and territoriality are factors that strengthen peer groups, influence student satisfaction, and affect the social climate of RHs.

### Congruence

The term *congruence* refers to the degree of connectedness between an individual's psychological need for support and affirmation and the social environment in which the person interacts. Holland (1985) identified six types of social environments: realistic, investigative, artistic, social, enterprising, and conventional. Holland found that the more closely a person's personality fit the characteristics of one of the social environments, the happier the person was with the environment and the more that environment reinforced the behaviors associated with it. Therefore, students with high need for creative expression might be most compatible with an artistic environment that values their creative energy and reinforces artistic expression consistent with the characteristic of that environment.

Holland (1985) believed that the degree of compatibility between students' perceptions, values, attitudes, beliefs, and career aspirations and the interpersonal environment in living units was a predictor of how satisfied they will be and the degree to which they will connect with other students. A high degree of incongruence between the social environment and the student is likely to present the highest degree of dissatisfaction, conflict, and polarization. A highly progressive student placed in a peer environment with highly conservative students is unlikely to find the social environment to be a good fit.

Congruence or environmental fit is also a function of the compatibility between students' personalities and social environments. Students' needs can either enhance or detract from their experiences depending on the congruence of their needs with their social environments (Moos, 1987). A student who has a high need for order, organization, and cleanliness may be most comfortable in an environment in which everything is in its proper place, beds are made, and noise distractions are minimal. If the student lives in an environment where others have similar needs for order, the student will likely find the environment compatible with his or her personal needs. In contrast, if a student lives in an environment in which the majority of people are sloppy, careless, loud, and disorderly, this incongruence between personal needs and the environment is likely to place a student under stress and produce dissonance and dissatisfaction.

### Environmental Press

The degree to which a particular environment can be characterized by the behaviors of the residents is the press of that environment (Stern, 1970). A living unit characterized by intense study, carefully observed study hours, and frequent conversations about academic topics could be described as having a strong academic environmental press. In contrast, a living unit composed of students focused on human rights activism might be described as having an environmental press toward social justice. A high degree of congruence between a student's personality and environmental press produces the highest level of satisfaction and is the most growth-producing environment for the student (Holland, 1985; Strange & Banning, 2001). The degree of fit between these two variables affects the social climate and student satisfaction (Moos, 1987).

## Territoriality

Human territorial behavior regulates social interactions, defines group membership, and signals nonmembers that a particular space is occupied (Altman & Chemers, 1980). Most animals mark territory. It gives social clues to warn that the territory is taken, hence avoiding conflicts over resources and mating. Well-defined territories provide security to members and allow them to take ownership of an area (Harris, 1998). Altman and Chemers (1980) identify three types of territory: primary, secondary, and public. In an RH, these types equate to a student's room (primary), the student's living unit (secondary), and the public space in the RH where the student lives (public). Benfield (2008) studied territorial formation in an honors living unit of 110 students assigned to a new RH. The students had not previously met their roommates, and all of the students were assigned to two-person rooms. He tracked changes in territorial behavior over the first 11 weeks of the semester and found that the development of territorial markers took more than 3 weeks to develop. However, once primary territories were formed and social group attachments established, they helped create positive outcomes associated with college satisfaction, successful adjustment, reduced stress, and positive well-being.

Kastenbaum (1984) investigated territorial behavior among roommates and found, as expected, that the more territorial students were the worse their relationships were with their roommates. Good roommate relationships required the ability to share. Men tend to be more territorial than women (Mercer & Benjamin, 1980) and clearly defined social boundaries help to identify territory.

## Developing Residence Hall Community

A common goal of residence life programs is to help students create a sense of community in their living units. The meaning of community may vary, but it generally refers to a psychological attachment and sense of belonging among students who live together. Hillary (1955) reviewed 94 definitions of the term *community*. He consolidated the ideas expressed in these definitions into a single definition: "a group of individuals engaged in communal interaction, possessing common interests and goals, who show concern for and a sensitivity to the needs of others, and are primarily interested in furthering the group's goals over all others" (p. 118).

Developing a sense of community in RHs is important for students because living units are bases of emotional support and are gateways to developing stronger institutional relationships (Berger, 1997). Students who fail to connect with others in their living units often feel isolated and are at increased risk of leaving college (Eshbaugh, 2008; Tinto, 1993). Community is also important because people are social beings and need the support and encouragement of others. Acceptance as community members helps students develop self-esteem and resolve developmental tasks associated with establishing stable identities (Chickering & Reisser, 1993; Jones & Abes, 2013; Moos, 1987). Students who have strong senses of community are more likely to remain in college, to develop trusting relationships with other people, to become more involved in college activities, and to develop lifelong friendships while in college (Astin, 1993; Ledbetter, Griffin, & Sparks, 2007; Tinto, 1993).

McCarthy, Pretty, and Catano (1990) found that students who did not feel a sense of community in their RHs experienced higher levels of emotional and physical exhaustion than students who did. McCluskey-Titus et al. (2002) conducted a multi-institutional study about community development and academic achievement in RHs. They found a strong positive association between having a sense of belonging within a living unit and involvement in social activities. They also found that students who expressed greater senses of belonging in the living units were more likely to report increased intellectual development and better studying behaviors. Students who express greater identification with community also report higher levels of social integration in their living units (Berger, 1997).

In single-gender RHs, men have an easier time establishing community than women. Chiricosta, Work, and Anchors (1996) and Wang et al. (2003) found a stronger sense of community and greater involvement in activities among men in all-male RHs than among women in all-female RHs. The reasons for these findings may be that men need less community support from friends than women do or that men and women have different expectations about the intensity of community experiences (Eshbaugh, 2008).

Conventional RHs with limited privacy, short corridors, and designated group space are environments that support the development of community. Apartment-style buildings, buildings with long corridors, and buildings that do not identify territorial boundaries make it more difficult to develop community. However, limiting privacy does not necessarily lead to greater community among students. Banning (1997) pointed out that "privacy and community are not opposites" (p. 4). Privacy is a function of students' abilities to exercise control over their environments. Constant social interaction is stressful and leads people to withdraw to find solitude.

## Elements Necessary to Establish Community

One of the ways to identify the elements necessary to form community is to examine how organizations with a strong sense of community function. Three college groups that have this are athletic teams, fraternities and sororities, and U.S. military Reserve Officers' Training Corps (ROTC) units. Athletic team members have frequent contact, depend on each other for performance in sporting events, and are united in their commitment to achieve their goals. In addition, athletes' frequent social interaction outside of practice reinforces their commitment to the community-focused experience of team membership.

Fraternities and sororities have some of the same elements. They use membership selection, initiation rituals, social status, and Greek letters to mark their distinctiveness from other groups. There is an unspoken competition among fraternities and among sororities. This competiveness is most evident during rush (recruitment), Greek week activities, intramural activities, and discussions about the relative social statuses of various Greek organizations. More important to the establishment of a Greek community are the communal experiences of these groups. Social events and philanthropic commitments frequently require participation of all members. These events unite members in a common purpose and provide a shared experience. Living and eating in a fraternity or sorority house, participating in weekly chapter meetings and occasional ceremonies, and sharing membership secrets bind members together in what the organizations refer to as brotherhood or sisterhood. However, fraternities and sororities are never as strong as when they perceive that they are under attack by another group or by the university administration. Under these circumstances, fraternity and sorority members develop increased solidarity in support of their organizations.

ROTC units also develop a sense of community. Rising before dawn to exercise, wearing uniforms on campus, participating in weekend military exercises, and attending summer leadership and training programs have the effect of forming close associations among the men and women who are part of these organizations. They experience a common bond facilitated by the time they spend together, their reliance on each other for the accomplishment of goals, and commitment to the military. Organizations such as marching band or orchestra have some of these same unifying experiences, including long hours of practice, dedication to a common goal, and the visual distinction that comes with wearing uniforms or concert formalwear.

RH living units do not have the same degree of control as athletic teams, fraternities and sororities, or ROTC units, but they have other advantages. Among these are the housing assignment process, options for special interest group housing, frequency of contact, and residence life staff trained to help create community experiences.

There are eight propositions that support the development of a sense of community or belonging in RHs. They do not have equal value: some are more important than others are, and not every factor must exist at the same level or at the same time. Strength in one factor may be sufficient to substitute for the absence of another.

1. The closer students live to each other in an RH, the more likely it is that they will meet and become friends (Cullum & Harton, 2007; McPherson, Smith-Lovin, & Cook, 2001; Priest & Sawyer, 1967; Stinebrickner & Stinebrickner, 2006).

2. The greater the homogeneity of students in the living unit, the more likely they are to develop friendship and community (Astin, 1993; Holland, 1985; Newcomb, 1962; McPherson et al., 2001; Micomonaco, 2011).

3. The more satisfied students are with the quality of the RH living environment, the more likely they are to commit themselves to the community (Brown & Devlin, 2003; Devlin, 2007).

4. The more clearly defined the social and physical bounders are within a living unit, the more likely students are to develop community (Altman, 1975, 1976; Altman & Chemers, 1980; Benfield, 2008).

5. A living unit organized around a special lifestyle topic or academic program is more likely to develop community than a living unit to which students are randomly assigned (Blimling, 1993; Inkelas & Weisman, 2003; Pascarella & Terenzini, 1991; Pike, 1999).

6. The more time students spend together, the greater the chances are that they will develop friendships and a sense of

community (Lazarsfeld & Merton, 1954; McPherson et al., 2001).

7. The degree to which students in a living unit participate in community activities contributes to friendships and a sense of community within that living unit (McCluskey-Titus et al., 2002; Moos, 1987).

8. Community and peer acceptance significantly influences the likelihood of students remaining in college, reporting high levels of college satisfaction, and reducing students' levels of emotional and physical stress (Berger, 1997; Eshbaugh, 2008; Ledbetter, Griffin, & Sparks, 2007; McCarthy, Pretty, & Catano, 1990; McCluskey-Titus et al., 2002; Tinto, 1993).

## Barriers to Community

Although RHs start with many advantages in helping to form community among students, barriers exist, one of the most difficult of which to overcome is residential design flaws. Some buildings make it difficult to establish community among students. Features identified in Chapter 6, such as long corridors, high-rise buildings, and poorly maintained facilities, increase student dissatisfaction and make it more difficult for students to commit themselves to other students in the RH. Large living units make it more difficult to form community than smaller ones. Policy issues also influence how students perceive the environment. Highly restrictive policies and excessively noisy environments increase student dissatisfaction and draw students away from committing to community (Arboleda et al., 2003).

Student organizations compete for members' allegiance and can pull students away from commitment to the RH living group. Marching bands, debate teams, sports teams, student governments, identity groups, and fraternities and sororities are among the student organizations that demand strong student commitment and consume large amounts of time. Students may choose to invest their time and energy in one of these groups instead of the living unit. In doing so, they may form a closer sense of community through those group affiliations than through their involvement in the RH. Students make connections with many groups. It is important that students develop senses of community on campus, but the groups that are the sources of their strongest attachments do not have to be the students in their living units.

Students can be members of multiple communities, but the degree of investment will vary. Some students prefer to consider their RH living units as spaces they go to sleep and study but not participate. Students who have committed relationships may spend all of their free time with their significant others, while other students may find that their closest personal relationships are with the students in their RH and they spend most of their free time there.

## How to Create Community in Residence Halls

If residence life professionals do nothing other than assign students to RHs and leave everything else to chance, students will make friends, relationships within living units will develop, and some degree of community will exist. Living together predisposes students to make connections and spend time with one another. Community is not an all-or-nothing proposition. Although it is a laudable goal to have every student in a living unit connected in a meaningful way to every other student in that unit, it may be unrealistic. Therefore, the immediate goals in creating community are to make students feel welcome, become acquainted with one another, and identify common interests.

Efforts to form community should focus on the living unit. RHs housing more than 150 students—the number of people that Dunbar (2004, 2010) found to be the maximum for community—are probably too large for students to have frequent, meaningful interaction.

The first step in deciding how to build community is to define the physical boundaries of the community. Where physical boundaries do not exist, partitions, doors, paint, murals, lounges, and common space can be added to identify the parameters of the territory controlled by the living group. Group identification can be aided by the adoption of a name for the living unit and the establishment of a selection process for assignment to the living unit. Some RHs already enjoy positive campus reputations because of their locations, recent construction, or association with prestigious academic programs.

The best chance to foster close attachments are with first-year students starting the first few weeks of the fall term. It is not the only time; it is just the most opportune time. This period is when students establish patterns of study, work, and socializing and when they are most open to expanding their networks of friends.

One of the keys to developing community among residents is the degree to which students are engaged in mutually shared experiences. Students living at one end of a long RH corridor may never meet students living at the other end unless there is some event that brings them together. To increase residential community, some institutions link summer orientation and fall room assignments. Other programs make housing assignments so that students enrolled in first-year seminars or common core classes live together. These efforts increase the likelihood that students will know each other and bond to form community. The same applies to housing assignments based on academic majors, particularly those with highly structured curricula, such as nursing and engineering, where students take many of the same basic core courses together and routinely see each other in classes.

Experiences available exclusively to members of a living unit also help to establish group identification. As one example, consider the bonds that develop among students who participate in a university-sponsored study abroad program. The international experience reinforces their group identity as students at the institution. In these programs, students share new experiences, have uncommitted time to engage in informal social conversations, are similar ages, and have a common interest—the topic of the study abroad program. An alternative spring break trip, where a group of students participate in a service learning program together, is another example of a unifying common experience that strengthens group affiliation and a sense of community.

Special lifestyle units and special interest floors offer students common experiences that define group membership and encourage community. These units have the added benefit of affirming students' commitment to the group while furthering their interest in the lifestyle or special interest topic.

Common experiences increase the level of trust among students and the depth of their knowledge about each other. When trust does not exist, confidence-building courses, trust-building workshops, and informal student counseling can help students process their feelings and develop stronger relationships within the group.

Connections among students need to be maintained through frequent communication so that the sense of mutually shared experience and belonging can be sustained. Social media is the usual way this happens because it allows students to stay engaged and learn about group activities with minimal effort in a venue in which they already engage.

Friendly competition among living units gives students a chance to participate in and root for their community. It reinforces a collective sense of identity and focuses the community members on achieving a common goal. At Oxford University in the United Kingdom, most of the residential colleges sponsor crew teams. The colleges regularly compete against one another and take pride in the accomplishment of their teams. Competition like this helps to define the community and affirms bonds among students.

# What Works, What Doesn't, and Why

Students make friends with other students who are most like them, live near them, share common interests, experience the same activities, and with whom they enjoy spending time. Residence life staff can create the conditions that lead to the development of a strong sense of community among students in a living unit, but ultimately students must engage and invest something of themselves for a sense of community to develop.

Personality plays a role in creating friendships and developing a sense of connection among students. Extroverted students have an easier time making connections and uniting with others in a sense of community (DeNeui, 2003; Lounsbury & DeNeui, 1996). Students who struggle with interpersonal skills, who are unsure of themselves, or who shy away from initiating contact with others have a harder time fitting in. Residence life staff may need to spend additional time with these students to help them create opportunities for inclusion and coach them on how to get involved.

Living in a college RH with a group of people with whom you share a common bond can be one of the most rewarding experiences of a person's life. Sometimes the right group of circumstances comes together and students form a sense of community that sustains them throughout college. However, there is no guarantee that this will happen. When there is no sense of community or when the peer environment has become negative, it is the responsibility of the residence life staff to intervene and change the environment. How to manage RHs to advance student learning and other educational objectives is what residence life professionals are trained to do, and it is the subject of the next chapter.

# 8

# Managing Student Life in Residence Halls to Support Student Learning

Residential learning environments do not happen by themselves. They are created intentionally to achieve specific outcomes. For most housing and residence life (HRL) programs, the desired outcome is student learning. How they achieve it requires successfully managing five dimensions of the RH experience: (1) developing and using residential curriculums and learning experiences; (2) employing instructional methods; (3) managing the learning environment; (4) providing advocacy and institutional representation; and (5) conducting and using assessment. This chapter addresses the first four of these dimensions; conducting and using assessment is the subject of the next chapter. Table 8.1 provides an overview of the first four dimensions of managing student life in residence halls (RHs) and a brief summary of key issues under each dimension.

The educators responsible for managing student life in RHs are resident directors (RDs). Although senior housing officers (SHOs) are responsible for managing RH systems, in many ways their role is to support RDs in their direct work with students. This same relationship exists between faculty and academic deans. Faculty members are responsible for educating students in their classes; academic deans support them with the resources needed to do that. RDs are the classroom instructors of the modern American RH.

**Table 8.1 Managing Student Life and Learning in Residence Halls**

| Developing and Using Residential Curriculums and Learning Experiences | Employing Instructional Methods | Managing the Learning Environment | Providing Advocacy and Institutional Representation |
|---|---|---|---|
| Engagement | Involvement | Milieu management | Liaison with other departments |
| Student conduct | Role modeling | Student safety and welfare | Parent relationships |
| RHA | Integration of in-class and out-of-class experience | Building maintenance | Advocate for students who need support |
| Programs | Intervention | Building services | Provide feedback to supervisors about student concerns |
| Activities | Setting adult role expectations | Security | Advocate for improving the quality of student life |
| Special housing assignment programs | Sense of community | Emergency management | |
| Learning | Direct instruction | | |
| Communities | Counseling | | |
| Interaction with faculty | Advising student groups | | |
| First-year housing | Structuring the peer environment | | |
| | Direct feedback and support | | |
| | Crises management | | |

Their goal is education, and the process by which they accomplish it is the subject of this book.

## Developing and Using Residential Curriculums and Learning Experiences

Many educators view programming as the primary means of educating students in RHs and have developed programming models to support these efforts (Blimling, 2010; Schuh & Triponey, 1993; Upcraft, 1982). Resident assistants (RAs) usually are expected to follow the models by completing a number of programs each semester that present information on topics such as wellness, study skills, relationships, and campus involvement.

Traditional models of educational programming have a place in RHs, but some of these approaches are no longer robust enough to capture the interest of students and engage them in a meaningful way. A contemporary approach to educating students in RHs needs a broader perspective than programming. The challenge is not how to program but how to engage students in a way that captures their energy, imagination, and commitment. Educational efforts focused on traditional programming topics such as birth control, eating disorders, time management, and human sexuality are available online.

Speakers on current topics can be overshadowed by a plethora of 24-hour television broadcasts, news alerts on cell phones, YouTube videos, and blogs. What once passed for programming has been replaced by a level of electronic engagement that not only does a better job than most programs ever did but also is available whenever and wherever a student wants to access the information on the Internet.

Competition for students' time has never been greater. Studying, Internet, television, video gaming, recreation, cell phone and texting communications, and students' social lives all compete for the time they are not in class or working. Add to those options commitments related to student clubs and organizations, such as marching band, orchestra, or the debate team, and students have a generous number of ways to spend their out-of-class time.

Educational engagement in RHs needs to have immediate relevance to capture students' interests. It needs to provide more than simply offering information to engage students in a way that results in learning. That is, efforts to engage students in the RHs should offer an educational experience that is not available elsewhere.

One way to think about educating students in RHs is to consider the combined effort as a residential curriculum. In the same way that faculty design courses to meet the educational requirements of an academic degree, residence educators can create learning experiences to meet the educational goals of RHs. Among the first to write about residential curricula were Kerr and Tweedy (2006), who explored the effectiveness of traditional RH programming at the University of Delaware. Although Delaware's residence life professionals did a good job attracting students to attend the many hundreds of programs they offered throughout the academic year, Kerr and Tweedy concluded that the numbers of students in attendance and the numbers of programs offered were not good indications of what students learned. The authors also questioned who should lead educational programming. Many institutions rely on RAs to lead programming, but RDs, who frequently have master's degrees in college student affairs, have the training and expertise to create the most effective learning experiences for students.

The residence life staff at Delaware began the process of establishing a residential curriculum by focusing on five of the institution's educational goals, which led to the development of learning outcomes and a set of competences connected with each outcome. A set of strategies or pedagogical approaches and lesson plans was established for each competency-based learning experience. The residence life staff used qualitative feedback from students about their learning experiences and other benchmark indicators from standardized instruments to assess the effectiveness of their efforts and make improvements accordingly.

The idea of intentional goal-directed learning experiences designed to create a curriculum-based approach to educational engagement is grounded in progressive theory and research about student learning (Barr & Tagg, 1995; Blimling, Whitt, & Associates, 1999; Hamrick, Evans, & Schuh, 2002; Keeling, 2004, 2006; Kuh, Kinzie, Bridges, et al., 2006; Kuh et al., 2005). Traditional approaches to managing the learning environments of RHs have usually taken a passive approach through which information and entertainment programs are made available based on student interest and availability of people to lead the sessions or activities. Under the intentional goal-directed approach, the focus is on developing programs that advance a particular learning goal, such as civic responsibility. Programs are designed to meet the goal. Differences between the passive and intentional approaches to student learning are summarized in Table 8.2.

The curriculum-based approach is one type of intentional goal-directed approach that places the responsibility for education in RHs with professionals who have the knowledge and expertise to design learning experiences appropriate for students' stages of psychosocial/cognitive development. As educators, residence life professionals plan the curriculum for the academic year in much the same way that a classroom instructor plans a syllabus. Activities are sequenced to achieve stated learning outcomes. Some programs are designed to encourage students to meet other students and make friends and thus advance the goal of fostering community development. Other programs create learning experiences designed to advance students' understanding and knowledge about topics, such as social justice or environmental stewardship. Critical to this approach is a focus on intentionally constructed learning experiences designed to further institutional student learning goals.

**Table 8.2 Passive and Active Approaches to Student Life and Learning in Residence Halls**

| Features of the Passive Approach | Features of the Intentional Approach |
| --- | --- |
| Involvement offered to students who might be interested | Participation in experientially based learning activities are expected and encouraged |
| Provide information or entertainment | Focused on enhancing understanding and critical thinking |
| Offered without consideration of skills students may learn through their involvement | Designed to develop functionally transferable skills |
| Frequently feature students as audience members | Strengthens group interaction and social skills |
| Problems handled by staff with little or no input from residents | Solves actual problems with student involvement |
| Individual students learning with little support for collaboration | Collaborative and cooperative learning are a primary method of student learning |
| No intentional efforts made to create a sense of community | Development of a sense of community among students is a goal |
| Voluntary student involvement and unsolicited student participation beyond serving as audience members | Involvement and engagement is encouraged and expected |
| No effort made to develop programs that increase informal time with faculty | Increased student–faculty interaction is encouraged and available |
| No assessment of student learning | Assessment of student learning occurs regularly |

| Features student accountability, judicial processes, documenting violations, sanctions, involvement of campus police, and punitive measures to address conduct violations | Addresses student conduct violations through adult conversations, systemic change, mediation, counseling, and the encouragement of responsible behavior |
|---|---|

Another characteristic of the curriculum-based approach is that educational goals are established for RHs collectively rather than each RH developing a different set of learning goals. Although RDs may take different approaches to accomplishing an institution's educational goals, all RDs are working toward achieving the same goals with RH students. The parallel for this approach in the academic curriculum is an undergraduate course required as part of the core curriculum, such as English composition or precalculus. Instructors may take different approaches, but each instructor must cover the same basic material.

However, teaching through the RH experience is different from classroom instruction; traditional lecture-style teaching has limited utility in RHs. Students are in class throughout the week, and few want to spend their time sitting through another lecture or similar classroom experience. Residence life educators must learn to use experiential learning activities, community development, the peer environment, and their knowledge of students' contemporary interests to engage them in light of the competing demands on their time. Designing a curriculum-based approach to RH programming can be broken down into the following five steps:

1. Identify learning goals: Educational goals are broad statements of overall direction. They frequently come from institutional mission statements, institutional strategic learning goals, departmental mission statements, or national educational documents, such as learning goals recommended

by the Association of American Colleges and Universities
(AACU, 2007).

2. Specify strategic learning objectives: Learning objectives are a
collection of specific learning outcomes that further the
achievement of educational goals.

3. Plan educational activities: Educational experiences, such
as workshops, community service projects, problem-solving
experiences, team-based learning, and involvement projects
that produce student learning are the ways that residence life
educators plan to meet strategic learning objectives.

4. Create program lesson plans: Lesson plans create blueprints
for activity that include the desired learning outcome and how
that outcome will be measured. Learning plans also ensure that
details of the event are complete, time is well spent, and the
learning objectives are achievable through the planned activity.

5. Assess learning outcomes: Feedback is helpful in understanding
how students experienced a learning activity, but it often fails
to satisfy the broader question about what students learned
or whether the program advanced the learning objective. A
number of qualitative and quantitative assessment methods
available to assess student learning are discussed in Chapter 9.

Among the institutions that have implemented a curriculum-
based approach to programming are the University of Delaware
(Kerr & Tweedy, 2006; Kerr, Tweedy, & Diesner, 2007; Student
Life Committee of the Faculty Senate, 2008), Miami University
(Miami University Office of Residence Life, 2013), Saint Louis
University (Saint Louis University Housing and Residence Life,
n.d.), and Valparaiso University (Valparaiso University Office of
Residential Life, 2007). The educational objectives of these programs
have similarities and differences. Valparaiso's educational goals focus
on community relations, intellectual awakening, and personal development. Miami's goals include academic success, community

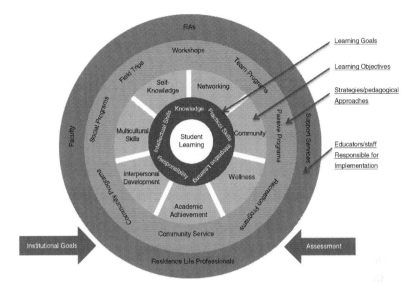

**Figure 8.1    Curriculum-Based Programming Model**
    Learning Goals—(1) knowledge of human cultures and the physical and natural world, (2) intellectual and practical skills, (3) personal and social responsibility, and (4) integrative learning—adapted from: Association of American Colleges and Universities. (2007). College learning for the new global century. Washington, DC: Author.

engagement, intrapersonal development, and cultural proficiency. Saint Louis's approach centers on community responsibility, understanding self and others, and life skills. Delaware has 12 outcomes to promote student learning in a variety of areas including civic engagement, equity, sustainability, and citizenship.

    Figure 8.1 depicts a curriculum-based educational model for student learning in RHs. At the center of the model is learning by students. The next ring of the circle represents learning goals adapted from AACU's (2007) goals for education: knowledge of human cultures and the physical and natural world; intellectual and practical skills; personal and social responsibility; and integrative learning. This list of learning goals will vary with institutional goals. The next ring (third from center) of the circle represents learning objectives that may help students realize one or more of the learning goals. Strategies or pedagogical approaches are fourth from center. At the outer ring of the circle are the educators and staff responsible for implementing the residential curriculum. Residence life professionals take a leadership role in this model, with RAs helping them. Faculty-in-residence, faculty advisory boards, and faculty who teach in residential learning communities also help achieve the residential learning outcomes. The support services professionals represented in this model include many of the collaborative partnerships residence life maintains with other departments, such as counseling centers, academic affairs, cultural centers, housing operations, and physical plant operations that provide direct and indirect services that make educational programs in RHs possible. The model shows input from institutional goals and assessment of the learning objectives.

Curriculum-based programming can use existing organizational structures such as the Residence Hall Association (RHA) to achieve some of the learning outcomes in the model. RHA and similar residential student organizations provide learning experiences that teach functionally transferable skills, such as how to run a meeting, debate ideas, work within a policy structure, organize others, and follow-through on projects. The primary purpose of these organizations is to engage students in the organizational process to advance the learning of students in the organization. Student members of the organization benefit through their participation. The interaction that occurs among these students as they work collectively to accomplish projects is where the most effective learning occurs.

Residence life educators interested in using a curriculum-based approach to student learning should work with faculty to decide what to teach and how to teach it. The faculty is responsible for the curriculum, and they should be partners in the process. At the University of Delaware, residence life professionals take their curriculum recommendations to a university-wide faculty committee that works with RH educators to design the residential curriculum and approve it before the HRL department implements it (Student Life Committee of the Faculty Senate, 2008).

The curriculum-based approach offers a number of advantages, but it is not the only way to engage students in active learning in RHs. Other approaches to student learning in RHs focus on connecting what students learn in the classroom with their experience in RHs. This approach works particularly well in special housing programs, such as a living unit for engineering students, where students share a common course curriculum and the design of the residential learning experience complements what they learn from their coursework. Yet another approach is to offer students experiential learning opportunities to help them develop skills in areas such as leadership, diversity, mediation, negotiation, job searching, personal health, and test taking.

Each approach to student learning is based in an assumption about how students learn best. The curriculum approach is structured to engage students in activities that advance institutional learning outcomes. The integrative approach, focused on connecting students' in-class and out-of-class learning, acknowledges the importance of integrated learning and the primary and complementary roles of faculty and residence life professionals in that process. The learning opportunities approach, which offers students a rich set of varied learning experiences and lets them choose the skills and experiences they want, acknowledges students' responsibility for their own learning and the role of residence life educators as guides, instructors, teachers, and mentors in that process. All of these approaches can advance student learning in RHs, and more than one approach might work successfully on a particular college campus.

Another source of planned learning in RHs comes from residential academic enrichment programs. Research on programs like living and learning centers (LLCs), special lifestyle programs, and honors housing is discussed in Chapter 4. Many of these programs have partnerships with faculty to enrich the RH experience and advance student learning. RDs usually work as parts of teams of educators focused on helping students learn. In addition to their responsibility for the general management of RHs, including supervision of RAs and other building staff, other roles might include co-teaching courses, organizing field trips and community service activities, providing assessment data, and working directly with students to help shape their learning experiences.

## Employing Instructional Methods

No matter how enthusiastic RDs are at the start of the fall term, the demands of their jobs are exhausting and the hours are long. Student conduct issues, roommate squabbles, RA supervision, residents with psychological difficulties, overly protective parents, administrative meetings, and routine crises take their toll on RDs over the course of the academic year. It is easy to forget that the primary responsibility of an RD is that of educator.

To fulfill their educational responsibilities, RDs should have the skills necessary to employ the following instructional methods to engage students in individual and group learning.

### Involvement

Involvement is the first step in helping students get the most from their RH experiences. Involvement leads to engagement that captures the intellectual and perhaps emotional interests of students (Astin, 1984; Kuh et al., 2005). Generally, the more involved students are, the more engaged they are; the more engaged they are, the more they learn. Pascarella and Terenzini (2005) explained that "individual effort or engagement is the critical determinant of the impact of college" (p. 602). Because of this, institutional effectiveness in shaping cocurricular, curricular, interpersonal, and academic experiences for students is critical to student learning.

### Role Modeling

Students look to RAs and RDs as representatives of the institution. How these individuals behave in RHs makes impressions on students. Language, self-control, emotional maturity, and friendliness are all subject to scrutiny by students. Little goes unnoticed in a community where everyone lives together, and students freely share information and opinions with others in person and on Facebook, Twitter, and other social networking sites.

## Integrating In-Class and Out-of-Class Experiences

RHs should help students integrate what they learn in different spheres of their college experiences. RDs can help this process by finding ways to integrate students' in-class and out-of-class experiences. Curricular-based educational programs, students teaching other students, partnerships with faculty, and partnerships with other student affairs departments can help students integrate their learning. Classes taught in RHs, special housing assignment programs, roommate matching programs, and residentially based service-learning activities are examples of integrated learning opportunities.

## Direct Intervention

Students' lives in RHs are often on public display. As a result, they can reveal the need for intervention. The challenge for RDs is to know when to intervene, when to wait, and how to intervene if there is a need to do so. Typical intervention issues in RHs include eating disorders, substance abuse problems, anger management issues, deep depression, parental conflicts, relationship violence, broken romantic relationships, roommate conflicts, psychological problems, academic difficulties, and stress. Reynolds (2013) developed a slightly different list of common problems encountered by student affairs practitioners, and among the top were stress, time management, anxiety, transition to college, student entitlement, academic difficulties, and financial concerns.

## Setting Adult Role Expectations

Identity development during the college years is primarily about growing into adulthood, and students generally want to be treated as adults. RDs help students move into adult roles by giving them feedback about their behavior, both positive and negative, and by having adult conversations with them about their responsibilities as adults. Treating students like adults, even when they are still wrestling with issues of late adolescence and frequently underperform adult role expectations, sets a standard of expected conduct that helps students grow and mature.

## Creating a Sense of Community

It is not enough for RDs to wait for community to develop in RHs. They need to work with RAs to engage students in unifying activities that help students connect with each other. Community is also based on a sense of trust and fairness in the way the RH is operated. The manner in which RDs approach conflicts between living units or between RAs and residents helps establish an atmosphere of mutual trust and connectedness.

RDs also need to address behavior that isolates residents or makes some people feel less welcome. Homophobic, racist, or sexist language and behavior have a debilitating effect and inhibit some residents' full membership in the community. Tolerating this behavior is corrosive to community, and if it is not addressed the RH experience fails to teach the important lesson that students live in a pluralistic world. Therefore, RDs must take affirmative action to correct behavior that erodes community as much as they must work to find ways for students to connect, develop friendships, and build a sense of community.

## Direct Instruction

RDs are educators with the principle task of constructing a learning environment. Much of that work is done through creating learning experiences, managing the environment, collaborating with other educators, and involving students. However, RDs are often called upon to provide direct instruction in programs for students and in training for staff. Most institutions use RDs to help with RA training; RDs prepare presentations and other learning experiences that help RAs acquire information and skills they need to perform their duties. Direct instruction is the most traditional form of classroom teaching, and RDs as educators must master this skill.

## Counseling

One of the ways that RDs help students is by one-on-one counseling. They learn elementary counseling skills as part of most student affairs graduate programs. They meet with students to listen, analyze, and provide feedback. However, they do not do psychotherapy, have ongoing therapeutic relationships, or attempt to provide diagnoses. RDs can help students think through many of the normal developmental problems of late adolescence and early adulthood and can provide guidance about relationships, strategies for academic success, time management, and personal conduct. They usually do not have sufficient training and expertise to help students with complex psychological problems, self-destructive behaviors, deep depression, or other mental health problems. In these circumstances, RDs must know when and how to refer students to mental health professionals. Their skill set also should include early identification of students in need of help and the ability to persuade them to seek professional assistance.

## Advising Student Groups

Most RHs have student councils or advisory groups that are part of a campus-based RHA. Some RHs also have judicial boards that adjudicate violations of RH policies and recommend sanctions to administrative officers when appropriate. Advising these groups requires the RD to allow the learning experience to unfold in ways that give students responsibility for the organization. Advising is done through a combination of providing information, posing questions, offering suggestions for consideration by the students, and providing students with feedback about their leadership styles or approaches. In RH judicial hearings, advising also includes making sure that the rights of the accused student are respected and that institutional adjudicatory processes are followed. Essentially, advising in this capacity is teaching through a case study approach and is an important skill for RDs and other student affairs professionals.

Dunkel, Schuh, and Chrystal-Green (2014) wrote about the importance of advisors in shaping the student learning experience. Although advisors play a number of roles, the authors believe that the three most common are mentor, supervisor, and educator. Involvement in student organizations helps students learn functionally transferable skills, such as how to conduct a meeting or how to reach consensus. It also has a strong association with students developing self-confidence, self-esteem, communication skills, and persisting in college (Dunkel et al.). Time invested in advising student groups is time invested in helping students learn.

### Structuring the Peer Environment

LLCs, honors housing, and special lifestyle units are examples of programs that organize the peer environment to achieve specific educational outcomes. To the extent that RDs are included in developing or managing these programs, they are socially engineering the residential environment to advance student learning. Roommate matching is another example of structuring the peer environment to achieve an outcome that might be educational or is an attempt to reduce roommate conflicts. The organizational knowledge necessary to manipulate the peer environment to achieve educational outcomes takes an understanding of adolescent behavior, peer groups, college transition experiences, group processes, and familiarity with research on successful and unsuccessful student learning experiences in RHs.

### Direct Feedback and Support

Instructional methods are not always complicated. Sometimes instruction requires direct feedback to students or RAs about behavior or performance. Students want to know other people's views about them, and they usually value RDs' opinions. RDs need to spend time observing students' interactions, including the relationships between RAs and residents, and decide when feedback is appropriate. Erikson (1968) observed that direct feedback is an important component of resolving identity issues during adolescence and suggested that feedback be coupled with the consequences of actions—both good and bad.

**Crisis Management**

Managing the everyday crises of college students is one of the roles for which RDs have frontline responsibility. Life events such as the death of a family member, broken romantic relationships, excessive alcohol consumption, drug experimentation, suicidal ideation and behavior, and relationship violence are all-too-frequent sources of crises among college students. Some RDs have mostly uneventful academic years, while other RDs handle multiple crises throughout the academic year. Managing crises involves helping students get the support they need from appropriate offices and services and providing students with emotional support during and after events. In addition, it involves managing the emotional environment of the living unit where the student is a member or, if the circumstance is serious enough, the emotional environment of the entire RH.

RAs look to RDs for direction, feedback, reassurance, and support during crises. Even when RAs have the necessary training and experience, crisis management is the responsibility of RDs, usually with the help of other student affairs professionals. A suicide or sexual assault in an RH affects the entire building. A student hospitalized because of alcohol poisoning or a mental health challenge leaves residents concerned and RAs wondering if they did what was right. These crises are often complicated by the fact that to maintain confidentiality RDs can share only a limited amount of information with students and RAs. Therefore, RDs must learn to navigate the roles of being supportive, quashing inaccurate information, reassuring students, and not disclosing information that compromises students' privacy.

## Managing the Learning Environment

RHs are small communities that need RDs to manage the quality of the social climates, including culture and atmosphere, and the basic functioning of the buildings themselves. The manners in which RDs handle these responsibilities help give RHs personalities that range from warm and inviting to cold and hostile. The managerial aspects of the environment can be organized into four categories: student conduct, building operations, building security and safety, and building services.

### Student Conduct

Holding students accountable for violations of institutional policy has long been one of the duties assigned to RDs. Although confronting students with conduct violations can be unpleasant, it is a necessary part of maintaining a learning environment in RHs. The question is not whether RDs should enforce institutional policies but how they should go about doing it. Disciplinary conversations are opportunities to engage students in discussion about their personal conduct, decision making, commitment to the institution, and the long-term repercussions of their behavior on goals they have set for themselves. Disciplinary counseling engages students in meaningful dialogue, the results of which are likely to produce some level of student learning, even when students seem resistant.

A relatively small percentage of students who violate institutional policies are caught and held accountable for their behaviors. What happens to students who violate institutional policies may or may not set an example for other students, but that is not the goal. Rather, the purposes of addressing conduct violations are fostering student learning and maintaining positive environments for all students.

There are three components of student conduct in RHs: enforcement, process, and outcome. Assessment could be added as a fourth category, but student conduct assessment usually concerns the judicial processes or recidivism rates and tends to be idiosyncratic. Because students spend much of their free time in RHs, RDs see students at their best and at their worst. Occasionally, students act out and it becomes necessary for RDs to intervene. RDs need to develop judgment about what behaviors to confront, what to ignore, when to make referrals to the student conduct office, when to involve senior residence life supervisors, when to involve the campus police, and when matters can best be resolved with adult conversation and offering advice.

Level of enforcement is a matter of professional judgment. There are two primary schools of thought about how to enforce institutional policies in RHs. One approach advocates for enforcement of all violations. Under this philosophy, students are accountable, campus police are involved when appropriate, and parents receive notice of alcohol and drug violations when students are under the age of 21. The second school of thought takes a more holistic approach. As a first step, it explores questions about what students should learn through their RH experiences. It then structures the educational experience in RHs, including the level of enforcement, to achieve that goal. Increasing the level of enforcement in RHs can eliminate most behavioral infractions, but the trade-off for a high level of enforcement may be student alienation, which inhibits community and curtails student growth and development.

For example, consider enforcement efforts to stop the use of marijuana in RHs. A strict no-tolerance policy that employs RAs as rule enforcers and involves search warrants, campus police, harsh disciplinary sanctions, parental involvement, and student arrests is likely to increase the risk of detection and make the consequences so severe that students will significantly reduce their use of using marijuana in the RHs and move their use to other locations. The trade-off for this level of enforcement is likely to be the deteriorated quality of the residential social climate created by such a rigorous level of enforcement. Although RHs could be essentially marijuana-free, the rigorous level of enforcement would likely decrease the quality of the residential social climate and drive a wedge between residence life staff and students, increase the risk of students experimenting with less detectable and perhaps more dangerous drugs, and attract RAs who are more interested in controlling other students than in building community. Involvement of campus police means that students could be charged with civil or criminal violations and be forced to pay fines and court costs. In addition, these students would likely need to disclose their arrests (convicted or not) when applying for professional positions in medicine, law, pharmacy, education, accounting, military service, law enforcement, and other professions.

Few institutions go to these extremes to enforce policies prohibiting the use of marijuana or underage drinking, the two most frequent violations among undergraduates. The alternative to no-tolerance enforcement is not abdication of enforcement but rather some other standard. Setting the appropriate level of enforcement takes professional judgment. For example, a suspicion that students are using marijuana for the first time might warrant an adult conversation with the RD, who would explain the policy and how repeated violations will be addressed. Repeated or public use may warrant referral to the institution's office of student conduct for appropriate disciplinary action. Continued use or sale of small amounts of marijuana may require students to leave the university for a semester or two until they demonstrate the ability to follow institutional policies.

RDs have a responsibility to follow institutional policies for how to enforce student conduct violations. If they disagree with those policies or can offer better ways to handle infractions, they have a responsibility to share this information with their supervisors and work within the system to change policies in ways that will benefit students. If their efforts are unsuccessful, they have the option to seek employment at an institution that shares their professional opinions. They do not have the option to ignore institutional policies with which they disagree.

## Building Operations

The degree to which buildings are maintained affects students' perceptions of the environment (Foubert, Tepper, & Morrison, 1998; Strange & Banning, 2001). As discussed in Chapter 6, a poorly maintained physical environment creates a perception that no one cares about the environment and that because no one cares the environment can be treated in a careless way. Even when RDs do not supervise housekeeping and maintenance personnel assigned to their buildings, they have a commitment to the students to press those responsible for building maintenance to maintain high-quality physical settings. Seldom do RDs have the authority to make significant financial decisions about building maintenance and repair; however, they do have the responsibility to bring problems about the physical condition of their RHs to the attention of those with the authority to act and to press them for needed changes to improve the quality of the living environment for students.

## Building Security and Safety

Most RHs have some form of security that usually starts with electronic swipe-card access at exterior doorways. Some RHs have people who monitor the main entrances. Uniformed security officers, part-time staff, or student workers are often employed for this purpose. The amount of time a person sits at the front desk or control point varies with the campus and its location. In urban areas, it is common to have buildings monitored 24 hours a day, 7 days a week. In rural and suburban areas where there is less crime, it is common to have a student located near the front entrance during the evening hours to provide building security but otherwise to leave the front entrance unattended during the day. Some RHs have video cameras located near doorways and lobbies for additional security.

RDs often have responsibility for scheduling students to work evening hours as night security for the building. When they do not have this responsibility, they still need to ensure that whoever has the duty to provide security treats residents as welcome members of the community and knows how to respond to problems. RDs also assign a duty schedule for the RAs and ensure that they are trained to handle routine student concerns and that they know how to respond to more serious problems including when to contact the RD or campus police for assistance.

Fire prevention and building maintenance are two other aspects of safety. RHs are usually equipped with fire suppression equipment, smoke detectors, fire pull stations, fire extinguishers, and addressable alarm systems that sound warnings, flash lights, broadcast messages, and automatically alert fire departments of fires, including their locations. Fire code officials and institutional safety officers normally maintain this equipment. However, RDs have the responsibility to ensure that students know what to do in the event of an emergency. They also have a responsibility to address fire hazards, such as the use of open flames in RH rooms.

A poorly maintained building can present safety risks. Loose stair treads, poorly secured window frames, rickety stair railings, improperly functioning elevators, and propped fire and exterior doors are examples of safety hazards that require immediate attention. RDs have the responsibility to ensure that needed repairs are completed and that resident behaviors do not conflict with safety and security measures.

## Building Services

RHs offer a wide variety of services, ranging from 24-hour front desk operations that distribute student mail and receive packages for residents to laundry pick-up and delivery and campus and community shuttle services. There is no requirement that institutions provide hotel-like services to students in RHs. However, if the institution chooses to provide these services and students are willing to pay for them, students have a right to expect the institution to deliver what it promised and perform the tasks well. RDs are the institution's representatives, and even when they have no direct responsibility for services offered they have an institutional responsibility to make sure that students receive contracted services.

## Providing Advocacy and Institutional Representation

RDs serve as liaisons between students and other university departments. Because of their close daily contact with students, RDs often have a better understanding of students' interests, concerns, and attitudes than other educators do. As they listen to students, hear their concerns, and observe their activities, RDs develop insight into the student experience in ways that few others have the opportunity to do. RDs need to share what they learn with other student affairs professionals, including what they observe and the concerns students express to them. SHOs and senior student affairs officers need this information to inform their decisions and to make changes when necessary to improve the quality of student life.

RDs also serve as advocates for students. This role is often the result of a student experiencing some type of personal crisis, such as a parent conflict or a financial, mental health, or academic problem. The advocacy role for RDs includes not only helping students work through their problems but also contacting offices and other student affairs professionals who can intervene and provide assistance. In the case of a student struggling academically, the advocacy role might include meeting with the student's academic advisor or helping the student enter a tutoring program. For students who have already exhausted financial aid options at the institution, RDs may find themselves coaching students about how to find on-campus jobs.

RDs also serve as liaisons with parents and guardians. During move-in, parents frequently meet RDs and want to know that they can call RDs if an emergency occurs or if they have concerns. This is a common RD responsibility, but often RDs find that the information parents want or the amount of control parents want to exercise is something that they cannot provide under the institution's confidentiality policies. Even when students waive certain rights to confidentiality for their parents, other student affairs professionals may need to make decisions about what information to share.

Most educators are highly respectful of students. They are genuinely interested in the education of students and act with honor and integrity toward them. Occasionally employees exploit their relationships with students and treat them disrespectfully or in a manner that constitutes harassment. In these rare circumstances, RDs, like other student affairs professionals, have a responsibility to students and the institution to ensure that the matter is addressed.

## Concluding Thoughts

Managing a college RH is difficult. It requires knowledge of psychosocial and cognitive development, peer group influences, person–environmental interaction theory, and cognitive learning strategies. Comfort with social media, knowledge of contemporary college culture, and the ability to connect with students from many racial, ethnic, cultural, and social backgrounds are prerequisites for the job. The around-the-clock schedule of the position demands high energy, nearly constant availability, and the capacity to make good judgments with little information during crises. Only some of the necessary skills and knowledge necessary can be gleaned through reading, workshops, and professional development programs. Experience teaches the rest. Work as an RA, graduate resident assistant, and RD provides the experiential context for success as an educator responsible for student learning in RHs.

Managing a college RH is not a solitary process. Every RD needs advice and guidance from experienced residence life supervisors and the support and help of RAs. Student learning is an institutional commitment in which RHs play a part. What students learn in RHs is not more or less important than what students learn through their other college experiences. Learning is learning, no matter whether it occurs in the classroom or in the RH. RH administration is a means of creating a learning environment; administration is not an end in itself.

Part of what makes managing an RH as a learning environment difficult is that RHs, campus cultures, institutional policies, and institutional personalities are different. What works well in one type of RH, with one group of students, at a particular institution may or may not work well in a different university with different students. And what worked well one year may not necessarily work well the next year with different students and different RAs. Student learning environments are constructed new each academic year and are shaped by the social, physical, and interpersonal dynamics operating in each RH. Creating a positive learning experience in an RH at the start of the academic year is not enough to guarantee that it will be sustained throughout the year. Managing an RH takes constant attention, careful observation, collaborative participation, and the knowledge of when to intervene, when to observe, when to ask for help, and when to try a different approach.

No matter what efforts RDs make to improve student learning in RHs or how well they manage the environments, provide educational programs, or supervise staff, there is no way to determine how successful they are without some form of program assessment. A host of qualitative and quantitative assessment methods and techniques are available to provide feedback and guidance about how to improve the quality of the educational experience in RHs. The next chapter discusses the assessment process.

# 9

# Assessing and Improving Residence Life Programs

Prior to the Family Educational Rights and Privacy Act of 1974 (FERPA), deans of men and women maintained extensive written records on students that included information about student behaviors, activities, awards, leadership positions, character, and personal problems. Deans' records amounted to qualitative assessments of students' out-of-class activities and their progress toward graduation.

Most institutions stopped collecting and recording this type of personal information after FERPA was enacted because the files contained confidential reports made by staff. The information was for internal use only and was never intended for release to students. However, FERPA opened these files to students so that they could see their personal records and challenge the accuracy of the information they contained. Despite changes in protocol, records of student conduct hearings and student leadership positions survived. Some institutions adopted Brown and Citrin's (1977) suggestion for creation of student development transcripts, which have since grown into electronic databases that capture various pieces of data about student involvement.

Housing and residence life (HRL) professionals have for many years collected information about occupancy rates, numbers of students applying for rooms, annual cost of room damage, room change requests, and RH departure rates. Institutions use this information to determine housing rates and to estimate the number of rooms needed based on the percentage of students who enrolled and persisted. When coupled with other financial data this management information allows for planning and provides a measure of operational efficiency and management success. However, assessment of student learning does not have such easily quantifiable metrics and is more complicated to evaluate. The overall process of assessing student learning answers a series of basic research questions posed by Schuh and Associates (2009, pp. 15–17):

1. What is the issue at hand?
2. What is the purpose of the assessment?
3. Who should be studied?
4. What is the best assessment method?
5. How should we collect our data?
6. What instrument should we use?
7. How should we analyze the data?
8. How should we report the results?

Assessment of student learning in RHs is a process that can be organized into six stages: (1) establish learning outcomes; (2) develop learning strategies; (3) select inquiry methods; (4) collect evidence; (5) analyze evidence; and (6) report and use evidence. Figure 9.1 shows this process as a loop because the results of assessment are used to establish new learning outcomes and improve the quality of student learning experiences in RHs. Although the assessment loop may appear as a series of discrete actions, it is actually highly interactive. Decisions made at one stage in the process affect other stages, and assessment results may lead educators to conduct additional studies to understand or to qualify results. This chapter addresses each of the six stages in the assessment loop to provide a framework and model for assessment in RHs.

**Figure 9.1    Assessment Loop**

## Establish Learning Outcomes

A number of sources identify learning goals for RHs. The Council for the Advancement of Standards in Higher Education (CAS, 2009) associates six learning and development outcomes with RHs: (1) knowledge acquisition, construction, integration, and application; (2) cognitive complexity; (3) intrapersonal development; (4) intrapersonal competency; (5) humanitarianism and civic engagement; and (6) practical competency. The Association of American Colleges and Universities (AACU, 2007) applies four learning outcomes for higher education to RHs: (1) knowledge of human cultures and the physical and the natural world; (2) intellectual and practical skills; (3) personal and social responsibility; and (4) integrative learning. A Google search of "residence hall goals" results in hundreds of examples of educational goals in use by college and universities throughout the United States. Common among these are community engagement, multicultural proficiency, intellectual advancement, personal development, and life skills.

Although researching goals from national associations and other institutions is informative, the place to start when creating learning goals for RHs is with the institution's mission statement or a similar institutional document focused on learning outcomes. The learning outcomes identified by a housing and residence life (HRL) program must be achievable and measurable. RHs contribute to student learning in many ways (see Chapter 6); however, much of the effect of RHs on student learning is indirect (Pascarella & Terenzini, 1991, 2005), and some of the assumptions about the positive influences of RHs are not supported by research.

Given enough time, resources, and appropriate methods, most types of student learning can be measured. However, some learning outcomes, such as cognitive complexity or moral development, require specialized testing, significant time, and a research design that might not be practical for HRL programs. Therefore, part of the criteria for selection of outcomes to be achieved must be that the outcomes are measurable within the context of available resources, skill level, time commitment, and interest of residents.

## Develop Learning Strategies

Learning strategies are the means employed to achieve the learning outcomes identified by the HRL program. These are the interventions educators use to affect change in the RH environment or directly influence students. If HRL leaders want to develop a sense of community among students, residence life educators need to decide what strategies they will use to nurture the development of community. Team sports, group projects, social activities, service learning, confidence-building courses, and life skills workshops are examples of strategies HRL professionals adopt to help achieve this goal. The success of each of these experiences can be independently and collectively measured with satisfaction surveys, interviews, focus groups, and a host of other quantitative and qualitative research methods.

## Select Inquiry Methods

The two methodological approaches to social science research are qualitative and quantitative. Qualitative research answers the question of why something happened or how people think about a subject. It provides deeper insight into an issue and answers questions that quantitative research cannot. Qualitative research uses interviews, focus groups, and natural observation to gain a better understanding of a phenomenon or to explain it. It is the best research approach for developing an understanding of an issue, to uncover the underlying motivations behind behavior, or to highlight perspectives of different groups (Creswell, 2013).

Quantitative research describes an experience or association using statistical analyses. This research approach quantifies behaviors, attitudes, opinions, beliefs, and other variables. It answers questions about how many, how much, to what degree something was achieved, how probable it is that a treatment effect will cause a particular outcome, or how likely it is that two variables are associated. It can be used to determine how much students learned from an experience or to test a research hypothesis. Quantitative data can be generalized from samples to larger populations, and results can be compared between years and among institutions using the same instrument.

The question asked and the purpose of the assessment determines the appropriate research method. If the HRL program wants to know the degree of student satisfaction or dissatisfaction with an RH, the answer requires a quantitative approach. However, if the HRL program wants to know why some students are satisfied and others are not, the answer usually requires a qualitative approach (Hoy, 2010). Not all assessment requires elaborate research. Sometimes a well-constructed opinion survey is all that is needed. However, if the purpose of the assessment is summative, meaning that the goal is to measure the amount of learning or the quality of the learning experience that took place in RHs, a more elaborate methodological approach is usually required. What distinguishes one of these approaches from the other is whether the information was collected to improve an ongoing learning experience or if it was to assess the proficiency of a completed learning experience.

Both quantitative and qualitative approaches use rigorous methods to design and execute studies, and both add value to the assessment process. Frequently, HRL researchers employ a mixed methods approach that starts with describing various outcomes associated with the RH experience. They then use this information to structure questions for a qualitative study to gain a better understanding about why desired outcomes were or were not realized. Sometimes the opposite happens; qualitative research is used to gain a better understanding of a phenomenon under investigation, and quantitative analysis is employed to test hypotheses formed through the qualitative process.

## Collecting Evidence

Collecting evidence or data may seem straightforward; however, it can be complicated. Quantitative research involves many decisions to ensure a representative sample, a high response rate, and timing so as not to be influenced by extraneous factors that could affect the results. Quantitative data are normally collected from samples of a population using surveys, questionnaires, nonparticipant observation, and the administration of standardized tests (Hoy, 2010).

Qualitative information is usually gathered through unstructured and structured interviews, document analysis, observation, case studies, and phenomenological analysis (Creswell, 2013). Collecting this information involves selecting the right participants, recording and transcribing interviews, scheduling participants, and finding time when current events do not shape participants' opinions.

Quantitative RH instruments often use self-reported nonparity scaling techniques such as Likert scales (5- to 9-point ranges, such as strongly agree to strongly disagree) or semantic differential scales (5- to 9-point ratings that pose two opposite adjectives, such as good–bad, friendly–unfriendly). This approach queries students' opinions, judgments, or the degree to which they like or dislike something. It does not objectively evaluate their knowledge or reason.

Some quantitative designs use objective testing instruments, such as the Collegiate Assessment of Academic Proficiency (ACT, 2013), which measures students' academic achievement. A typical research design using an instrument like this might include a pretest of student scores on this examination, followed by their involvement in a living and learning community (LLC) or residential learning community and then a posttest using the same instrument. To the extent that other extraneous variables can be controlled, such designs might show whether students who participated in a particular academically enriched RH program performed better than students in a comparison group.

Two of the most popular instruments used in RH assessment are the University Residence Environmental Scale (URES; Moos & Gerst, 1974), and the ACUHO-I/EBI Resident Assessment (ACUHO-I/EBI, 2013).

## URES

Moos and Gerst (1974) developed the URES instrument from Moos's (1974) theoretical work about how human environments function. The instrument is based on the consensus of students' perceptions in a living unit that together define the social climate of that environment. Using this approach, Moos and Gerst studied social climates in residential environments by focusing on the context and intensity of relationships (involvement, emotional support); personal growth (independence, traditional social orientation, competition, academic achievement, intellectuality); and systems maintenance and system change (order and organization, student influence, innovation). They used these three environmental constructs and the associated behaviors to measure RH social climates. The URES consists of 100 items divided into 10 subscales. Each of the subscales measures a dimension of the living group climate.

### Relationship Dimension

1. Involvement—the degree of commitment to the living group and the amount of interaction and feeling of friendships among the living group.

2. Emotional support—the extent of concern for other students in the living unit including efforts to aid each other with academic and personal problems, and the emphasis placed on open and honest communication among the group members.

### Personal Growth Dimension

3. Independence—the diversity of residence behavior that is permitted by the social group without social sanctions versus the degree of socially proper and conformist behavior.

4. Traditional social orientation—the amount of stress students place on dating, going to parties, and other traditional heterosexual interactions among students.

5. Competition—the degree to which a variety of activities, such as dating and grades, are viewed by group members as competitive.

6. Academic achievement—the extent to which strictly classroom and academic accomplishments of concern are promoted within the living unit.

7. Intellectuality—the emphasis on cultural aesthetics and other scholarly intellectual activities in the living group as distinguished from strictly classroom academic achievement.

## System Maintenance and System Change Dimension

8. Order and organization—the amount of formal structural organizational rules, schedules, and established procedures enforced within the living unit.

9. Student influence—the extent to which student residents perceive that they control the living unit by formulating and enforcing policies.

10. Innovation—organizational and individual spontaneity of behaviors and ideas, including the variety of activities and number of new activities and programs, within the living unit.

Moos (1976, 1987) believed that personality and other psychological issues are important aspects in seeking to understand human behavior but offer only partial explanations. Understanding the social climate and the physical environment is necessary to understand human behavior. The URES is used widely in efforts to compare the effectiveness of special assignment programs.

### ACUHO-I/EBI Resident Assessment

This instrument was developed as a joint project between ACHUO-I and the Educational Benchmarking Institute (EBI), which is a for-profit corporation (Mosier & Schwartzmuller, 2002). Designed specifically for use in RHs, the ACUHO-I/EBI Resident Assessment provides the most comprehensive analysis of the residential experience available today; it covers a wide range of residence life issues, including student satisfaction with facilities, services provided, room assignment and room change processes, safety and security, dining services, and the college/university overall. The Resident Assessment covers social climate variables, including tolerance for fellow residents, respect for fellow residents, and sense of community in the living unit. Specific learning outcomes associated with personal interactions; diversity; time management, study, and problem-solving; and personal growth are assessed. The instrument summarizes various scales to provide an index of resident satisfaction, learning experiences, and overall program effectiveness for the full resident experience.

Institutions can compare results of the Resident Assessment between years as well as results of their benchmarked peers, including peers they select and those within their Carnegie Classifications. The statistical tools provided with the program allow institutions to compare student responses from individual living units, by RH, area of the campus, and a number of other variables that may reveal significant differences. The ACUHO-I\EBI Resident Assessment is a sophisticated instrument that is useful for both RH management and institutional accreditation purposes.

## Analyze Evidence

Assessment data are analyzed to answer assessment questions concerning learning outcomes and other pertinent variables. This analysis needs to answer the basic question of all research—the so what? question. It may be interesting to learn that 65 percent of students in an RH took a survey and rated the sense of community in that building as a 3.5 on a 7-point Likert scale. However, such findings do not answer the so what? question without researchers providing context. This can be a comparison against a standardized mean to give a percentile ranking, or it could be a comparison with another group. To find that students in one RH rated community as a 3.5 while students in another RH rated community at a 6.5, both on a 7-point Likert scale with 7 as high, gives context to the question. If further analysis revealed that roommates, resident assistants (RAs), and participation in organized intramural team sports contributed to higher ratings, the so what? question is answered, at least in part, and useful information for improving community in RHs is gathered. Other forms of comparison might include significant differences between a pretest and posttest, such as attitudes toward underrepresented religious groups before and after a workshop, or other learning experiences designed to address prejudice.

Researchers use an array of statistical tests to analyze quantitative data. Results from these tests show a probability level representing the likelihood that no relationship exists or, more precisely, the probability of falsely rejecting a null hypothesis of no relationship. Often research results show an effect size indicating the magnitude of the treatment's effect. When combined with inferential statistics or $p$-values, effect sizes improve the interpretation of results. Results of quantitative analysis are generalizable to similar populations. Therefore, it is reasonable to assume that results from a reliable instrument with high validity from a sufficiently large and representative sample of students living in an RH is generalizable to other students in that RH and to other RH populations with a similar demographic profile.

Qualitative research relies on trustworthiness to validate results from interviews and other sources of information. A number of techniques are used to validate trustworthiness of qualitative studies including independent corroboration, confirmability analysis of the results, and negative case analysis. Qualitative research results are in narrative form and usually include extensive text quotations from study participants. This approach provides rich deep textual analysis and evidence for the interpretations made by the researcher.

## Report and Use Evidence

All of the work that goes into assessment has little meaning if it sits on a shelf and is not used to improve student learning. Collecting data for future analyses may have long-term value, but assessment results are most meaningful when linked to current circumstances.

The information from an assessment must be presented in a way that quickly summarizes the main findings in an executive summary; graphically illustrates quantifiable findings in easily accessible charts, tables, and diagrams; and presents numbers that can be easily understood by people with only a passing knowledge of statistics.

Assessment reports should be written with several audiences in mind. Among these are the senior student affairs officer, other senior officers of the institution, regional accreditation agencies, institutional trustees, student affairs professionals in other departments, faculty, students, and the public. Even when the HRL program does not intend to widely communicate the results of the report, it should be written with the assumption that at some point the information may be public.

It is not necessary to reveal everything in an assessment. Some results are useful only to a limited number of people or do not show any significant findings. Not all results have equal value, and dumping everything into a report can overshadow the most noteworthy findings. However, HRL programs should not intentionally shelter relevant information because it was uncomplimentary of the HRL program. Negative results are useful when they define a problem that HRL professionals can analyze and find ways to solve.

Reporting assessment information has a political dimension. If some RHs did well and others showed substandard performance, the public reporting of this information reflects on the resident directors (RDs) and area coordinators responsible for those buildings. Although the performance information should be shared with the HRL professionals responsible for each building, the results are tantamount to a staff evaluation and should be treated with the same level of confidentiality.

The same applies to reporting results of special assignment programs in RHs with shared responsibility between student affairs and academic affairs. If the assessment performance of an LLC or honors program is unsatisfactory, a private meeting with the faculty and HRL professionals involved is appropriate. A public reporting of the results might compromise the program and interest of both faculty and students to engage in it.

Reporting is only the first step in looking at results. The real test is putting the knowledge to use to improve student learning. Supervisors should take the opportunity to speak with RDs about their successes and failures based on the assessment findings. Those conversations should analyze why certain efforts succeeded and how those successes can be used to improve other efforts. Where learning goals were not met, strategies should be analyzed and modifications made to address the deficiencies.

Doing the same program each year when results of an assessment show significant deficiencies is a poor allocation of resources. Assessment provides a way to identify needed changes and adjust strategies and resources. Programmatic efforts can outlive their usefulness, and the result of an assessment provides evidence of when that has happened. Special assignment programs and special interest floors are often created to address the interests of students at a particular moment in time. A new generation of students may not share these same interests. The personnel and financial resources from such programs can be reallocated to more productive programmatic efforts that advance student learning. Assessment results are one source of information to help make that decision.

Critical events analyses or debriefings after completing assignments or projects allow for review of what worked, what did not work, and why. The goal is to learn from every assignment or project and incorporate that knowledge into the next endeavor. The focus of these meetings is always on how to learn and improve. Each element of the project or operation is analyzed by multiple experts in an objective way to identify both productive processes and areas of needed improvement.

A similar process should occur in HRL programs but often does not because no sooner does the semester end than summer conferences, orientation, new RD training, and vacations begin. HRL work is difficult, and most HRL professionals need to decompress after the semester. Frequent turnover among RDs and RAs adds another layer of complexity to the assessment process and the opportunity to apply experience in an RH the following year.

Regardless of these obstacles, time needs to be allocated to debrief the academic year. When assessment results are available, teams of people with different perspectives should come together and review results with the goal of improving student affairs practices that contribute directly to the achievement of the learning goals for the HRL program. These debriefing sessions have the added advantage of teaching less experienced staff members about successful programs and engaging them as professional peers who offer valuable insights and ideas.

The debriefing sessions should result in information that can be applied to the HRL program the following year. Outcomes from these meetings may result in a determination that learning objectives cannot be accomplished through the HRL program or that the expenditure of resources is too large for the results received.

## Establishing a Culture of Assessment

Higher education has gone through periods in its history where it produced reports showing how many students graduated, the SAT scores of the incoming first-year students, or how well students performed on selected standardized tests like the Graduate Record Exam (GRE) or the Medical College Admission Test (MCAT). Annually college administrators sent information to the U.S. Department of Education to comply with reporting requirements of the Integrated Postsecondary Education Data System (IPEDS). HRL professionals followed institutional expectations and produced similar types of information quantifying the number of educational programs conducted in RHs, the percentage of students who returned to live in RHs for a second year, and number of student conduct violations that occurred in RHs. Data were collected primarily for record keeping and for inclusion in annual reports.

However, those days have passed. What changed was ranking systems used by the media to sort the best institutions from the rest and demands from state and federal agencies for more accountability as to how many students are graduating and what students are learning.

Responding to public criticism about the rising cost of higher education and student dissatisfaction with aspects of their education, in 2006 the U.S. Department of Education began to demand greater accountability from higher education, and a commission was appointed to study it. A highly critical report was issued that called for greater institutional accountability for student learning and graduation rates.

Higher education moves slowly; it took several years before higher education accrediting agencies began requiring evidence that institutions were serious about assessing what students learned. However, the increased assessment demands from regional accrediting agencies have not persuaded the U.S. Department of Education that students are learning enough or graduating at acceptable rates, particularly at for-profit postsecondary institutions. In 2014, the Department of Education proposed additional reporting requirements for postsecondary institutions so that it could identify colleges that provide good value and those that do not. The criteria they established aligned with three principles: access, affordability, and outcomes. Proposed outcome measures include graduation and transfer rates, earnings of graduates, and completion of advanced degrees.

Publically ranking institutions by the value they offer students will bring public pressure on institutions to perform. Institutions that fail to show good value will suffer damage to their reputations, and they will be pressed by institutional stakeholders to do better. If a culture of assessment does not exist at institutions with poor ranking, the Department of Education's proposed value-based ranking system may force them to develop one.

What is interesting about this new initiative is that the proposed data are not grades or test scores but instead focus on skills and abilities students demonstrate in the workplace as measured by annual earnings and admission to graduate programs. Students who lived in RHs learn many of the social, interpersonal, and group communication skills necessary for success in the workplace. Research is already available that shows the strong association between living in an RH and persistence in college (Huhn, 2006; Noble et al., 2007; Pascarella & Terenzini, 1991, 2005; Schudde, 2011). There is every reason to believe that students who live in RHs will also show success in the workplace after graduation.

However, the contributions RHs make to the education of students will go unnoticed if HRL programs do not provide the data demonstrating the contribution that RHs make to educating students. The only way this will happen is if HRL administrators make assessment part of the culture by expecting it as a normal part of the duties and responsibilities of HRL professionals. Ideally, HRL departments would have one or more people within the department with high-level statistical and research skills to guide assessment throughout the academic year. These individuals not only would bring the level of professionalism needed to produce the most useful information but also would be accepted by the community of assessment professionals who now serve in institutional research departments, state higher education offices, and regional accrediting agencies.

## What Works, What Doesn't, and Why

Both quantitative and qualitative assessments have value and need to be used based on the questions investigated. Qualitative assessments often provide the most insightful and useful information in a comprehensive assessment program. Quantitative assessments are widely understood measurements and offer the opportunity to compare results from previous years and with other institutions. Attaching a number to something seems to make it more authentic. Numbers invoke the authority of analytic inquiry and scientifically based knowledge (Boyle, 2001), even when those numbers are based only on correlations and probabilities. Numbers may be far less valuable than the information obtained from a robust qualitative study, but an overall HRL program assessment needs to include some quantitative information, even if it is only to ask how satisfied students are with the program. Numbers can add credibility to results and are a way to quantify the value of the contribution made by HRL programs to the student experience.

Assessment is foremost a management tool. It is not a substitute for educational decision making, and in most circumstances it gives only a glimpse of the student experience. Many institutions do some form of assessment in the spring term. The results are seen as an evaluation of how the program performed the previous academic year. Spring terms are complicated for many reasons and may not be the best time for assessment. Students are frequently tired of the academic pressure, bored with eating in dining halls, stressed from the daily pressures of sharing RH rooms, and motivated to seek greater independence away from the oversight of RAs and RDs. A better time for assessment may be the fall term, when problems can be identified early and corrected before the end of the academic year. If an RD is experiencing difficulty, supervisors are likely to hear about it, but often this information is anecdotal. Assessments are more objective and can provide the type of information supervisors and RDs need to salvage an RH experience that is going astray. The problem with waiting until the end of the academic year to make these determinations is that the students who shared their opinions are gone by the time changes can be made. With the start of the fall term, new students enter the RHs, and a new community experience begins to form.

Ideally, assessment should be an ongoing process, not a one-time end-of-the-year event. Despite the benefit of multiple assessments, the practical reality is that students are inundated with surveys, tests, evaluations, and assessments from academic departments, institutional research offices, other students, and random others who gain access to student emails. Students quickly get survey weary and stop responding to requests.

HRL professionals are educators who learn and teach; assessment is part of the learning process for HRL professionals. They devote their professional lives to helping students grow into better adults and to helping students succeed during and after college. To do that, they must think as educators and use data and other evidence to improve the learning experience for students.

# 10

# The Future of Residence Halls

For the past two decades, higher education in the United States has been buffeted by waves of reform. It started in mid-1990 with efforts to hold universities more accountable for graduation rates and other quality indicators that produced institutional rankings by the media and increased state and federal reporting requirements. Taxpayer concerns and the financial demands of Medicaid, pension funds, and correctional institutions reduced state funding to public higher education (Mahtesian, 1995). The 2008 recession further reduced state funding and drove unemployment rates up and endowment equity down. State and local support for higher education fell every year from 2000 to 2011, dropping from 71 percent to 57 percent (Chakrabarti, Mabutas, & Zafar, 2012). During this period, public funding per student, excluding loans, dropped 21 percent (SHEEO, 2012). Starting in 2008, state funding got worse. State support for higher education declined by an average of 28 percent by 2013 (Weissman, 2013).

State universities responded to budget cuts by increasing tuition and fees. Full-time undergraduate tuition and fees at public four-year institutions increased by an average of 42 percent from 2006–07 to 2011–12; tuition and fees at private institutions increased by an average of 28 percent (College Board, 2012). The Federal Reserve Board concluded that there was an "economically meaningful relationship between public funding and public institution tuition changes but mainly since the recession began and especially for the group of states with larger higher education funding cuts" (Chakrabarti et al., 2012, para. 6). The Federal Reserve Board and Congress responded to the 2008 recession by lowering interest rates and stimulating the economy with government spending. Collectively, these actions drove down borrowing costs for new construction and other economic investments.

Higher education usually experiences increases in enrollment during times of economic recession, and this trend accelerated with the educational demands of the job market (SHEEO, 2012). Between 2001 and 2011, the number of 18- to 24-year-olds attending college increased from 28.0 million to 31.1 million, an 11 percent increase, and the percentage of all 18- to 24-year-olds in the United States enrolled in college rose from 36 percent in 2001 to 42 percent in 2011 (NECS, 2013).

Enrollment growth and low interest rates allowed universities and private developers to borrow money to construct new RHs, apartments, and other buildings that had self-generated revenue. Debt at the 500 higher education institutions rated by Moody's Investor Services, an international credit rating agency, doubled between 2000 and 2011 during a time when donor pledges and giving at colleges declined by more than 40 percent relative to the amount they owed (Martin, 2012). In 2011, Moody's estimated that the 500 higher education institutions they rated had $205 billion in outstanding debt (Corkery, 2012).

Both institutional debt increase and the amount of money universities spent on student services increased. Desrochers and Kirshstein's (2014) review of higher education spending from 2002 through 2012 found that the fastest-growing salary expenditure per full-time equivalent student came from an increase in student services and the personnel to staff those services. They note that "personnel expenditures within student services suggest that some of the 'administrative bloat' reflects widespread investments in midlevel professionals providing non-instructional student assistance" (p. 18). Although they found that total higher education employment rose more than 25 percent, most of that growth was attributable to enrollment increases.

From 2000 to 2010, the population of students in higher education became more diverse. The number of white students increased by 24 percent, black students by 78 percent, Hispanic students by 90 percent, Asian/Pacific Islanders by 33 percent, and Native Americans by 0.5 percent (NCES, 2013). In addition, higher education saw significant changes in performance-based funding, technology used by students, the emergence of social media, expanded globalization, increased use of online education, and more governmental oversight. In this chapter, I examine each of these areas and the influence each is likely to have on the future of RHs in the next decade.

## Changing Student Population

NCES (2013) projects a 14 percent increase in postsecondary enrollment from 2010 to 2021. However, the biggest changes will come in the demographic composition of students. Table 10.1 depicts the annual expected enrollment growth in students by race/ethnicity from 2010 through 2021 (NCES, 2012c). The greatest enrollment increases will come from students who are currently underrepresented in higher education. Projected increases are 4 percent white, 25 percent black, 42 percent Hispanic, 20 percent Asian/Pacific Islander, and 1 percent American Indian/Alaska Native (NCES, 2012b). The change in the demographic profile of students reflects a change in the U.S. population. Nearly half of the children born in the United States in 2012 are nonwhite (National Vital Statistics Report, 2013) and by 2043 the U.S. Census (2012) projects that the U.S. population will be 43 percent white, 15 percent black, 31 percent Hispanic, 8 percent Asian, and 3 percent other racial/ethnic groups.

Different areas of the United States will experience different degrees of diversity. Already, California, Hawaii, New Mexico, and Texas no longer have a racial majority, while many of the states in the Midwest and West will remain predominantly white well into

**Table 10.1 Actual and Projected Numbers for Enrollment of U.S. Residents in all Postsecondary Degree-Granting Institutions, by Race/Ethnicity: Fall 2010 through Fall 2021 (in thousands)**

| | | Race/Ethnicity | | | | |
|---|---|---|---|---|---|---|
| Year | Total | White | Black | Hispanic | Asian/Pacific Islander | American Indian/Alaska Native |
| Actual | | | | | | |
| 2010 | 20,307 | 12,930 | 3,088 | 2,785 | 1,303 | 200 |
| Projected | | | | | | |
| 2011 | 20,551 | 12,996 | 3,144 | 2,871 | 1,338 | 201 |
| 2012 | 20,782 | 13,042 | 3,216 | 2,959 | 1,364 | 201 |
| 2013 | 20,987 | 13,060 | 3,288 | 3,051 | 1,386 | 201 |
| 2014 | 21,209 | 13,073 | 3,372 | 3,159 | 1,405 | 201 |
| 2015 | 21,390 | 13,053 | 3,448 | 3,267 | 1,422 | 200 |
| 2016 | 21,613 | 13,066 | 3,527 | 3,379 | 1,442 | 200 |
| 2017 | 21,910 | 13,136 | 3,610 | 3,498 | 1,466 | 200 |
| 2018 | 22,248 | 13,236 | 3,694 | 3,626 | 1,492 | 201 |
| 2019 | 22,561 | 13,328 | 3,764 | 3,750 | 1,517 | 202 |
| 2020 | 22,822 | 13,388 | 3,824 | 3,868 | 1,540 | 202 |
| 2021 | 23,010 | 13,407 | 3,873 | 3,967 | 1,560 | 202 |

*Note:* Race categories exclude persons of Hispanic ethnicity. Because of underreporting and nonreporting of racial/ethnic data and nonresident aliens, some estimates are slightly lower than corresponding data in other published tables. Detail may not sum to totals because of rounding. Some data have been revised from previously published figures.

*SOURCE:* U.S. Department of Education, National Center for Education Statistics, Integrated Postsecondary Education Data System (IPEDS), "Fall Enrollment Survey" (IPEDS-EF:96–99); IPEDS Spring 2001 through Spring 2011, Enrollment component; and Enrollment in Degree-Granting Institutions by Race/Ethnicity Model, 1980–2010. (This table was prepared February 2012.)

the future (U.S. Census, 2012). Social stratification among higher education institutions will further influence the degree of diversity at particular institutions.

The significant change in the demographic profile of students entering higher education is evident by an analysis of current U.S.

Census data for children ages 4 to 17 who will reach college age in the next 14 years. In this population, the percentage of white and black college-age students will *decrease* by 14.8 and 8.9 percent, respectively; however, Hispanic students will *increase* by 13.7 percent, and all other racial/ethnic college-age students will increase by 14.6 percent (Meyers, 2014).

Population percentages alone do not determine who attends college. A full 82 percent of the high school graduates from high-income families went to college in 2012, 66 percent from middle-income families enrolled, but only 52 percent of students from low-income families enrolled (Lipka, 2014). This percentage difference has been consistent since 2002 (College Board, 2013a). A number of factors contribute to this gap, including variations in high school graduation rates, cost of college attendance, the types of institutions attended, and other socioeconomic factors. By 2019–20 white non-Hispanic students are projected to be approximately 55 percent of graduates; in 2008–09 they accounted for approximately 62 percent (WICHE, 2013).

As of 2012, the number of Hispanic students enrolled in college reached a new high of 2.4 million, or approximately 19 percent of all college students, while the number of non-Hispanics declined between 2011 and 2012 (Lopez & Fry, 2013). The number of Hispanic students could be higher if the federal government and more states allowed Hispanic undocumented high school students to attend college as in-state residents, making them eligible for lower tuition rates, and if these students were eligible for federal student financial assistance. Although some states have allowed undocumented students who graduated from in-state high schools to enroll as in-state residents, they are still not eligible for federal student financial aid.

Greater student diversity in the future should improve student learning in residence halls (RHs). Research from the National Study of Student Learning (Pascarella, 1996) found that diversity experiences in the first year of college were particularly important in developing students' critical thinking skills and had long-term positive influence on students' cognitive growth throughout college. The study also revealed that racially oriented diversity experiences were particularly influential in enhancing the critical thinking skills of white students.

Pascarella and Terenzini (2005) found that diversity experiences also can improve students' academic skills and knowledge acquisition and may "enhance more general cognitive skills and intellectual development" (p. 194). In addition, their study showed that casual interactions with members of different racial and ethnic groups, like the type that occur in RHs, have statistically significant positive net effects on students' attitudes and values.

Increased racial diversity in RHs over a short period could lead to some lifestyle conflicts among students, but research on student attitudes and opinions suggest otherwise. Politically and ideologically current students are more liberal and more accepting of cultural differences than past generations, suggesting that any such lifestyle conflicts should be minimal and short-lived (Levine & Dean, 2012; Pew Research Center, 2014).

## Financial Constraints on Rising Costs of Higher Education

Student loan debt nearly tripled between 2005 and 2012 because of the increased number of students borrowing money and the larger amount of money each student borrowed (Lee, 2013). Over 70 percent of the students who graduated in 2012 had student loan debt averaging $29,400 each (Project on Student Debt, 2013). Current estimates of national student loan debt now exceed $1.2 trillion (Federal Reserve Board, 2014).

Room and board charges are a significant part of the debt students incur on residential campuses. At public four-year universities, they account for more than half the total charges students pay (College Board, 2013b). When these charges are included, the total cost of attending public four-year institutions rose more rapidly in the past decade (2003–04 and 2013–14) than in either of the two previous decades (College Board, 2014). Tuition and fees increased during this period by 5.2 percent per year above inflation, and room and board charges increased by an average of 2.6 percent per year above inflation—leading to a 3.8 percent average annual rate of growth above inflation (College Board, 2014). The rapid rate of increases has had the greatest impact on low-income families. For the poorest 20 percent of Americans, the cost of public higher education in 2011 was 114 percent of their annual income (Mettler, 2014). The published costs of attending many private universities (before tuition discounts) exceed the median household income of many families; the national average household income in the United States is $51,371, ranging from $71,122 in Maryland to $37,095 in Mississippi (U.S. Census, 2013). Even for families with higher incomes, the cost of paying for college is becoming too expensive. Cohen (2014) provides this example:

> Consider a family of four, earning $100,000 in income and having $50,000 in savings. The E.F.C. [expected family contribution] says that this family will contribute $17,375 each year to a child's college expenses. A $100,000 income translates into take-home pay of about $6,311 monthly. An E.F.C. of $17,375 means the family must contribute about $1,500 a month—every month for four years. But cutting family expenses by 25 percent every month is unrealistic. (para. 6)

Whether students attend a public four-year university or a private four-year university with a generous policy of tuition discounting, the real cost of attending college has continued to increase at a rate faster than inflation or annual family incomes.

There are many reasons for the increases. Some researchers believe that one of the main ones is the increased debt from new construction in auxiliary services such as residence halls (RHs), dining halls, stadiums, and recreation centers. Eaton and Habinek (2013) found that between 2002 and 2010 debt service payments at public research universities increased by 86 percent and overall spending on auxiliary services increased by 22 percent. By comparison, the rate of increase for instructional spending was only 11 percent. Total debt at public research universities in 2010 was 50 percent greater than it was in 2002, leaving public research universities with an average debt per student of $26,615 (Eaton & Habinek).

Faced with rising enrollments, student demand for higher-quality housing, and evidence that the quality of student housing influences student recruitment and retention (Cain & Reynolds, 2006), many housing and residence life (HRL) professionals took advantage of favorable construction costs and historically low interest rates to invest in new RHs and apartments. Abramson (2012) studied the construction of new student housing over a 10-year period (2003 through 2012). His analysis included 427 student housing projects totaling 57 million square feet and housing 171,000 students. The total cost of these projects exceeded $13 billion. Based on these data, Abramson estimated that the average RH was built to house approximately 374 students and cost approximately $69,000 per student, or $200 per square foot, at 2012 rates. He noted that during the 10-year period reviewed cost per square foot rose rapidly from $148 to $231 but declined in 2008 to stabilize nationally at around $200 per square foot.

HRL departments function much like independent not-for-profit businesses. Debt service payments on capital improvements, such as new RH construction, and other operating expenses, such as utilities and personnel, are paid from revenue generated by leasing rooms to students and summer conferences guests. Some universities operate under this auxiliary services model, while others centralize all institutional revenue, including revenue from student housing, and operating budgets are assigned to HRL departments.

Although some of the cost associated with the increase in higher education is attributable to debt incurred by HRL departments and other auxiliary services, business decisions like these are made in consultation with financial experts and are based on enrollment growth, housing demand, construction costs, interest rates, energy efficiency, and borrowing capacity. It is likely that over the life span of an RH these investments in student housing will provide a positive financial benefit to the institution. However, the challenge of the next decade is stabilizing the associated operating costs and maintaining occupancy during a time of changing enrollment patterns and demographics and more cost-conscious families (Harvey, 2014).

Higher education is under pressure to constrain spending and limit annual increases (Belkin & Thurm, 2012; Boehner & McKeon, 2003; Ginsburg, 2011), and these constraints apply to annual increases in room and board. Many universities have implemented programs to reduce operating costs through administrative staff reductions, restructuring, and consolidation (Belkin, 2013). Some private colleges are resetting their published prices by dropping the long-standing practice of tuition discounting and instead publish the actual net cost of attendance to attract more cost-conscious families (Lewin, 2013).

Moody's Investors Services (2013) rated the financial outlook for higher education as negative for 2014 because of continued price resistance to increased tuition and fees, declining federal research support, heightened competition for students, diminished donor support, and diminished state support for public institutions. It also cited regulatory oversight from federal and state agencies and the push to move to a performance based accountability system based on criteria such as retention, graduation, and job placement. Standard & Poor's Financial Services (2014), another international investment rating agency, also has a negative outlook on the financial health of colleges and universities. The reasons they give include "heightened scrutiny regarding affordability and the corresponding shift in demand, narrowing operating margins, and increased regulation" (para. 1).

The changing demographic profile of students in the next decade may change the number of students interested in living in RHs. Table 10.2 depicts the percentage distribution of undergraduates by local residence while enrolled (National Postsecondary Student Aid

**Table 10.2 Percentage Distribution of Undergraduates by Local Residence While Enrolled, Selected Characteristics**

| Institutional and Student Characteristics | On Campus | Off-Campus, Not with Parents | Off-Campus, with Parents |
|---|---|---|---|
| Total | 15.4 | 58.6 | 26.0 |
| Public | | | |
| 2-Year | 1.0 | 62.0 | 37.0 |
| 4-Year nondoctorate | 20.9 | 53.9 | 25.2 |
| 4-Year doctorate granting | 29.3 | 55.3 | 15.4 |
| Private | | | |
| 4-Year nondoctorate | 42.7 | 45.9 | 11.3 |
| 4-Year doctorate granting | 49.6 | 39.0 | 11.4 |
| Race/ethnicity | | | |
| White | 17.5 | 58.6 | 23.9 |
| Black | 13.5 | 65.3 | 21.2 |
| Hispanic | 7.5 | 55.4 | 37.1 |
| Asian | 17.4 | 50.7 | 31.9 |
| American Indian | 9.3 | 65.7 | 25.0 |
| Pacific Islander | 9.9 | 54.1 | 36.0 |
| Two or more races | 17.2 | 57.0 | 25.8 |
| Other | 9.7 | 63.1 | 27.2 |
| Dependence status | | | |
| Dependent | 27.5 | 32.6 | 39.8 |
| Independent | 2.0 | 87.4 | 10.6 |
| Age | | | |
| 18 or younger | 37.2 | 18.7 | 43.3 |
| 19–23 | 22.3 | 41.4 | 36.3 |
| Income | | | |
| Lowest 25 percent | 12.7 | 53.7 | 33.6 |
| Middle 50 percent | 13.1 | 58.4 | 27.3 |

| | | | |
|---|---|---|---|
| Highest 25 percent | 20.5 | 64.3 | 15.2 |
| Parent's education | | | |
| High school diploma or less | 8.6 | 65.9 | 25.5 |
| Some postsecondary education | 13.1 | 58.1 | 28.8 |
| Bachelor's degree or higher | 23.9 | 51.7 | 24.4 |

*Source:* U.S. Department of Education, National Center for Education Statistics, 2007–08 National Postsecondary Student Aid Study (NPSAS:08). Adapted from Table 3.9 (pp. 97–98) (National Postsecondary Student Aid Study, 2010); available at http://nces.ed.gov/pubs2010/2010205.pdf#page=97.

*Note:* Numbers may not add to 100 due to rounding and the elimination of some subcategories.

Study, 2010). Although Hispanic students are the fastest-growing student population, they are the least likely to lived on campus. In fact, students from all underrepresented groups are less likely to live on campus than are white students. One reason for this is that more first-generation college students come from underrepresented groups (NCES, 2012a). Among 5- to 17-year-olds in 2011, 61 percent were first-generation (NCES, 2012a). For the past three decades, a lower percentage of first-generation students lived on campus than non-first-generation students. The gap has remained relatively consistent; between 1975 and 2005, first-generation students at four-year universities were approximately 14 percent less likely to live on campus than were non-first-generation students (Saenz et al., 2007). Other reasons for the differences are related to socioeconomic factors and the greater likelihood of students from underrepresented groups to attend community colleges and for-profit universities, which usually do not have RHs (Baum, Ma, & Payea, 2013; Mettler, 2014). If white students become a smaller segment of the college-going population, as predicted, and students from underrepresented groups continue to live off-campus or continue to prefer attending community colleges, then some of the occupancy models that supported decisions to borrow money to build new RHs and apartments could be tested by the changing population of students and their choice of where to live and where to attend college.

## Performance-Based Funding and Educational Attainment

Many state legislatures have enacted or are considering performance-based funding for higher education, which usually includes graduation rates as one measure of performance (NCSL, 2014a). If the demographic projections for future enrollment are accurate and nothing is done to improve educational attainment rates of underserved students, future graduation rates are likely to decline. The Western Interstate Commission for Higher Education (WICHE) (2013) compared the educational attainment of younger workers (aged 25–34) to their older counterparts (aged 45–54). The study revealed not only that black, Hispanic, and American Indians/Alaska Natives graduate at much lower rates than whites or Asian/Pacific Islanders but also that "younger Hispanics have lower attainment rates than their older counterparts and while Black non-Hispanics are better educated than their elders, the difference is slight" (p. 3). Unless efforts are made to improve graduation rates of underserved students, the combination of demographic changes and lower attainment rates will jeopardize state funding in states with performance-based funding models.

The U.S. Department of Education (2014) has proposed a ranking system for higher education based on the value of the education offered at each institution. It will be based on data provided by institutions about access, affordability, and outcomes. Suggested outcome measures include graduation and transfer rates, earnings of graduates, and completion of advanced degrees; access measures may include the percentage of students receiving Pell Grants; and affordability measures may include net price and loan debt. The Department of Education is undertaking the value-ranking system in response to growing public pressure about the rising cost of higher education and concerns that many for-profit postsecondary institutions have very low graduation rates and are forcing students into significant debt for low-value degrees. Regardless of the reasons, associated institutional costs, or accuracy of the information collected, publication of a Department of Education ranking on the educational value of an institution's degree could have profound effects on institutional enrollments, tuition and fees, fundraising, and overall institutional reputation. If the reputation, financial health, or enrollment of an institution suffers, HRL programs also suffer.

## Public–Private Partnerships

Prior to the 1970s, many colleges and universities controlled students' off-campus living arrangements. Institutions abandoned this practice when the student–institutional relationship changed and most in loco parentis functions ended. It was not long after this change that private developers saw the financial opportunities in student housing. Their obstacles were land acquisition, financing, and competition from universities that had long enjoyed property tax exemptions, ownership of student housing with little or no debt, and policies that required students to live on campus for one or more years. Private developers took different approaches to circumvent these issues. One approach was to ignore universities and build low-cost, wood frame, garden-style apartments with amenities such as clubhouses, fitness centers, swimming pools, on-site parking, air conditioning, and private bedrooms. This model worked for many private developers, but others saw the benefit of developing public–private partnerships with universities.

As universities sought to expand and improve their student housing, they found interested partners among private companies who had access to capital and understood the student housing market. Universities with limited bonding capacity also saw in these partnerships the opportunity to offer students modern accommodations without assuming debt or using their bonding capacity to build RHs. In addition, some public universities were constrained by state budget cuts and state legislatures that would not approve new capital construction projects that added debt obligations to state agencies. A number of state legislators and trustees also held the opinion that whatever government could do, private enterprise could do better. Public–private partnerships seemed to offer an ideal way to tap the acumen of private business to benefit state-controlled universities. In this entrepreneurial climate, universities, and occasionally their foundations, began to view private developers as partners.

A survey by College Planning and Management found that 70 percent of the new buildings under construction in 2011 were developed by universities without any involvement from outside private partners (Moore, 2012). The remaining 30 percent were owned solely by private developers, jointly by universities and private developers, or by university foundations and operated by HRL departments. Earlier surveys by this same organization found a similar distribution (Moore, 2010).

A number of different public–private arrangements exist in student housing. Bernstein (n.d., para. 8–14) identified four of the most common structures:

> (1) University-owned land with ground lease to developer. This is the structure that has been most commonly implemented in our public–private partnerships. The developer obtains a long-term ground lease of a university-owned parcel of land and commits to financing, constructing, and managing the property. The university maintains fee ownership of the land, with the typical ground lease arrangement structured to last between 60 and 80 years. (2) University-owned land with ground lease to developer plus master lease. This structure

mirrors the previous arrangement but includes some additional risk mitigation for the developer. Under a master lease, the university extends a financial commitment to lease units within the project regardless of student demand. It is often the case that the master lease is negotiated for a multiyear period but does not typically extend through the length of the ground lease term. (3) Foundation-owned project and fee development. Under this arrangement, the university typically enters into a long-term ground lease with a 501(c)(3) foundation that is either independent or in some way affiliated with the institution. Tax-exempt bonds are issued to fund the project and are later repaid through project revenues. The developer receives a fee for services, which typically include coordinating bond financing, collaborating with the architect, managing construction, and finally, delivering the project. (4) Joint ownership. The final deal structure . . . involves the developer and university sharing some form of risk and return through joint ownership. This can involve the institution contributing either land or a building into the partnership in return for a percentage of equity within the partnership. The developer contributes the remaining equity that is needed to complete the project, while also obtaining project financing and assuming all construction risk.

Public–private partnerships have earned a place among the student housing options available to universities. In states that have made it difficult for public universities to borrow money, for universities with limited access to capital markets, or for institutions that have limited debt capacity but need additional student housing, partnerships with private developers may be good financial options. Large universities with good credit ratings, debt capacities, multiple sources of income, large HRL infrastructures, and access to land usually find that they can build and operate new student housing at the same or less cost without collaborating with private developers. However, they may wish to collaborate for certain types of projects, like family housing. Every institution and every business arrangement has its own set of parameters that determine the viability of partnerships.

There are examples of institutions that contract with private developers to build and manage all or part of their student housing, but there is no evidence that this is a trend. In the next decade, when universities explore opportunities to construct new RHs or apartments, they are likely to consider the option of partnership on a case-by-case basis.

HRL departments also maintain partnerships with many private businesses to provide maintenance and repair services for fire alarms, elevators, plumbing and electrical systems, video cameras, cable television, recycling, landscaping, windows, and roofs. They also pay licensing and maintenance fees on software to assist with room assignments, summer conference housing, and repair requests. Some HRL departments have found it more cost-effective to outsource housekeeping and some housing functions. As annual increases in room and board charges become more constrained by public pressure to reduce the rising cost of higher education, HRL departments may consider more outsourcing options—if they are more economical, provide the same or better quality of service, and allow institutions to retain control over the most important educational elements of RHs.

However, there is no evidence that partnerships or outsourcing of RH operating functions will significantly change the landscape of HRL departments in the next decade. The most likely scenario is that institutions will continue to make business judgments about cost efficiencies in RHs influenced not only by potential cost savings but also by the quality of the educational experience for students. Because of this, most residence life functions will likely remain under the control of the university, while some housing operational functions that can be performed more efficiently by private businesses may be outsourced.

## Expanded Use of Online Education

Researchers speculate that the traditional model of students leaving home to attend college will be changed by massive open online courses (MOOCs) and other forms of online education (Christensen & Horn, 2013; Friedman, 2013; Pappano, 2012). Advocates of this vision argue that higher education is too expensive and that the traditional residential universities have served their purpose and will soon be artifacts of the past. The future, they propose, is one in which distinguished faculty members from across the globe teach courses via the Internet and thousands of students enroll through online education distributors. Students will learn from home, save money, choose what to study from a list of courses offered by the best universities in the world, and collect the academic credits they need to obtain degrees. What graduates know (based on standardized tests), rather than where they attended college, will become the criterion for employment, making education at the most prestigious universities equal to that of the least reputable online marketers of degrees (Christensen & Horn; Friedman). Selingo (2013) compared the arguments being made by people who deny the future impact of online course delivery to arguments made by the newspaper industry before it underwent a massive transformation that closed many newspapers and forced others online.

Allen and Seaman (2013) found that the number of students taking online courses increased from 10 percent in 2003 to 32 percent in 2011. Their study also revealed that approximately 6.7 million students took at least one online course in 2012, a 9 percent increase from the previous year. The majority (69 percent) of academic leaders included in the study considered online instruction as critical to the long-term strategic plan of their institutions. However, the public is less convinced. A Pew Research Center (2011) survey found that only 29 percent of the public perceived online courses to be as valuable as classroom instruction.

MOOCs have received recent attention because of large enrollments, the high quality of the institutions offering them, and the fact that courses are free. In 2012, only 5 percent of institutions in the United States offered MOOCs, and another 9 percent were planning to do so (Allen & Seaman, 2013). However, interest in them appears to be waning. In 2012, 26 percent of academic leaders thought they were not a sustainable method for offering courses, and in 2013 that number increased to 36 percent (Allen & Seaman).

Three problems affect the success of MOOCs. The first is the financial model. There isn't one. Courses cannot be offered free for very long without a return on the investment of faculty and technical resources. Second, only a handful of institutions are accepting certificates of MOOC completion for course credit. And third, completion rates for MOOCs are very low. Kolowich (2014) found that only 5 percent of the 841,687 people who registered for 17 MOOCs at Harvard University and Massachusetts Institute of Technology (MIT) completed the courses and earned certificates; 36 percent of the registrants never viewed any of the course material, and 5 percent of registrants who viewed at least half of a course's content completed the course. These finding are similar to an earlier study at Pennsylvania State University that highlighted low MOOC completion rates (Kolowich, 2013).

What is often overlooked in discussions about online education is where students are living when they take courses. The traditional assumption has been that students are at home and not enrolled in a traditional two- or four-year college. Most online courses at four-year public and not-for-profit private universities are taken by students currently enrolled and attending their home institutions, which may be offering the course online (Gabrel,

2010). Online courses include the online-only model and the hybrid/blended model in which part of the instruction is in a traditional classroom setting and part is online. Some students living on campus enroll in several courses taught through classroom instruction and one or two courses taught either partially or fully online. Course time conflicts, graduation requirements, work schedules, convenience, and learning styles contribute to students' decisions to take courses online.

Public universities that experience significant cuts in state funding frequently use online education as a way to reduce instructional expenses and ease demand on overcrowded classrooms (Gabrel, 2010; Selingo, 2013). With online instruction, course enrollments are not restricted by physical classroom size, availability, or scheduling limitations.

HRL departments have nothing to fear in the next decade from an increase in online education. Students will still attend college and live with other students in RHs, not only because students want to leave home and be with other students but also because parents want their children to have the best opportunities to succeed, make friends, experience life, and build their futures. That is hard to do over the Internet, in online course chat rooms, or watching video lectures by people you never meet.

As long as RHs have good technology and fast internet connections, students will be able to use their RH's rooms as their classrooms. Sometime in the future, RHs could become the place students take most of their courses. Students will still have access to faculty and laboratories, but they may find that they learn as much in online courses as they do from sitting through lectures in auditoriums with hundreds of other students. Although this may seem plausible at large public universities, families spending upward of $60,000 annually on private colleges are likely to continue to demand low student-to-faculty ratios and high levels of personal interaction with faculty (Gabrel, 2010). This may be one of the reasons that online courses are more common at public universities and why selective private colleges are the least interested in this format (Allen & Seaman, 2013; Pew Research Center, 2011).

## Challenges of Expanding Technology

Today's traditional-age college students, 18 to 24 years old, have always been around technology. They are sophisticated users of the Internet, social media, and mobile technology. Students embrace new technologies as they emerge and tend to search for the newest and most innovative platforms available. A full 98 percent of undergraduates use the Internet, and 92 percent access the Internet wirelessly on either laptops or cell phones (Smith, Rainie, & Zickuhr, 2011). Virtually all college students own cell phones (96 percent), and more students use laptop computers (88 percent) than desktop computers (59 percent); many have both (Smith et al.).

Widespread cell phone use by students has made it easier for institutions to notify them of emergencies and campus crimes. Cell phones and swipe cards are routinely used to access RHs, elevators, vending machines, and sometimes individual student rooms. Extensive use of cell phones has allowed institutions to remove telephones and landlines from most student rooms, saving significant operating costs. Smartphones are used by 53 percent of students, most of whom (77 percent) use them as soon as they awaken in the morning (Payne, 2013). Future smartphone technology promises biometric security, constant health and fitness monitoring, 3D screen holograms, seamless voice control, built-in projectors, and flexible screens (Court, 2013; Poh, 2013). Students routinely use the camera and audio and video recording features of smartphone to document all types of behavior and post to social media sites. As wearable devices such as Google Glass become more common, more conflicts will likely arise over issues of privacy and appropriateness of content.

The rampant growth in technology and students' expectations for access to unlimited bandwidth is overwhelming the ability of residential networks to meet demand. Online video gaming, streaming video, music services, social media, and the presence of multiple mobile devices per user require extraordinary amounts of bandwidth. In RHs that do not have wireless access, many students install their own wireless routers, which present security and access problems.

Peer-to-peer file sharing of videos and music is a source of concern for the entertainment industry because it loses significant amounts of money on royalty payments each year. Although much of this practice has stopped, due in part to the efforts of university information technology (IT) professionals and aggressive entertainment industry lawyers, websites like Pandora, Spotify, Netflix, and YouTube now consume massive amounts of bandwidth on multiple mobile and fixed devices (New, 2013).

The demand for bandwidth, electrical power, and electrical outlets is likely to expand in the future and is already a significant challenge for colleges and universities (Daly, 2012). The devices that consume the most bandwidth on campus are (in order of demand) tablets, smartphones, iPods, game boxes, e-readers, video systems, handheld gaming consoles, smart TVs, wireless printers, and DVRs (Daly). According to the Association for Information Communication Technology Professionals in Higher Education (ACUTA), 90 percent of IT officers indicate that increased use of tablets is likely to consume the most bandwidth in coming years, which prompted 27 percent of campuses included in its study to limit the number of devices a student can use to connect to the campus network at one time (Daly). A subsequent study found that 61 percent of institution leaders expect the cost of providing residential networks to increase but that only 39 percent have realized increases in their operating budgets to address the demand (ACUTA & NACUBO, 2013). The methods IT officers use to control costs include offering students the option to pay for additional bandwidth (16 percent) and outsourcing portions of the residential network (22 percent) to private providers, such as cable companies (ACUTA & NACUBO).

How important is bandwidth to students? A total of 64 percent of students would consider moving from their RHs or apartments if the internet speed was too slow (Daly, 2012). Demand for bandwidth will continue to increase with the use of more mobile devices and cloud-based computing. HRL departments that provide substandard service in this area can expect to see students move to housing that better meets their technology needs.

## Continuing Use of Social Networking Sites

Most college students (81 percent) use social media as one of their primary means of communicating with friends and family (Pew Research Center, 2014). Many residence life professionals, including resident assistants (RAs), have social media connections with their residents. However, use of social media is not all positive. Students who are prone to text or post before thinking or who post confidential information about themselves or others frequently experience the consequences of those decisions. Most (90 percent) college students hold the view that people share too much information about themselves online; nevertheless, many students continue to do so (Pew Research Center).

Lepp, Barkely, and Karpinski (2014) found that student cell phone use and texting are negatively associated with grade point average (GPA) and positively associated with feelings of anxiety. Kalipidu, Costin, and Morris (2011) explored the use of social media use and attitudes related to self-esteem and college adjustment. They found that first-year students had stronger emotional connections to and spent more time on social media sites than upper-division students and that frequent use of social media sites in the first year of college was negatively associated with emotional and academic adjustment. However, with upper division students, frequent use of social media sites was positively associated with social adjustment and attachment to the university. The results suggest that the use of social media sites increases social integration with peers as first-year students reduce their interaction with high school friends and family members and make more friends in college by becoming more involved in campus activities. Number of friends on a social media site—not the amount of time spent using a site—was the primary predictor of college adjustment of the first-year students in this study.

A frequent criticism of social networking is that it promotes multitasking, which can decrease efficiency and productivity. Karpinski et al. (2013) investigated the impact of multitasking on social networks and GPAs among U.S. and European university students. They found a negative relationship between the use of social networks and GPA that was made worse by multitasking for U.S. students but not for European students. The researchers concluded that European students were less prone to disruptive multitasking, but the reason for this difference is unclear.

Manago, Taylor, and Greenfield (2012) examined a social media site that had a status update feature. They discovered that for university students, status updates served as a form of emotional disclosure that enhanced feelings of intimacy. Students in the study who had larger networks of friends were more satisfied with life and perceived greater social support than students with fewer friends on the social media site. The researchers believe that social networking sites help students satisfy their psychosocial needs for permanent relationships, which is highly valued in a transient environment. This assertion was reinforced by the finding that students with the highest numbers of long-term friends placed high value on social media sites as a source of social support.

Advances in communication technology have made it easier for college students to stay connected to their families. Ramsey et al. (2013) found that between 2009 and 2011 students' rates of in-person contact and telephone use to communicate with parents did not change but that use of texting and social network sites to contact parents increased significantly; use of email declined.

Students' telephone interaction with parents was associated with satisfaction, intimacy, support, and instructional assistance—all of which strengthened relationships between students and parents.

Despite the benefits and advantages of social media, indiscrete social media behavior can have long-term damaging effects. Concerns include violations of privacy and cyberbullying, and in some cases social media may become the source of a student conduct inquiry. Although most RAs and residence life professionals do not search students' social networking sites for evidence of misbehavior, when information reaches administrators about violations of university policy it can be difficult to ignore. If the evidence is credible and serious, university officials may have a duty to take formal action.

Social networking sites allow activists to inform and mobilize others for action. Fighting proposed tuition and fee increases or organizing protests against unpopular institutional decisions is facilitated by the open communication offered by the use of social networking sites. The examples shared in this section are just a few of the many ways social networking is part of college life. Residence life educators need to continue to understand and use this medium to communicate better with students and help students learn how to use these sites in ways that connect them to the university community and their friends without overexposing themselves in ways that may hurt them in future years.

## Globalization

As state budget cuts increase, public four-year universities have heavily recruited undergraduate international students who pay out-of-state tuition and do not receive federal financial aid (Lewin, 2012). Efforts to recruit international students have grown in intensity to the point that institutions have paid commissions to international agents to recruit students. This practice has become so widespread that in 2013 the National Association for College Admission Counseling (NACAC) changed its ethics standards to allow the practice, which it previously prohibited (Redden, 2013).

The Institute of International Education (2013) reported that the number of international students studying at U.S. institutions in 2013 was nearly 820,000—a 7.2 percent increase from the previous year. Figure 10.1 depicts the numbers of international students studying in the United States from 2002 through 2013. The rate of growth in international student enrollments started in 2007. Most international students come from China (29 percent), followed by India (12 percent), South Korea (9 percent), Saudi Arabia (5 percent), and Canada (3 percent). International students pursue many academic disciplines, but business and management (21.8 percent), engineering (18.8 percent), mathematics and computer science (9.5 percent), social sciences (8.9 percent), and physical and life sciences (8.4 percent) are the most frequent fields of study (Institute of International Education, 2013).

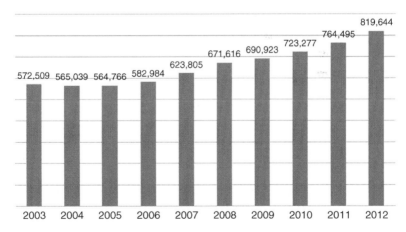

**Figure 10.1    International Student Enrollment in United States, 2003–2012**

*Data Source:* Institute of International Education. (2013). Open doors data. Available at http://www.iie.org/Research-and-Publications/Open-Doors/Data

International students add to the diversity of a university, bring new perspectives to a multitude of issues in classroom discussions, and enrich the global perspectives of U.S. students. However, undergraduate international students offer some special challenges, particularly for residence life professionals.

Institutions that close RHs between the fall and spring terms and after the end of the academic year need to arrange housing for international students who need housing during these times. This is less of a problem for upper-division students, who frequently live in on-campus apartments, but it can present a challenge for first-year undergraduates who live in traditional RHs and who need access to food services and other student services such as the health service, student center, counseling center, and recreation center.

Perhaps the greatest challenge for residence life professionals responsible for large numbers of undergraduate international students is the increased likelihood of emergencies, such as psychological health events or physical injuries. Although institutions commonly require international students to have medical insurance, assisting international students during crises places additional responsibility on residence life professionals to mobilize the resources necessary to communicate with parents when it becomes necessary to do so. Student affairs professionals who work in international student offices can assist with many of the challenges, such as finding translators to communicate with parents during an emergency and arranging visas for family members when situations require travel to the United States. Large institutions located in proximity to urban environments can adapt more easily to these challenges because of available institutional and community resources. Smaller institutions, particularly in rural areas, are those that are likely to be most challenged in providing the infrastructure necessary to fully address the needs of a large number of undergraduate international students.

More U.S. universities are establishing branch campuses in countries throughout the world. The countries with the largest numbers of U.S. branch campuses are China (13), Canada (9), United Arab Emirates (8), and Qatar (7) (Lane & Kinser, 2014). The principal purpose of these branch campuses is to educate host nation students, though some also serve as study abroad sites for U.S. students. International branch campuses are of varying sizes and complexity. Some offer academic work in one field, while others are complete campuses with multiple degree programs and student housing. Institutions that provide student housing frequently hire residence life professionals to provide educational programs and student support services. As enrollments on these campuses climb and more U.S. students study abroad, more of these campuses are likely to offer student housing.

## Increasing Governmental Oversight

Governmental regulation of higher education increased in the past two decades, and there is no reason to believe that it will decline in the next decade. The 2008 reauthorization of the Higher Education Act (HEA) of 1965, retitled the Higher Education Opportunity Act (HEOA) of 2008 (Public Law 110–315), created a host of new reporting requirements related to higher education, most directed at holding universities more accountable. A 2011 study of senior higher education executives found that 90 percent perceived the new provisions of the 2008 HEOA to be burdensome and 68 percent perceived it to be more burdensome than other federal, state, and nongovernmental regulations (Advisory Committee on Student Financial Assistance, 2011).

Changes to three laws that have the most impact on HRL departments are amendments to the American with Disabilities Act (ADA) of 1990, the Crime Awareness and Campus Security Act of 1990, and U.S. Department of Education guidance on compliance with provisions of Title IX. Congress created the Crime Awareness and Campus Security Act of 1990 (Title II of Public Law 101-542) and amended it in 1992, 1998, 2000, and 2008. In 1998, the act was renamed the Jeanne Clery Disclosure of Campus Security Policy and Campus Crime Statistics Act, and it is often referred to simply as the Clery Act.

When Congress amended the Clery Act in 2008 it added a number of new provisions, among them additional hate crimes, required clarification of the relationship between campus police and other law enforcement agencies, rules about emergency notification procedures, required publication of missing student notification procedures for institutions with on-campus student housing, fire safety reporting requirements for institutions with on-campus student housing, a definition of on-campus student housing, and requirements concerning disclosure of the results of disciplinary proceedings provided to alleged victims of crimes of violence or nonforcible sex offenses (U.S. Department of Education, Office of Postsecondary Education, 2011). Although most reportable student misconduct in RHs was included in the campus crime statistics, the modifications to the Clery Act now treat student housing as a separate subclassification and impose additional reporting requirements.

Congress passed the ADA of 1990 (Public Law 110-325) to ensure nondiscrimination against people with disabilities and to guarantee their access to public facilities. ADA was modified several times, most recently in 2008. Among the changes to the law in 2008 were an expanded definition of a disability, a directive that the term should be construed broadly, increased obligations on institutions to make accommodations, and limitations on what institutions could do to address behavior associated with a disability, including mental health disorders. One of the new regulations in this law concerns service animals and assistance animals. Service animals are defined specifically "as a dog that is individually trained to do work or perform tasks for a person with a disability" (U.S. Department of Justice, Office of Civil Rights, 2011, para. 2). HRL departments have permitted service dogs for many years as a reasonable accommodation to policies prohibiting animals in RHs. New is the inclusion of assistance animals to provide support. The assistance animal could be a dog, cat, potbellied pig, or any number of other animals that provide emotional support to a person with an emotional disability. The U.S. Department of Justice has gone so far as to issue regulations on the use of miniature horses as assistance animals (U.S. Department of Justice, Civil Rights Division, 2011).

Although ADA regulations do not specifically address assistance animals in student housing, the U.S. Department of Housing and Urban Development (HUD) has issued its interpretation, which applies to the Fair Housing Act and therefore to universities (2013). Under the HUD interpretation, reasonable accommodations must be made for assistance animals even when their presence violates provisions of the housing lease prohibiting animals or other people object to them. Because housing administrators are limited by regulations about what they can ask students to provide to verify their requests, the potential for abuse of this regulation in RHs and apartments is evident. More complicated yet is the difficulty presented when two students with disabilities—such as a student with severe allergies to animals—conflict with another student's emotional need to have a comfort animal. HUD goes so far as to provide guidance on how to resolve these conflicts.

The Title IX Education Amendment of 1972 was created to prohibit discrimination on the basis of sex, and there is a substantial case law about how it should be interpreted and implemented (Kaplin & Lee, 2009). On April 4, 2011, the U. S. Department of Education, Office of Civil Rights issued a letter that provided additional regulatory guidance about the interpretation and implementation of Title IX in higher education. The letter established a number of institutional obligations to respond to allegations of sexual harassment and sexual assault. The 19-page letter details procedures for investigation, adjudication, resolution, and legal recourses of appeal for complainants if they are not satisfied with the resolution of the allegations.

The Clery Act, ADA, and Title IX are not the only new laws and regulatory requirements imposed on higher education. State legislatures, local municipalities, and other governmental entities such as the Occupational Safety and Health Administration (OSHA) and the Environmental Protection Agency (EPA), which have authority to regulate public health, safety, building codes, and fire safety, also issue new regulations each year.

The public reaction to the rapid rise in the cost of higher education and the successful lobbying efforts of special interest groups with Congress and state legislators is evident among regulations imposed on universities through legislation and court challenges. Prominent among these are legislation and court rulings in seven states (Colorado, Idaho, Kansas, Mississippi, Oregon, Utah, and Wisconsin) allowing students and other people to carry concealed weapons on public university campuses (NCSL, 2014b).

Twenty-four-hour news coverage by television, bloggers, websites, and newspapers has exacerbated the regulatory pressure on higher education by sensationalizing events and exaggerating how pervasive an issue is within higher education. In this media-rich environment, events on one or two campuses are generalized as endemic to all of higher education. This rush to judgment by the media is the wellspring of efforts by often well-intentioned state and federal legislators who want to solve problems—real or not. At times, the clamor of state and federal legislative efforts to regulate higher education can be overwhelming. For example, the chair of the assembly committee responsible for higher education in one state recently proposed 20 new higher education laws aimed at cutting the cost of higher education and making institutions more accountable (Kelderman, 2014). Among the proposed legislation was a state law that would prohibit universities from requiring meal plans and a proposed law requiring the state's auditor to independently determine if each student fee a university charged actually benefited students.

Rationales constructed to support the creation of policies, laws, and regulations are not always wrong; however, they may be wrong for specific applications. The problem is determining when they will be wrong and managing the consequences. Imposing new accountability mechanisms is like prescribing new medicines that have random and possibly severe consequences. It should be done rarely, and only when all other options have been exhausted.

The culture of accountability and blame directed at higher education creates emotional uncertainty for administrators that can paralyze decision making. Worse yet, the fear of being the target of scrutiny and second-guessing that has followed many decisions in higher education has devolved into universities building policy walls as barricades against special interest groups seeking to place blame. In such environments, risk-taking is discouraged and professional judgments become hazardous. This environment is not good for higher education. Although terms like *accountability* and *transparency* seem harmless, the zealous application of such benevolent ideas can offer a road to institutional stagnation and impassivity.

Dennis Gabor (1964), the Noble Prize–winning physicist, wrote, "The future cannot be predicted, but futures can be invented" (p. 207). The challenge for HRL professionals is to help invent a future that allows students to learn, grow, and develop in environments that are not overly burdened by bureaucratic regulation. It starts by working with other university administrators to inform policymakers about the quality of student life and learning in RHs, stopping bad legislation, and managing new laws and regulations in ways that keep students' best interests at the center of decision making.

# References

Abma, J. C., Martinez, G. M., Mosher, W. D., & Dawson, B. S. (2004). Teenagers in the United States: Sexual activity, contraceptives use, and childbearing, 2002. *Vital Health Stat, 23*(24), 1–48.

Abramson, P. (2012, June). There's no place like home. *College Planning & Management*, 24–35. Available at http://collegeplanning.epubxp.com/i/74667/23

ACT. (2013). Collegiate Assessment of Academic Proficiency (CAAP). *CAAP Guide to Successful General Education Outcomes*.

ACUHO-I/EBI. (2013). ACUHO-I/EBI Resident Assessment. Available at http://www.webebi.com/assessments/resident-life

Advisory Committee on Student Financial Assistance. (2011). *Higher education regulations study: Final report*. Advisory Committee on Student Financial Assistance.

Aiello, J. R., Baum, A., & Gromley, F. P. (1981). Social determinants of residential crowding stress. *Personality and Social Psychology Bulletin, 7*(4), 643–649.

Allen, I. E., & Seaman, J. (2013). *Changing course: Ten years of tracking online education in the united states*. Babson Survey Research Group and Quahog Research Group.

Altman, I. (1975). *The environment and social behavior: Privacy, personal space, territory and crowding*. Monterey, CA: Brooks/Cole.

Altman, I. (1976). Privacy: A conceptual analysis. *Environment and Behavior, 8*, 7–29.

Altman, I., & Chemers, M. (1980). *Culture and environment*. Monterey, CA: Brooks/Cole.

Altus, D. (1996). A look at student housing cooperatives. In *Communities directory: A guide to cooperative living* (2nd ed.) (pp. 172–175). Langley, WA: Fellowship for Intentional Community.

Ambrose, S. A., & Lovett, M. C. (2014). Prior knowledge is more than context: Skills and beliefs also impact learning. In V. A. Benassi, C. E. Overson, & C. M. Hakala (Eds.), *Applying science of learning in education: Infusing psychological science into the curriculum* [e-book] (pp. 7–19). American Psychological Association (Division 2). Available at http://teachpsych.org/ebooks/asle2014/index.php

Amen, D. G. (1998). *Change your brain, change your life*. New York: Three Rivers Press.

American Academy of Sleep Medicine. (2008). Circadian rhythm sleep disorders. Darien, IL. Available at http://www.aasmnet.org/resources/factsheets/crsd.pdf

American College Health Association. (2012). *National College Health Assessment: Spring 2012 reference group executive summary*. American College Health Association (ACHA).

American College Personnel Association (ACPA). (1996). The student learning imperative: Implications for student affairs. Washington, DC. Available at http://www.myacpa.org/sli/sli.htm

American College Personnel Association (ACPA) and National Association of Student Personnel Administrators (NASPA). (1997). *Principles of good practice for student affairs: Statement and inventories*. Washington, DC: Author.

American College Personnel Association (ACPA) and National Association of Student Personnel Administrators (NASPA). (2010, July 26). *ACPA and NASPA Professional Competency Areas for Student Affairs Practitioners*. Washington, DC: Author. Available at http://www.naspa.org/regions/regioniii/Professional%20Competency.pdf

American Council on Education (ACE). (1937). *American Council on Education Studies, Series 1, Vol. 1, No. 3. The student personnel point of view*. Washington, DC: Author.

American Council on Education (ACE). (1949). *Student personnel point of view*. Series vi—student personnel work—number 13. Washington, DC: Author.

American Council on Education, Committee on Student Personnel Work. (1949). *The student personnel point of view* (rev. ed.). Washington, DC: Author.

Angelini, B. (1999). Designing residence hall facilities to support student learning. *Talking Stick, 16*(6), 10–15.

Antonio, A. L. (2001). Diversity and the influence of friendship groups in college. *Review of Higher Education, 25*(1), 63–89.

Antonio, A. L. (2004). The influence of friendship groups on intellectual self-confidence and educational aspirations in college. *Journal of Higher Education, 75*(4), 446–471.

Arboleda, A., Wang, Y., Shelley, M. C., & Whalen, D. F. (2003). Predictors of residence hall involvement. *Journal of College Student Development, 44*(4), 517–531.

Argon, J. (2009, June 1). 20th annual residence hall construction report. *American School & University*.

Arminio, J. (1994). Living learning centers: Offering college students an enhanced college experience. *Journal of College and University Student Housing, 24*(1), 12–17.

Arms, J. H., Cabrera, A. F., & Brower, A. M. (2008). Moving into student spaces: The impact of location of academic advising on student engagement among undecided students. *NACADA Journal, 28*(1), 8–18.

Arnett, J. (2005). The developmental context of substance use in emerging adulthood. *Journal of Drug Issues, 35*, 235–253.

Ash, S. E. (1987). *Social psychology*. Oxford, UK: Oxford University Press. (Original publication 1952).

Askell-Williams, H., Lawson, M. J., & Skrzypiec, G. (2012). Scaffolding cognitive and metacognitive strategy instruction in regular class lessons. *Instructional Science, 40*, 413–443.

Association of American Colleges and Universities. (AACU). (2007). *College learning for the new global century*. Washington, DC: Author.

Association for Information Communications Technology Professionals in Higher Education (ACUTA) and National Association of College and University Business Officers (NACUBO). (2013). *Second annual ACUTA/NACUBO state of ResNet report 2013*. ACUTA/NACUBO.

Astin, A. W. (1977). *Four Critical Years*. San Francisco: Jossey-Bass.

Astin, A. W. (1984). Student involvement: A developmental theory for higher education. *Journal of College Student Development, 25*(4), 297–308.

Astin, A. W. (1993). *What matters in college: Four critical years revised*. San Francisco, CA: Jossey-Bass.

Baker, D. E. (2004, May). A national set of competencies for paraprofessionals in residential college or living and learning programs (Unpublished doctoral dissertation). Louisiana State University, Baton Rouge.

Baker, R. W., & Siryk, B. (1999). *The student adaptation to college questionnaire manual*. Los Angles, CA: Western Psychological Services.

Balogh, C. P., Grimm, J., & Hardy, K. (2005). ACUHO-I construction and renovation data: The latest trends in housing construction and renovation. *Journal of College and University Student Housing, 33*(2), 51–56.

Balogh, C., Price, K., Day, J., & Moser, R. (2010). ACUHO-I construction and renovation data: The latest trends in housing construction and renovation. *Journal of College and University Student Housing, 36*(2), 82–91.

Banning, J. H. (1997). Designing for community: Thinking "out of the box" with porches. *Journal of College and University Student Housing, 26*(2), 3–6.

Banning, J. H., & Kuk, L. (2011). College housing dissertations: A bound qualitative meta-study. *Journal of College and University Student Housing, 37*(2), 90–105.

Barkhus, L., & Tashiro, J. (2010). Student socialization in the age of Facebook. In E. Mynatt (Ed.), *Proceedings of the SIGCHI Conference on Human Factors in Computing* (pp. 133–142). Atlanta, GA: ACM.

Barr, R. B., & Tagg, J. (1995, November/December). From teaching to learning—A new paradigm for undergraduate education. *Change*, 13–25.

Barr, V., Krylowicz, B., Reetz, D., Mistler, B. J., & Rando, R. (2011). *The association for university and college counseling center directors annual survey: Reporting period: September 1, 2010 through August 31, 2011.* Available at http://www.insidehighered.com/sites/default/server_files/files/DraftMonograph %202011%20Victor%2003162012%20Public%20Form.docx

Baum, A., & Gatchel, R. J. (1981). Cognitive determinants of reaction to uncontrollable events: Development of reactance and learned helplessness. *Journal of Personality and Social Psychology, 40*(6), 1078–1089.

Baum, A., Mapp, K., & Davis, G. E. (1978). Determinants of residential group development and social control. *Environmental Psychology and Nonverbal Behavior, 2*(3), 145–160.

Baum, S., Ma, J., & Payea, K. (2013). *Education pays 2013: The benefits of higher education of individuals and society.* San Jose, CA: College Board.

Bausch, K. C. (2001). *The emerging consensus in social systems theory.* New York: Springer.

Baxter Magolda, M. (1992). *Knowing and reasoning in college: Gender-related patterns in students' intellectual development.* San Francisco, CA: Jossey-Bass.

Baxter Magolda, M. (2001). *Making their own way: Narratives for transforming higher education to promote self-development.* Sterling, VA: Stylus.

Belch, H. A., & Mueller, J. A. (2003). Candidate pools or puddles: Challenges and trends in the recruitment and hiring of resident directors. *Journal of College Student Development*, 44(1), 29–46.

Belkin, D. (2013, December 30). Colleges trim staffing bloat: Amid tuition backlash and cuts in state subsidies, schools target efficiencies. *Wall Street Journal*.

Belkin, D., & Thurm, S. (2012, December 28). Dean's list: Hiring spree fattens college bureaucracy—and tuition. *Wall Street Journal*.

Benfield, J. A. (2008). A longitudinal assessment of privacy and territory establishment in a college residence hall setting (Doctoral dissertation: Colorado State University). ProQuest Dissertations and Theses, 208. Available at http://proquest.com/docview/304621265?accountid= 13626

Benjamine, D., Cesarini, D., Koellinger, P., & Visscher, P. (2013). GWAS of 126,559 individuals identifies genetic variants associated with educational attainment. *Science*. Available at http://ssgac.org/documents/FAQsRietvel detal2013Science.pdf

Bennett, M. A., & Benton, S. L. (2001). What are the buildings saying? A study of first-year undergraduate students' attributions about college campus architecture. *NASPA Journal*, 38(2), 159–177.

Berger, J. B. (1997). Students' sense of community in residence halls, social integration and first-year persistence. *Journal of College Student Development*, 38(5), 441–452.

Bernstein, B. (1972). *Class, codes and control: Volume 1*. London: Routledge & Kegan Paul.

Bernstein, D. I. (n.d.). Public private partnerships: It's the right time. National Association of College and University Business Officers (NACUBO). Available at http://www.nacubo.org/Business_Officer_Magazine/ Business_Officer_Plus/Bonus_Material/Public-Private_Partnerships_It% E2%80%99s_the_Right_Time.html

Blakemore, S.-J. (2012). Development of the social brain in adolescence. *Journal of the Royal Society of Medicine*, 105(3), 111–116.

Blakemore, S.-J., & Frith, U. (2005). *The learning brain*. Malden, MA: Blackwell.

Blimling, G. S. (1989). A meta-analysis of the influence of college residence halls on academic performance. *Journal of College Student Development*, 30(3), 298–308.

Blimling, G. S. (1993). The influence of college residence halls on students. In J. C. Smart (Ed.), *Higher education: Handbook of theory and research*, vol. 9 (pp. 248–307). New York: Agathon Press.

Blimling, G. S. (1998). The benefits and limitations of residential colleges: A meta-analysis of the research. In F. K. Alexander & D. E. Robertson (Eds.), *Residential colleges: Reforming American higher education* (pp. 39–76). Louisville, KY: Oxford International Roundtable.

Blimling, G. S. (2001). Uniting scholarship and communities of practice in student affairs. *Journal of College Student Development, 42,* 381–396.

Blimling, G. S. (2010). *The resident assistant: Applications and strategies for working with college students in residence halls,* 7th ed. Dubuque, IA: Kendall Hunt.

Blimling, G. S., & Schuh, J. H. (Eds.) (1981). *Increasing the educational role of residence halls.* New Directions for Student Services Sourcebook No. 13. San Francisco: Jossey-Bass.

Blimling, G. S., Whitt, E. J., & Associates. (1999). *Good practice in student affairs: Principles to foster student learning.* San Francisco, CA: Jossey-Bass.

Boehman, J. (2006). Affective, continuance, and normative commitment among student affairs professionals (Doctoral dissertation). North Carolina State University, Raleigh.

Boehner, J. A., & McKeon, H. P. (2003). *The college cost crisis: A congressional analysis of college costs and implications for America's higher education system.* Available at http://eric.ed.gov/?id=ED479752

Boland, P. A., Stamatakos, L. C., & Rogers, R. R. (1994). *Reform in student affairs: A critique of student development.* Greensboro, NC: ERIC Counseling and Student Services Clearinghouse, School of Education, University of North Carolina at Greensboro.

Bolman, L. G., & Deal, T. E. (2013). *Reframing organizations: Artistry, choice, and leadership.* San Francisco, CA: Jossey-Bass.

Borst, A. J. (2011). Evaluating academic and student affairs partnerships: The impact of living-learning communities on the development of critical thinking in college freshmen (Doctoral dissertation). Available from ProQuest Dissertations and Theses database (UMI No. 3461086).

Bowman, R. L., & Bowman, V. E. (1995a). Academic courses to train resident assistants. *Journal of College Student Development, 36*(1), 39–46.

Bowman, R., & Bowman, V. E. (1995b). Counseling issues encountered by RAs: An update and extension. *Journal of College and University Student Housing, 25*(2), 10–15.

Boyle, D. (2001). *The sum of our discontent: Why numbers make us irrational.* New York: Texere.

Boyton Health Services. (2007). University of Minnesota systemwide student health report. *Boyton Health Service,* University of Minnesota. Available at http://www.bhs.umn.edu/surveys/survey-results/Systemwide_Report_07.pdf

Brandon, A., Hirt, J., & Cameron, T. (2008). Where you live influences who you know: Differences in student interaction based on residence hall design. *Journal of College and University Student Housing, 35*(2), 62–78.

Braxton, J., Hirschy, A., & McClendon, M. (2004). *Toward understanding and reducing college student departure (ASHE-ERIC Education Report, Vol. 30, no. 3).* San Francisco, CA: Jossey-Bass.

Bresnahan, M. J., Guan, X., Sherman, S. M., & Donohue, W. A. (2009). Roommate conflict: Does race matter? *Howard Journal of Communications, 20*(4), 394–412.

Brody, J. E. (2013, June 17). Cheating ourselves of sleep. *New York Times.*

Bronfenbrenner, U. (1989). Ecological systems theory. In R. Vasta (Ed.), *Annals of child development: Six theories of child development: Revised formulations and current issues* (pp. 187–249). London, UK: JAI Press.

Bronfenbrenner, U., & Morris, P. A. (2006). The bioecological model of human development. In W. Damon & R. M. Learner (Eds.), *Handbook of child psychology,* 6th ed., *Theoretical models of human development* (vol. 1, pp. 793–828). New York: Wiley.

Bronson, P., & Marryman, A. (2013). *Top dog: The science of winning and losing.* New York: Twelve.

Brooks, R. (2002). Transitional friends? Young people's strategies to manage their friendships during a period of repositioning. *Journal of Youth Studies, 5*(4), 449–467.

Brower, A. M. (2008). More like a home than a hotel: The impact of living-learning programs on college high-risk drinking. *Journal of College and University Student Housing, 35*(1), 32–49.

Brown, B. B. (1990). Peer groups and peer culture. In S. S. Feldman & G. R. Elliott (Eds.), *At the threshold: The developing adolescent* (pp. 171–196). Cambridge, MA: Harvard University Press.

Brown, G., & Devlin, A. S. (2003). Vandalism: Environmental and social factors. *Journal of College Student Development, 44*(4), 502–516.

Brown, G., & Devlin, A. S. (2003). Vandalism: Environmental and social factors. *Journal of College Student Development, 44*(4), 502–516.

Brown, L. M., & Gilligan, C. (1992). *Meeting at the crossroads.* Cambridge, MA: Harvard University Press.

Brown, R. D. (1972). *Student development in tomorrow's higher education—A return to the academy, Student Personnel Series No. 16.* Washington, DC: American College Personnel Association.

Brown, R. D., & Citrin, R. S. (1977). A student development transcript: Assumptions, uses, and formats. *Journal of College Student Personnel, 18*(3), 163–168.

Brubacher, J. S. (1977). *On the philosophy of higher education.* San Francisco, CA: Jossey-Bass Publishers.

Brugha, T. S., Weich, S., Singleton, N., Lewis, G., Babbington, P. E., Jenkins, R., et al. (2005). Primary group size, social support, gender and future mental health status in a prospective study living in private households throughout Great Britain. *Psychological Medicine, 35*(5), 705–714.

Buboltz, W. C., Brown, F., & Soper, B. (2001). Sleep habits and patterns of college students: A preliminary study. *Journal of American College Health, 50*(3), 131–135.

Bureau of Labor Statistics. (2013, April 5). The job market for recent college graduates in the United States. *United States Department of Labor.* Available at http://www.bls.gov/opub/ted/2013/ted_20130405.htm

Burnett, S., Bird, G., Moll, J., Frith, C., & Blakemore, S.-J. (2009). Development during adolescence of neural processing of social emotions. *Journal of Cognitive Neuroscience, 21,* 1736–1750.

Butler, K. (2006, July 4). The grim neurology of teenage drinking. *New York Times.*

Cain, D., & Reynolds, G. L. (2006, May–June). The impact of facilities on recruitment and retention of students. *Facilities Manager,* 46–53.

Carnevale, A. P., & Cheah, B. (2013). *Hardtimes: College majors, unemployment and earnings.* Washington, DC: Georgetown Public Policy Institute.

Casey, B. J., Jones, R. M., & Hare, T. A. (2008). The adolescent brain. *Annals of the New York Academy of Sciences, 1124,* 111–126.

Centers for Disease Control and Prevention (CDC). (2013, November 13). Attention-deficit/hyperactivity disorder (ADHD). *CDC.* Available at http://www.cdc.gov/ncbddd/adhd/data.html

Chafin, C. N. (2006). The impact of a living and learning community and inquiry guided learning on first year students' emotional intelligence and academic achievement (Doctoral dissertation). Available from ProQuest Dissertations and Theses database (UMI No. 3247014).

Chakrabarti, R., Mabutas, M., & Zafar, B. (2012). Soaring tuitions: Are public funding cuts to blame? *Federal Reserve Bank of New York.* Available at http://libertystreeteconomics.newyorkfed.org/2012/09/soaring-tuitions-are-public-funding-cuts-to-blame.html#.U7xFg41dUaA

Chickering, A. (1974). *Education and indentity*. San Francisco, CA: Jossey-Bass.

Chickering, A. W., & Reisser, L. (1993). *Education and identity* (2nd ed.). San Francisco, CA: Jossey-Bass.

Chiricosta, S., Work, G., & Anchors, S. (1996). The relationship between gender and feelings of community in residence halls. *Journal of College and University Student Housing, 26*(2), 35–39.

Choy, S. (2001). *Students whose parents did not go to college: Postsecondary access, persistence, and attainment*. Washington, DC: National Center for Education Statistics.

Christensen, C. M., & Horn, M. B. (2013, November 1). Innovation imperative: Change everything—Online education as an agent of transformation. *New York Times: Education Life*.

Clark, E. A., Jackson, S., & Everhart, D. (2012). Residential density: The effects of tripling college students. *Journal of College Student Development, 53*(3), 477–481.

Clark, T. A. (1920). Housing problems. *Secretarial notes second annual meeting National Association of Deans and Advisers of Men, 47*. National Association of Deans and Advisers of Men.

Cobb, N. J. (2010). *Adolescence: Continuity, change, and diversity* (7th ed.). Sunderland, MA: Sinauer Associates.

Cohen, S. (2014, March 20). A quick way to cut college costs. *New York Times: Opinion Pages*.

College Board. (2012, July). Trends in tuition and fees, enrollment, and state appropriations for higher education by state. Available at http://trends .collegeboard.org/sites/default/files/analysis-brief-trends-by-state-july-2012.pdf

College Board. (2013a, October). *How college shapes lives: Understanding the issues*. Available at http://www.unh.edu/news/docs/UNHsocialmedia.pdf

College Board. (2013b, March). *Trends in college pricing 2013*. Available at https://trends.collegeboard.org/sites/default/files/college-pricing-2013-full-report-140108.pdf

College Board. (2014). Trends in higher education: Average rates of growth of published charges by decade. Available at https://trends.collegeboard. org/college-pricing/figures-tables/average-rates-growth-tuition-and-fees-over-time

Collins, D., & Hirt, J. B. (2006). The nature of professional life for residence hall administrators. *Journal of College and University Student Housing, 34*(1), 14–24.

Corkery, M. (2012, December 30). Pressure to rein in tuition squeezes colleges. *Wall Street Journal.*

Cory, W. J. (1861). *Eaton Reform (Vol. 2)* London: Longman, Green, Longman, and Roberts.

Council for the Advancement of Standards in Higher Education (CAS). (2009). *CAS Professional Standards for Higher Education* (7th ed.). Washington, DC: Author.

Council of Student Personnel Associations. (1983). Student development services in postsecondary education. In G. L. Saddlemire & A. L. Rentz (Eds.), *Student affairs—a professions heritage: Significant articles, authors, issues and documents* (pp. 384–395). Carbondale, IL: American College Personnel Association Media Press.

Court, D. (2013, September 3). Future of smartphones: How will the next generation of mobile phones improve? *Tech Advisor.* Available from http://www.pcadvisor.co.uk/opinion/mobile-phone/3466728/future-of-smartphones/

Cowan, N. (2001). The magical number 4 in short-term memory: A reconsideration of mental storage capacity. *Behavior and Brain Science, 24,* 87–185.

Cowley, W. H. (1934). The history of student residential housing. *School and Society, 40,* 705–712, 758–764.

Cowley, W. H. (1949). Some history and a venture in prophecy. In E. G. Williamson (Ed.), *Trends in student personnel work* (pp. 12–27). Minneapolis: University of Minnesota Press.

Cox, B. E., & Orehovec, E. (2007). Faculty-student interaction outside the classroom: A typology from a residential college. *Review of Higher Education, 30*(4), 343–362.

Cranford, J. A., McCabe, S. E., Boyd, C. J., Lange, J. E., Reed, M. B., & Scott, M. S. (2009). Effects of residential learning communities on drinking trajectories during the first two years of college. *Journal of Studies on Alcohol and Drugs, 16,* 86–95.

Credé, M., & Niehorster, S. (2012). Adjustment to college as measured by the adaptation to college questionnaire: A quantitative review of its structure and relationships with correlates and consequences. *Educational Psychology Review, 24*(1), 133–165.

Creswell, J. W. (2013). *Qualitative inquiry and research design: Choosing among five approaches.* Los Angles, CA: Sage.

Crisp, R. J., & Turner, R. N. (2011). Cognitive adaptation to the experience of social and cultural diversity. *Psychological Bulletin, 137*(2), 242–266.

Crookston, B. B. (1973). Education for human development. In C. F. Warnath (Ed.), *New Directions for College Counseling* (pp. 47–65). San Francisco, CA: Jossey-Bass Publishers.

Crookston, B. B. (1974). A design for an intentional democratic community. In D. A. DeCoster & P. Mable (Eds.), *Student development and educaton in college residence halls* (pp. 55–67). Washington, DC: American College Personnel Association.

Cross, J. E., Zimmerman, D., & O'Grady, M. A. (2009). Residence hall room type and alcohol use among college students living on campus. *Environment and Behavior, 41*(4), 583–603.

Cullum, J., & Harton, H. (2007). Cultural evolution: Interpersonal influences, issue importance, and the development of shared attitudes in college residence halls. *Personality and Social Psychology Bulletin, 33*, 1327–1339.

Dahl, R. E., & Lewin, D. S. (2002). Pathways to adolescent health sleep regulation and behavior. *Journal of Adolescent Health, 31*(6), 175–184.

Daly, J. (2012, August 13). Increase in devices causing bandwidth trouble on campus: How can IT departments keep up? [infographic] *Edtech Magazine.* Available at http://www.edtechmagazine.com/higher/article/2012/08/increase-devices-causing-bandwidth-trouble-campus-infographic

Davidson, D. L. (2012). Job satisfaction and recruitment of entry-level residence life and housing staff. *Journal of College and University Student Housing, 38*(2), 78–90.

DeCoster, D. A., & Mable, P. (1974). Residence education: Purpose and process. In D. A. DeCoster & P. Mable (Eds.), *Personal development and community development in college residence halls.* Washington, DC: American College Personnel Association.

Deluga, R. J., & Winters, J. J. (1991). Why the aggravation? Reasons students become resident assistants, interpersonal stress, and job satisfaction. *Journal of College Student Development, 32*, 546–552.

Deming, W. E. (1982). *Out of crisis.* Cambridge, MA: MIT Center for Advanced Engineering Study.

DeMore, S. W., Fisher, J. D., & Baron, R. M. (1988). The equity-control model as predictor of vandalism among college students. *Journal of Applied Social Psychology, 18*, 80–91.

DeNeui, D. L. (2003). An investigation of first-year college student's psychological sense of community on campus. *College Student Journal, 37*(2).

Desrochers, D. M., & Kirshstein, R. (2014). Labor intensive or labor expensive? Changing staffing and compensation patterns in higher education.

*American Institutes for Research.* Available at http://www.deltacostproject
.org/sites/default/files/products/DeltaCostAIR_Staffing_Brief_2_3_14.pdf

Devlin, A. S. (2007). Vandalism in college residence halls: The picture from archival data. In *Proceedings of the 38th Annual Conference of the Environmental Design Research Association* (pp. 79–84). Available at http://www.edra.org/sites/default/files/publications/EDRA38-Devlin_1.pdf

Devlin, A. S., Donovan, S., Nicolov, A., Nold, O., & Zandan, G. (2008). Residence hall architecture and sense of community: Everything old is new again. *Environment and Behavior, 40*(4), 487–521.

Dewey, J. (1922). *Human nature and conduct.* New York: Holt.

Diamond, A. (2007). Consequences of variations in genes that affect dopamine in prefrontal cortex. *Cerebral Cortex, 17*, i161–i170.

Doumas, D. M., Turrisi, R., Ray, A. E., Esp, S. M., & Curtis-Schaeffer, A. K. (2013). A randomized trial evaluating a parent based intervention to reduce college drinking. *Journal of Substance Abuse Treatment, 45*(1), 31–37.

Doyle, T., & Zakrajsek, T. (2013). *The new science of learning: How to learn in harmony with your brain.* Sterling, VA: Stylus.

Duke, A. (1996). *Importing Oxbridge: English residential colleges and American universities.* New Haven, CT: Yale University Press.

Dunbar, R. I. (2004). *The human story: A new history of mankind's evolution.* London: Faber and Faber.

Dunbar, R. I. (2010). *How many friends does one person need? Dunbar number and other evolutionary quirks.* London: Faber and Faber.

Duncan, G., Boisjoly, J., Kremer, M., Levy, D., & Eccles, J. (2005). Peer effects in drug use and sex among college students. *Journal of Abnormal Child Psychology, 33*, 375–385.

Dunkel, N. W., & Schelber, P. J. (1992). Competency development of housing professionals. *Journal of College and University Student Housing, 22*(2), 19–23.

Dunkel, N. W., Schuh, J. H., & Chrystal-Green, N. E. (2014). *Advising student groups and organizations* (2nd ed.). San Francisco, CA: Jossey-Bass.

Dunning, D. (2007). *Self-insight: Roadblocks and detours on the path to knowing thyself.* New York: Taylor & Francis.

DuPaul, G. J., Weyandt, L. L., O'Dell, S. M., & Varejao, M. (2009). College students with ADHD: Current status and future direction. *Journal of Attention Disorders, 13*(3), 234–250.

Eagle, J. (2007). Postsecondary access and success for first-generation college students. *American Academic*, 3(1), 25–48.

Eaton, C., & Habinek, J. (2013). Why America's public universities—not just their students—have a debt problem. *Scholars Strategy Network*. Available at http://www.scholarsstrategynetwork.org/sites/default/files/ssn_key_findings_eaton_and_habinek_on_public_universities_wall_street_problem.pdf

Edwards, K. E., & McKelfresh, D. A. (2002). The impact of a living learning center on students' academic success and persistence. *Journal of College Student Development*, 43(2), 395–402.

Einarson, M. K., & Clarkberg, M. E. (2004, November 5). Understanding faculty out-of-class interaction with undergraduate students at a research university (CHERI working paper no. 57). *Cornell.edu*. Available at http://digitalcommons.ilr.cornell.edu/cheri/20/?utm_source=digitalcommons.ilr.cornell.edu%2Fcheri%2F20&utm_medium=PDF&utm_campaign=PDFCoverPages

Eisenberg, D., Golberstein, E., & Whitlock, J. (2014). Peer effects on risky behaviors: New evidence from college roommate assignments. *Journal of Health Economics*, 33, 126–138.

Eisenberg, D., Golberstein, E., Whitlock, J. L., & Downs, M. F. (2013). Social contagion of mental health: Evidence from college roommates. *Health Economics*, 22(8), 965–986.

Eligon, J. (2013, June 14). In student housing, luxuries overshadow studying. *New York Times*.

Eliot, L. (2009). *Pink brain blue brain: How small differences grow into troublesome gaps—and what we can do about it*. New York: Houghton, Mifflin, Harcourt.

Ellett, T. E., Belch, H. A., St. Onge, S. R., Wilson, M. E., Dunkel, N. W., Klein, S., et al. (2008). *Recruitment and retention of entry-level staff in housing and residence life: A report on activities supported by the ACUHO-I commissioned research program*. Columbus, OH: Association of College & University Housing Officers—International (ACUHO-I).

Ellett, T., & Schmidt, A. (2011). Faculty perspectives on creating community in residence halls. *Journal of College and University Student Housing*, 38(1), 26–39.

Ellis, B. J., Giudice, M. D., Dishion, T. J., Figueredo, A. J., Gray, P., Griskevicius, V., et al. (2012). The evolutionary basis of risky adolescent behavior: Implications for science, policy, and practice. *Developmental Psychology*, 48(3), 598–623.

Ender, S. C., & Newton, F. B. (2000). *Students helping students: A guide for educators on college campuses.* San Francisco, CA: Jossey-Bass.

Ender, S. C., Newton, F. B., & Caple, R. B. (1996). Contributions to learning: Present realities. In S. Ender, F. Newton, & R. B. Caple (Eds.), *Contributing to learning: The role of student affairs* (pp. 5–17). San Francisco, CA: Jossey-Bass.

Erikson, E. (1968). *Identity, youth and crises.* New York: Norton.

Eshbaugh, E. M. (2008). Brief report: Gender, social support and loneliness among residence hall students. *Journal of College and University Student Housing, 25*(2), 24–33.

Evans, G. W., & McCoy, J. M. (1998). When buildings don't work: The role of architecture in human health. *Journal of Environmental Psychology, 18,* 85–94.

Evans, N. J., Forney, D. S., Guido, F. M., & Renn, K. A. (2010). *Student development in college: Theory, research, and practice* (2nd ed.). San Francisco, CA: Jossey-Bass.

Everett, J. W., & Zobel, P. D. (2012). Promoting student connections and retention through an on-campus residential learning community for first-year underrepresented and low-income (AC 2012–3993). Paper presented at the American Society for Engineering Education (ASEE) 119th annual conference and exposition.

Federal Reserve Board. (2014, January). Consumer credit—G.19. *Federal Reserve Board.* Available at http://www.federalreserve.gov/releases/g19/Current/

Fedorovich, S., Boyle, C. R., & Hare, D. R. (1994). Wellness as a factor in the selection of resident assistants in university student housing. *Journal of College Student Development, 35,* 248–254.

Feldman, K. A., & Newcomb, T. (1969). *The impact of college on students* (vol. 1) San Francisco, CA: Jossey-Bass.

Feldman, W., & Feldman, P. (2005). Academic achievement: Developers and managers target off-campus student housing opportunities. *Journal of Property Management, 70,* 30–33.

Ficano, C. C. (2012). Peer effects in college academic outcomes—gender matters! *Economics of Education Review, 31,* 1102–1115.

Finning-Kwoka, S. M. (2009). The effect of a sophomore year experience on-campus living-learning community: Participants' sense of meaning in life, academic self-efficacy, and satisfaction (Doctoral dissertation). Available from ProQuest Dissertations and Theses database (UMI No. 3355138).

Flanagan, D. (1975). The effects of college and university residential programs on students (Unpublished manuscript). ERIC Document Reproduction Services No. ED 11 252.

Foster, G. (2006). It's not your peers, and it's not your friends: Some progress toward understanding the educational peer effect mechanism. *Journal of Public Economics, 90,* 1455–1475.

Foster, N. E., Halpern, A. R., & Zatorre, R. J. (2013). Common parietal activation in musical mental transformations across pitch and time. *NeuroImage, 75,* 27–35.

Foubert, J. D., Tepper, R., & Morrison, D. R. (1998). Predictors of student satisfaction in university residence halls. *Journal of College and University Student Housing, 27*(1), 41–46.

Frazier, W., & Eighmy, M. (2012). Themed residential learning communities: The importance of purposeful faculty and staff involvement and student engagement. *Journal of College and University Student Housing, 38*(2), 10–27.

Fredrickson, B. L. (2001). The role of positive emotions in positive psychology: The broaden-and-build theory of positive emotions. *American Psychologist, 56*(3), 218–226.

Freudenberger, H. J., & North, G. (1985). *Women's burnout: How to spot it, how to reverse it, and how to prevent it.* New York: Doubleday.

Fried, J. (2010). Intentional democratic communities: Residential education for civic engagement. *Journal of College and University Student Housing, 36*(2), 56–67.

Friedman, T. (2013, January 26). Revolution hits the universities. *New York Times.*

Gabor, D. (1964). *Inventing the future.* New York: Alfred A. Knopf.

Gabrel, T. (2010, November 4). Learning in dorm, because class is on the Web. *New York Times.*

Gallagher, R. P. (2010). National Survey of Counseling Center Directors 2010. American Counseling Association (ACCA) Monograph Series Number 85. International Association of Counseling Services, Inc.

Gallup. (2014, May 6). The 2014 Gallup-Purdue Index Report. *Gallup.com.* Available at http://www.gallup.com/strategicconsulting/168791/gallup-purdue-index-inaugural-national-report.aspx

Gamson, Z. F. (1987). Academic counterrevolution: The roots of the current movement to reform undergraduate education. *Educational Policy, 1*(4), 429–444.

Gardner, H. (1999). *Intelligence reframed: Multiple intelligence for the 21st century.* New York: Basic Books.

Gardner, J. N., & Jewler, A. J. (1989). *College is only the beginning.* Belmont, CA: Wadsworth.

Gardner, J. N., Van der Veer, G., & Associates. (1998). *The senior year experience.* San Francisco, CA: Jossey-Bass.

Gardner, M., & Steinberg, L. (2005). Peer influence on risk-taking, risk preference, and risky decision-making in adolescence and adulthood: an experimental study. *Developmental Psychology, 41,* 625–635.

Garrett, M. D., & Zabriskie, M. S. (2003). The influence of living-learning program participation on student-faculty interaction. *Journal of College and University Student Housing, 32*(2), 38–44.

Gates, G. J. (2012). LGBT identity: A demographer's perspective. *Loyola of Los Angles Law Review, 45*(3), 693–714.

Gates, G. J., & Newport, F. (2012, October 18). Special report: 3.4% of U.S. adults identify as LGBT. *Gallup Politics.* Available at http://www.gallup.com/poll/158066/special-report-adults-identify-lgbt.aspx

Gellin, A. (2003). The effects of undergraduate student involvement on critical thinking: Meta-analysis of the literature 1991–2000. *Journal of College Student Development, 44*(6), 746–762.

Gerst, M., & Moos, R. (1972). The social ecology of university residences. *Journal of Educational Psychology, 63,* 513–525.

Ginsburg, B. (2011). *The fall of the faculty: The rise of the all-administrative university.* New York: Oxford University Press.

Gladwell, M. (2005). *Blink: The power of thinking without thinking.* New York: Little, Brown and Company.

Glassman, J. B., Burkhart, B. R., Grant, R., & Vallery, G. C. (1978). Density, expectations, and extended task performance: An experiment in the natural environment. *Environment and Behavior, 10*(3), 299–315.

Glenn, N., & Marquardt, E. (2001). *Hooking up, hanging out, and hoping for Mr. Right: College women on mating and dating today.* New York: Institute for American Values.

Godley, J. (2008). Preference or propinquity? The relative contribution of selection and opportunity to friendship homophily in college. *Connections, 28*(2), 1–16.

Godshall, R. (2000). Creating communities. *American Schools and Universities, 72*(12), 150–154.

Goetz, R. D. (1983). Authoritarianism and ego development in four-year and two-year college students: A one-year impact study (Doctoral dissertation). *University of Washington, Dissertation Abstracts International, 44*(8), 2414A.

Golde, C. M., & Pribbenow, D. A. (2000). Understanding faculty involvement in residential learning communities. *Journal of College Student Development, 41*(1), 27–40.

Golding, W. (1954). *Lord of the flies.* New York: Conward, McCann, & Geoghegan.

Goldman, B. A., & Hood, S. J. (1995). Residence hall longevity and transfer rates of living learning residence hall students versus other residence hall students. *Journal of College and University Student Housing, 25,* 38–40.

Gonzales, N., & Dodge, K. A. (2010, April 26). Family and peer influences on adolescent behavior and risk-taking. Available at http://www.iom.edu/~/media/Files/Activity%20Files/Children/AdolescenceWS/Commissioned%20Papers/dodge_gonzales_paper.pdf

Grant, A. (2013). *Give and take: A revolutionary approach to success.* New York: Viking.

Grayson, P. J. (1997). Place of residence, student involvement, and first year marks. *Canadian Journal of Higher Education, 27*(1), 1–24.

Griffith, D., & Segar, T. C. (2006, March 21). Non-cognitive competencies: How entry-level housing professionals can make a difference. Presentation given at the annual convention of the American College Personnel Association, Indianapolis, IN. Available at http://www.tomsegar.com/acpa2006/NCC-ACPA2006.pdf

Grill, C. N., Fingerhut, A. W., Thadani, V., & Machón, R. A. (2012). Residential learning communities centered within a discipline: The psychology early awareness program. In K. Buch & K. E. Barron (Eds.), *Special Issue: Discipline-centered learning communities: Creating connections among students, faculty, and curricula.* New Directions for Teaching and Learning (Issue 132) (pp. 43–55). New York: John Wiley.

Hall, E. T. (1976). *Beyond culture.* Garden City, NY: Anchor Books.

Hamrick, F. A., Evans, N., & Schuh, J. H. (2002). *Foundations of student affairs practice: How philosophy, theory, and research strengthen educational outcomes.* San Francisco, CA: Jossey-Bass.

Hand, H. C. (1938). *Campus activities.* New York: McGraw-Hill.

Harris, J. R. (1998). *The nurture assumption.* New York: Touchstone.

Hartig, T., Mang, M., & Evans, G. (1991). Restorative effects of natural environment experiences. *Environment and Behavior, 23,* 3–26.

Harvey, D. C. (2010). The space for culture and cognition. *Poetics, 38,* 184–203.

Harvey, T. (2014, March 18). Affordability tops annual "hopes and worries" survey of applicants. *Chronicle of Higher Education.* Available at http://chronicle.com/blogs/headcount/affordability-tops-annual-hopes-and-worries-survey-of-applicants/37727

Hasson, R., & Fine, J. G. (2012). Gender differences among children with ADHD on continuous performance tests: A meta-analytic review. *Journal of Attention Disorders, 16*(3), 190–198.

Hattie, J., & Timperley, H. (2007). The power of feedback. *Review of Educational Research, 77*(1), 81–112.

Hattie, J. A., & Yates, G. C. (2014). Using feedback to promote learning. In V. A. Benassi, C. E. Overson, & C. M. Hakala (Eds.), *Applying science of learning in education: Infusing psychological science into the curriculum* (pp. 45–58). American Psychological Association (Division 2). Available at http://teachpsych.org/ebooks/asle2014/index.php

Hawkins, L. (1980). A comparative analysis of selected academic and nonacademic characteristics of undergraduate students at Purdue University by type of housing (Doctoral dissertation), Dissertation Abstracts International 41 (6-A):245 (University Microfilms No. 80-27,284).

Hawley, P. H. (2011). The evolution of adolescence and the adolescence of evolution: The coming of age of humans and the theory about the forces that made them. *Journal of Research on Adolescence, 21*(1), 307–316.

Henry, K. B., & Schein, H. K. (1998). Academic community in residence halls: What differentiates a hall with a living/learning program. *Journal of College and University Student Housing, 27*(2), 9–14.

Higher Education Research Institute. (2010). *Incoming college students rate emotional health at record low, annual survey finds.* Los Angles, CA: Higher Education Research Institute, ULCA Graduate School of Education.

Higher Education Research Institute (2012). The American freshmen: National norms fall 2012, research brief. *Cooperative Institutional Research Program at the Higher Education Research Institute.* Available at http://www.heri.ucla.edu/monographs/theamericanfreshman2012.pdf

Hillary, G. (1955). Definitions of community: Areas of agreement. *Rural Sociology, 20*(2), 111–123.

Hiller, A. A., & Beversdorf, D. Q. (2006). The effects of auditory stressors on cognitive flexibility. *Neuroscience, 12*(4), 228–231.

Hiller-Sturmhofel, S., & Swartzwelder, H. S. (2004–2005). Alcohol's effects on the adolescent brain—what can be learned from animal models. In *Focus on young adult drinking* (Vol. 28, pp. 213–221). Washington, DC: National Institutes of Health/National Institute on Alcohol Abuse and Alcoholism.

Hogg, M., & Vaughan, G. M. (2002). *Social psychology* (3rd ed.). London, UK: Prentice-Hall.

Holahan, C. J., & Wilcox, B. L. (1978). Residential satisfaction and friendship in high—and low- rise student housing: An interactional analysis. *Journal of Educational Psychology, 70*(2), 237–241.

Holahan, C. J., Wilcox, B. L., & Culler, R. E. (1978). Social satisfaction and friendship formation as a function of floor level in high-rise student housing. *Journal of Applied Psychology, 63*(4), 529–531.

Holland, J. (1985). *Making vocational choices: A theory of vocational personalities and work environments.* Englewood Cliffs, NJ: Prentice-Hall.

Holt-Lunstad, J., Smith, T. B., & Layton, J. B. (2010). Social relationships and mortality risk: A meta-analytic review. *PLoS Medicine, 7*(7), e1000316.

Hosoda, M., Stone-Romero, E. F., & Coats, G. (2003). The effects of physical attractiveness on job-related outcomes: A meta-analysis of experimental studies. *Personnel Psychology, 56*(2), 431–462.

Hoy, W. K. (2010). *Quantitative research in education: A primer.* Thousand Oaks, CA: Sage.

Huang, E. T. (1982). Impacts of environmental design on residential crowding. *Dissertation Abstracts International, 43*(3), 948A.

Hughey, A. W. (1983). Effects of living accommodations of high proximity on the self-perceptions of college students living in university housing facilities. *Psychological Report, 53*, 1013–1014.

Huhn, C. (2006, August 1). *The "housing effect" on first-year outcomes.* 1–7. Madison, WI: Academic Planning and Analysis, Office of the Provost, University of Wisconsin—Madison.

Humphreys, H. J. (2010). The psychosocial effect of residentially-based learning communities on first-year honors students in a highly selective private university (Doctoral dissertation). Boston College, Boston, MA. ProQuest, UMI Dissertation Publishing.

Hunter, D. E., & Kuh, G. D. (1989). Elizabeth A. Greenleaf: Having some fun getting the job done. *Journal of Counseling and Development, 67*, 322–331. (Reprinted in P. Heppner (Ed.) (1990), *Pioneers in counseling and human development: Personal and professional perceptions.* Washington, DC: American Association for Counseling and Development.)

Hutchins, R. M. (1943). *Education for freedom*. Baton Rouge: Louisiana State University Press.

Inkelas, K. K. (2000). Participation in living-learning programs at the University of Michigan: Benefits for students and faculty (CRLT occasional paper no. 15). *Center for Research on Learning and Teaching, University of Michigan*. Available at http://www.crlt.umich.edu/sites/default/files/resource_files/CRLT_no15.pdf

Inkelas, K. K., & Associates. (2007). *The National Study of Living-Learning Programs 2007 Report of Findings*. College Park, MD: Author.

Inkelas, K. K., Johnson, D., Lee, Z., Daver, Z., Longerbeam, S. D., Vogt, K., et al. (2006). The role of living-learning programs in students' perceptions of intellectual growth at three universities. *NASPA Journal*, 43(1), 115–143.

Inkelas, K. K., & Soldner, M. (2011). Undergraduate living-learning programs and student outcomes. In J. C. Smart & M. B. Paulsen (Eds.), *Higher Education: Handbook of theory and research* (vol. 26) (pp. 1–55). New York: Springer.

Inkelas, K. K., Vogt, K. E., Longerbeam, S. D., Owen, J. E., & Johnson, D. (2006). Measure outcome of living-learning programs: Examining college environments and student learning and development. *Journal of General Education*, 55(1), 40–76.

Inkelas, K. K., & Weisman, J. L. (2003). Different by design: An examination of student outcomes among participants in three types of living-learning programs. *Journal of College Student Development*, 44(3), 335–368.

Inman, P., & Pascarella, E. T. (1998). The impact of college residence on the development of critical thinking skills in college freshmen. *Journal of College Student Development*, 39, 557–568.

Institute of International Education. (2013, November 11). Data from the 2013 open doors report. *Institute of International Education*. Available at http://www.iie.org/en/Research-and-Publications/Open-Doors

Jacob, B., McCall, B., & Stange, K. M. (2013). College as country club: Do colleges cater to students' preferences for consumption? (Working Paper 18745). Cambridge, MA: National Bureau of Economic Research.

James, S. D. (2012, May 14). Gap year: Congrats! You're accepted to college, now go away. *ABC News*.

Johnson, J. L. (2001). Learning communities and special efforts in the retention of university students: What works, what doesn't, and used to read current worth the investment? *Journal of College Student Retention*, 2(3), 219–238.

Jones, D. P. (2002). College housing professionals at the crossroads. *Journal of College and University Housing Officers, 31*(1), 8–12.

Jones, S. R., & Abes, E. S. (2013). *Identity development of college students: Advancing frameworks for multiple dimensions of identity.* San Francisco, CA: Jossey-Bass.

Kalipidu, M., Costin, D., & Morris, J. (2011). The relationship between Facebook and the well-being of undergraduate college students. *Cyberpsychology, Behavior, and Social Networking, 14*(4), 183–189.

Kandel, E. R. (2013, April 12). What the brain can tell us about art. *New York Times.*

Kanoy, K. W., & Bruhn, J. W. (1996). Effects of a first-year living-learning residence hall on retention and academic performance. *Journal of the Freshman Year Experience and Students in Transition, 8,* 7–23.

Kaplin, W. A., & Lee, B. A. (2009). *A legal guide for student affairs professionals* (2nd ed.). San Francisco: Jossey-Bass.

Karlin, R. A., Rosen, L. S., & Epstein, Y. M. (1979). Three into two doesn't go: A follow-up on the effects of overcrowded dormitory rooms. *Personality and Social Psychology, 5,* 391–395.

Karotkin, D., & Paroush, J. (2003). Optimum committee size: Quality-versus-quantity dilemma. *Social Choice and Welfare, 20*(3), 429–441.

Karpinski, A. C., Kirschmer, P. A., Ozer, I., Mellott, J. A., & Ochwo, P. (2013). An exploration of social networking site use, multitasking, and academic performance among United States and European university students. *Computers in Human Behavior, 29*(3), 1182–1192.

Kastenbaum, D. R. (1984). Territorial behavior and interpersonal relations in a university residence environment (Unpublished doctoral dissertation). State University of New York, Buffalo. Dissertation Abstracts International, 44B,11.

Kaya, N., & Weber, M. J. (2003). Cross-cultural differences in the perception of crowding and privacy regulation: American and Turkish students. *Journal of Environmental Psychology, 23*(3), 301–309.

Keeling, R. P. (2004). *Learning reconsidered: A campus-wide focus on the student experience.* Washington, DC: American College Personnel Association & National Association of Student Personnel Administrators.

Keeling, R. P. (2006). *Learning reconsidered 2: A practical guide to implementing a campus-wide focus on the student experience.* Washington, DC: American College Personnel Association and University Housing Officers-International, & National Association of Student Personnel Administrators, & National Intramural-Recreation Sports Association.

Kelderman, E. (2014, March 28). Lost in translation: N.J. lawmakers and higher ed try to understand each other. *Chronicle of Higher Education*. Available at http://chronicle.com/article/Lost-in-Translation-NJ/145589/

Kelling, G. L., & Wilson, J. Q. (1982, March). Broken windows: The police and neighborhood safety. *The Atlantic*. Available at http://www.theatlantic.com/magazine/archive/1982/03/broken-windows/4465/

Kerr, K. G., & Tweedy, J. (2006). Beyond seat time and student satisfaction: A curricular approach to residential education. *About Campus, 2*(5), 9–15.

Kerr, K. G., Tweedy, J., & Diesner, M. (2007). Residential curriculum: A strategy for citizenship development (University of Delaware Office of Residence Life). Paper presented at the ACPA/NASPA Joint Meeting, Orlando, FL.

Ketchum, K. (1988). Factors that attract black and white students to and deter them from the resident assistant position. *Journal of College and University Student Housing, 18*, 16–20.

Kim, C. (2007, September 17). Pricey dorms for cheap co-op housing. *U.S. News & World Report, 143*(9).

Kimmel, M. (2008). *Guyland: The perilous world where boys become men.* New York: Harper Collins.

Kindlon, D. (2007). *Alpha girls: Understanding the new American girl and how she is changing the world.* New York: Rodale.

King, P. M., & Kitchener, K. S. (1994). *Developing reflective judgment: Understanding and promoting intellectual growth and critical thinking in adolescents and adults.* San Francisco, CA: Jossey-Bass.

Kinsey Institute. (2014, May 9). Kinsey's Heterosexual-Homosexual Rating Scale. *Kinsey Institute.* Available at http://www.kinseyinstitute.org/research/ak-hhscale.html

Kirschner, P. A., & Karpinski, A. C. (2010). Facebook in academic performance. *Computers in Human Behavior, 26*(6), 1237–1245.

Knez, I. (2000). Effects of indoor lighting, gender, and performance on mood and cognitive performance. *Environment and Behavior, 32*(6), 818–832.

Kohl, J. L. (2009). The association of critical thinking and participation in living and learning programs: Residential honors compared to civic/social leadership programs and non-participation in living and learning programs (Doctoral dissertation). University of Maryland.

Kohlberg, L. (1969). Stage and sequence: the cognitive-developmental approach to socialization. In D. Goslin (Ed.), *Handbook of socialization theory and research* (pp. 347–480). New York: Rand McNally.

Kolb, D. (1984). *Experiential learning: Experience as the source of learning and development.* Englewood Cliffs, NJ: Prentice Hall.

Kolb, D. A., Boyatzis, R. E., & Mainemelis, C. (1999). Experiential learning theory: Previous research and new directions. Department of Organizational Behavior, Waterhead School of Management, Case Western Reserve University, Cleveland, OH. Available at http://www.d.umn.edu/~kgilbert/educ5165-731/Readings/experiential-learning-theory.pdf

Kolowich, S. (2013, November 20). MOOCs are largely reaching privileged learners, survey says. *Chronicle of Higher Education.* Available at http://chronicle.com/blogs/wiredcampus/moocs-are-reaching-only-privileged-learners-survey-finds/48567

Kolowich, S. (2014, January 22). Completion rates aren't the best way to judge MOOCs, researchers say. *Chronicle of Higher Education.* Available at http://chronicle.com/blogs/wiredcampus/completion-rates-arent-the-best-way-to-judge-moocs-researchers-say/49721

Komarraju, M., Musulkin, S., & Bhattacharya, G. (2010). Role of student-faculty interactions in developing college students' academic self-concept, motivation, and achievement. *Journal of College Student Development, 51*(3), 332–342.

Komives, S. (1991). The relationship of hall directors' transformational and transactional leadership to select resident assistant outcomes. *Journal of College Student Development, 32,* 509–515.

Kraft, U. (2006, June–July). Burned out. *Scientific American Mind,* 28–33.

Kremer, M., & Levy, D. (2008). Peer effects and alcohol use among college students. *Journal of Economic Perspectives, 22*(3), 189–206.

Kretovics, M. A., & Nobles, J. (2005). Entry-level hiring practices used in college and university housing: Competencies recruited versus competencies hired. *Journal of College and University Student Housing, 33*(2), 44–50.

Krum, T. E., Davis, K. S., & Galupo, M. P. (2013). Gender-inclusive housing preferences: A survey of college-age transgender students. *Journal of LGBT Youth, 10*(1–2), 64–82.

Kuh, G. D., Cruce, T. M., Shoup, R., Kinzie, J., & Gonyea, R. M. (2008). Unmasking the effects of student engagement on first-year college grades and persistence. *Journal of Higher Education, 79*(5), 540–563.

Kuh, G. D., Kinzie, J., Bridges, B. K., & Hayek, J. C. (2006). What matters to student success: A review of the literature. *National Postsecondary Education Cooperative (NPEC).* Available at http://nces.ed.gov/npec/papers.asp

Kuh, G. D., Kinzie, J., Buckley, J. A., Bridges, B. K., & Hayek, J. C. (2006). What matters to student success: A review of the literature (commissioned report for the national symposium on postsecondary student success:

spearheading a dialog on student success. *National Postsecondary Education Cooperative.* Available at http://nces.ed.gov/npec/pdf/kuh_team_report.pdf

Kuh, G., Kinzie, J., Buckley, J., Bridges, B., & Hayek, J. (2007). *Piecing together the student success puzzle: Research, propositions, and recommendations* (ASHE Higher Education Report, Vol. 32, no. 5). San Francisco, CA: Jossey-Bass.

Kuh, G. D., Kinzie, J., Schuh, J. H., Whitt, E. J., & Associates. (2005). *Student success in college: Creating conditions that matter.* San Francisco, CA: Jossey-Bass.

Kuh, G. D., Schuh, J. H., Whitt, E. J., & Associates. (1991). *Involving colleges: Successful approaches to fostering student learning and development outside the classroom.* San Francisco, CA: Jossey-Bass.

Laar, C. V., Levin, S., Sinclair, S., & Sidanius, J. (2005). The effect of university roommate contact on ethnic attitudes and behavior. *Journal of Experimental Social Psychology, 41*(4), 329–345.

Lack, L. C. (1986). Delayed sleep and sleep loss in university students. *Journal of American College Health, 35,* 105–110.

Lacy, W. B. (1978). Interpersonal relationships as mediators of structural effects: College student socialization in a traditional and an experimental university environment. *Sociology of Education, 51*(3), 201–211.

Laitman, L., & Stewart, L. P. (2012). Campus recovery. In H. R. White & D. L. Rabiner (Eds.), *College drinking and drug use* (pp. 253–271). New York: Guilford Press.

LaNasa, S. M., Olson, E., & Alleman, N. (2007). The impact of on-campus student growth of first-year student engagement and success. *Research in Higher Education, 48*(8), 941–966.

Lane, J. E., & Kinser, K. (2014, March 17). Research & news about educational institutions moving across borders. *Global Higher Education.* Available at http://www.globalhighered.org/branchcampuses.php

LaVine, M. (2010). Socialization and student development: The living-learning community an integration of theory and practice. *Future Focus, 31*(2), 25–36.

LaVine, M., & Mitchell, S. (2006). A physical education learning community: Development and first-year assessment. *Physical Educator, 63*(2), 58–68.

Lazarsfeld, P. F., & Merton, R. K. (1954). Friendship as social process: A substantive and methodological analysis. In M. Berger, T. Abel, & C. H. Page (Eds.), *Freedom and control in modern society* (pp. 18–66). New York: Van Nostrand.

Ledbetter, A. M., Griffin, E., & Sparks, G. G. (2007). Forecasting "friends forever": A longitudinal investigation of sustained closeness between best friends. *Personal Relationships, 14*, 343–350.

Lee, D. (2013). *Household debt and credit: Student debt.* Federal Reserve Bank of New York. Available at http://www.newyorkfed.org/newsevents/ mediaadvisory/2013/Lee022813.pdf

Lee, C. H., & Kalyuga, S. (2014). Expertise reversal effects and its instructional implications. In V. A. Benassi, C. E. Overson, & C. M. Hakala (Eds.), *Applying science of learning in education: Infusing psychological science into curriculum* (pp. 31–44). American Psychological Association (Division 2). Available at http://teachpsych.org/ebooks/asle2014/index.php

Leonard, K., Quigley, B., & Collins, R. (2002). Physical aggression in the lives of young adults: Prevalence, location, and severity among college and community samples. *Journal of Interpersonal Violence, 17*, 533–550.

Lepore, S. J., Evans, G. W., & Palsane, I. M. (1991). Social hassles and psychological health in the context of crowding. *Journal of Health and Social Behavior, 32*, 357–367.

Lepp, A., Barkely, J. E., & Karpinski, A. C. (2014). The relationship between cell phone use, academic performance, anxiety, and satisfaction with life in college students. *Computers in Human Behavior, 31*, 343–350.

Levine, A., & Dean, D. R. (2012). *Generation of a tightrope: A portrait of today's college student.* San Francisco, CA: Jossey-Bass.

Levitz, J., & Belkin, D. (2013, June 6). Humanities fall from favor. *Wall Street Journal.*

Lewin, T. (2012, February 4). *Taking more seats on campus, foreigners also pay the freight. New York Times.* Available at http://www.nytimes.com/2012/02/05/ education/international-students-pay-top-dollar-at-us-colleges.html? pagewanted=all&_r=0

Lewin, T. (2013, December 25). Getting out of the discount game, small colleges lower price. *New York Times.*

Li, L., Maximova, E., Saunders, K., Whalen, D. F., & Shelley, M. C. (2007). The influence of custodial, maintenance, and residence life services on student satisfaction in residence halls. *Journal of College and University Student Housing, 34*(2), 43–52.

Light, R. J. (2001). *Making the most of college: Students speak their minds.* Cambridge, MA: Harvard University Press.

Lipka, S. (2014, January 19). Demographic data lets colleges peer into the future. *Chronicle of Higher Education.* Available at http://chronicle.com/article/ Demographic-Data-Let-Colleges/144101/

Littlejohn, S., & Smith, A. R. (2005). *Theories of human communication* (8th ed.). Belmont, CA: Thomson Wadsworth.

Lloyd-Jones, E. (1952). Personnel work and general education. In N. B. Henry (Ed.), *General education (fifty-first yearbook, part 1)* (pp. 214–229). Chicago, IL: National Society for the Study of Education and the University of Chicago Press.

Logan, C. R., Salisbury-Glennon, J., & Spence, L. D. (2000). The learning edge academic program: Toward a community of learners. *Journal of the First-Year Experience, 12*(1), 77–104.

Long, L. D., & Kujawa, K. (2012). *Experience of students in transitional housing.* East Lansing, MI: Campus Living Services and Residence Life, Michigan State University.

Longerbeam, S. D., & Sedlacek, W. E. (2006). Attitudes toward diversity and living-learning outcomes among first and second year college students. *NASPA Journal, 43*(1), 40–55.

Lopez, M. H., & Fry, R. (2013, September 4). Among recent high school grads, Hispanic college enrollment rate surpasses that of whites. *Pew Research Center.* Available at http://www.pewresearch.org/fact-tank/2013/09/04/hispanic-college-enrollment-rate-surpasses-whites-for-the-first-time/

Lorden, L. P. (1998). Attrition in the student affairs profession. *NASPA Journal.*

Lounsbury, J. W., & DeNeui, D. (1996). Collegiate psychological sense of community. *Journal of Community Psychology, 24*(4), 381–394.

Lund, H. G., Reider, B. D., Whiting, A. B., & Prichard, J. R. (2010). Sleep patterns and predictors of disturbed sleep in a large population of college students. *Journal of Adolescent Health, 46*(2), 124–132.

Mable, P. (1991). Professional standards: An introduction and historical perspective. In W. A. Bryan, R. B. Winston Jr. & T. K. Miller (Eds.), *Using professional standards in student affairs* (New Directions for Student Services No. 53) (pp. 5–18). San Francisco, CA: Jossey-Bass.

Magolda, P., & Gross, K. E. (2009). *It's all about Jesus! Faith as an oppositional collegiate subculture.* Sterling, VA: Stylus.

Mahtesian, C. (1995, July). Higher ed: The no-longer sacred cow. *Governing,* 20–26.

Manago, A. M., Taylor, T., & Greenfield, P. M. (2012). Me and my 400 friends: The anatomy of college students' Facebook networks, their communication patterns, and well-being. *Developmental Psychology, 48*(2), 369–380.

Mander, B. A., Reid, K. J., Baron, K. G., Tjoa, T., Parrish, T. B., Paller, K. A., et al. (2010). EEG measures index neural and cognitive recovery from sleep deprivation. *Journal of Neuroscience, 30*(7), 2686–2693.

Mark, N. P., & Harris, D. (2012). Roommates race and racial composition of white college students ego network. *Social Science Research, 41*, 331–342.

Martin, A. (2012, December 13). Building a showcase campus, using an I.O.U. *New York Times*. Available at http://www.nytimes.com/2012/12/14/business/colleges-debt-falls-on-students-after-construction-binges.html?pagewanted=all&_r=0

Martinez, M. (2005, January 2). Neighbors say the attitude's too liberal at Berkeley co-op—noise, drugs and flying animal flesh among complaints. *Houston Chronicle*, A-11.

Maslow, A. H. (1954). *Motivation and personality*. New York: Harper.

May, E. P. (1974). Type of housing and achievement of disadvantaged university students. *College Student Affairs Journal, 8*(2), 48–51.

McCabe, S. E., Boyd, C. J., Cranford, J. A., Slayden, J. A., Lange, J. E., Reed, M. B., et al. (2007). Alcohol involvement and participation in residential learning communities among first-year college students. *Journal of Studies on Alcohol and Drugs, 68*, 722–726.

McCarthy, M. E., Pretty, G. M., & Catano, V. (1990). Psychological sense of community and student burnout. *Journal of College Student Development, 31*(2), 211–216.

McCluskey-Titus, P., Oliver, R. S., Wilson, M. E., Hall, L. M., Cawthon, T. W., & Crandall, P. D. (2002). The relationship between community and academic achievement in residence halls. *Journal of College and University Student Housing, 30*(2), 12–16.

McPherson, M., Smith-Lovin, L., & Cook, J. M. (2001). Birds of a feather: Homophily in social networks. *Annual of Review of Sociology, 27*(1), 415–444.

Mercer, G., & Benjamin, M. L. (1980). Spatial behavior of university undergraduates in double occupancy rooms: An inventory of effects. *Journal of Applied Social Psychology, 10*, 32–44.

Metha, R., Shu, R. J., & Cheema, A. (2012). Is noise always bad? Exploring the effects of ambient noise on creative cognition. *Journal of Consumer Research, 39*(4), 784–799.

Mettler, S. (2014). *Degrees of inequality: How the politics of higher education sabotaged the American dream*. New York: Basic Books.

Meyers, J. (2014, January 19). Prospectus: Who will reach college age in the next 14 years? *Chronicle of Higher Education*. Available at http://chronicle.com/article//144061/#00/0-1

Miami University Office of Residence Life. (2013, May 23). Residential Curriculum. Miami, OH. Available at http://www.units.muohio.edu/saf/reslife/reslife/whatwedo/rescurric.php#LPM

Micomonaco, J. (2011). Living-learning communities as an intervention to improve disciplinary retention and learning outcomes in engineering education (Doctoral dissertation). Michigan State University, East Lansing.

Milem, J. F. (1998). Attitude change in college students: Examining the effect of college peer groups and faculty reference groups. *Journal of Higher Education, 69*(2), 117–140.

Miller, G. A. (1956). The magical number seven, plus or minus two: Some limits on our capacity for processing information. *Psychological Review, 63,* 81–97.

Miller, T. K., & Prince, J. S. (1976). *The future of student affairs.* San Francisco, CA: Jossey-Bass.

Misra, R., & McKean, M. (2000). College students' academic stress and its relation to their anxiety, time management, and leisure satisfaction. *American Journal of Health Studies, 16*(1), 41–52.

Moffatt, M. (1989). *Coming of age in New Jersey: College and American culture.* New Brunswick, NJ: Rutgers University Press.

Moody's Investors Services. (2013, November 25). 2014 outlook—US higher education, not-for-profits and independent schools. *Moody's Investor Services.* Available at http://facilities.georgetown.edu/document/1242807545994/11-25-2013_Higher+Education+Not+for+Profit+Outlook+2014.pdf

Moore, D. (2010, May). And the survey says. *College Planning and Management,* 6–8.

Moore, D. (2012, June). And the survey says. *College Planning & Management (2012 College Housing Report).* Available at http://webcpm.com/research/2012/06/college-housing.aspx

Moore, L. J., & Ostrander, E. R. (1980). Physical and social determinants of student satisfaction in university residence halls: The theme dorm concept. *Housing and Society, 7*(1), 26–34.

Moos, R. (1974). *The social climate scales: An overview.* Palo Alto, CA: Consulting Psychologist Press.

Moos, R. (1976). *The human context: Environmental determinants of behavior.* New York: John Wiley.

Moos, R. (1987). *Evaluating educational environments.* San Francisco, CA: Jossey-Bass.

Moos, R., & Gerst, M. (1974). *The university residence environmental scale manual.* Palo Alto, CA: Consulting Psychologist Press.

Mosher, W., Chandra, A., & Jones, J. (2005). *Sexual behavior and selected health measures: Men and women 15–44 years of age, United States, 2002. Advanced data from vital health statistics.* Hyattsville, MD: National Center for Health Statistics.

Mosier, R. E., & Schwartzmuller, G. J. (2002). Benchmarking in student affairs. In B. E. Bender & J. H. Schuh (Eds.), *Using benchmarking to inform practice in higher education* (New Directions for Higher Education no. 118) (pp. 79–92). San Francisco, CA: Jossey-Bass.

Murray, J. L., Snider, B. R., & Midkiff, R. M. (1999). The effects of training on resident assistant job performance. *Journal of College Student Development, 40*(6), 744–747.

Myers-Levy, J., & Zhu, R. J. (2007). The influence of ceiling height: The effect of priming on the type of processing that people use. *Journal of Consumer Research, 34*(2), 174–186.

Nasser, H. E. (2012, April 12). Geek chic: "Brogrammer?" Now, that's hot. *USA Today Tech.* Available at http://usatoday30.usatoday.com/tech/news/story/2012–04–10/techie-geeks-cool/54160750/1

Nathan, R. (2005). *My freshman year: What a professor learned by becoming a student.* Ithaca, NY: Cornell University Press.

National Center for Education Statistics (NCES). (2009a). *ELS 2002: Survey design and sample.* Washington, DC: U.S. Department of Education National Center for Education Statistics.

National Center for Education Statistics (NCES). (2009b). *About IPEDS.* Washington, DC: Department of Education National Center for Education Statistics.

National Center for Education Statistics (NCES). (2012a). *Condition of education, 2012.* Washington, DC: U.S. Department of Education.

National Center for Education Statistics (NCES). (2012b, February). Figure 21. Actual and projected numbers for enrollment of U.S. residents in all postsecondary degree-granting institutions, by race/ethnicity: Fall 1996 through fall 2021. *U.S. Department of Education Institute for Education Science National Center for Education Statistics.* Available at https://nces.ed.gov/programs/projections/projections2021/sec5c.asp

National Center for Education Statistics (NCES). (2012c, February). Table 29. Actual and projected numbers for enrollment of U.S. residents in all postsecondary degree-granting institutions, by race/ethnicity: Fall 1996 through fall 2021. *U.S. Department of Education Institute of Education Sciences National Center for Education Statistics.* Available at http://nces.ed.gov/programs/projections/projections2021/tables/table_29.asp?referrer=list

National Center for Education Statistics (NCES). (2013). *Projections of education statistics to 2021 (fortieth edition) (NCES 2013–008). U.S. Department of Education, National Center for Education Statistics.* Washington, DC: U.S. Government Printing Office.

National Conference of State Legislatures (NCSL). (2014a, March 5). Performance-based funding for higher education. *NCLS.org.* Available at http://www.ncsl.org/research/education/performance-funding.aspx

National Conference of State Legislatures (NCSL). (2014b, March). Guns on campus. *NCSI.org.* Available at http://www.ncsl.org/research/education/guns-on-campus-overview.aspx

National Postsecondary Student Aid Study. (2010, September). 2010220: Profile of undergraduates students: Trends from selected years, 1995–96 to 2007–08. *U.S. Department of Education Center for Education Statistics.* Available at http://nces.ed.gov/pubs2010/2010220.pdf

National Vital Statistics Report. (2013, December 30). Births: Final data for 2012. *CDC.* Available at http://www.cdc.gov/nchs/data/nvsr/nvsr62/nvsr62_09.pdf

New, J. (2013, February 11). Digital devices invade campus, and networks feel the strain. *Chronicle of Higher Education.* Available at http://chronicle.com/article/Digital-Devices-Invade-Campus/137217/

Newcomb, T. M. (1962). Student peer group influence. In N. Sanford (Ed.), *The American college* (pp. 469–488). New York: John Wiley & Sons.

Newman, C. J. (1933). *On the scope and nature of university education.* New York: E.F. Dutton & Co. Inc.

Nidiffer, J. (2000). *Pioneering deans of women.* New York: Teachers College Press.

Noble, K., Flynn, N. T., Lee, J., & Hilton, D. (2007). Predicting successful college experiences: Evidence from a first year retention program. *Journal of College Student Retention, 9*(1), 39–60.

North American Students of Cooperation (NASCO). (2008). *NASCO cooperative organizer's handbook: 2008 edition.* Ann Arbor, MI: Author.

North American Students of Cooperation (NASCO). (2014, April). NASCO history and locations. *NASCOCoop.* Available at http://www.nasco.coop/properties

Norwalk, K., Norvilitis, J. M., & MacLean, M. G. (2009). ADHD symptomatology and its relationship to factors associated with college adjustment. *Journal of Attention Disorders, 13*(3), 251–258.

Nowotny, O., Julian, J., & Beaty, R. (1938). Student co-operative projects. In *Secretarial Notes Twentith Annual Meeting of the National Association of Deans and Advisers of Men* (pp. 40–49). National Association of Deans and Advisers of Men.

O'Malley, P. M. (2004–2005). Maturing out of problematic alcohol use. In *Focus on young adult drinking* (pp. 202–204). Washington, DC: National Institute on Alcohol Abuse and Alcoholism/National Institutes of Health.

Ong, S.-E., Petrova, M., & Spieler, A. C. (2013). Demand for university student housing: An empirical analysis. *Journal of Housing Research, 22*(2), 142–164.

Orme, R. (1950). *Counseling in residence halls.* New York: Teachers College, Columbia.

Pace, C. R. (1984). *Measuring the quality of college student experiences: An account of the development and use of the college student experience questionnaire.* Los Angeles, CA: Higher Education Research Institute, Graduate School of Education, University of California.

Padgett, R. D., Johnson, M. P., & Pascarella, E. T. (2012). First-generation undergraduate studeents and the impacts of first year of college: Additional evidence. *Journal of College Student Development, 53*(2), 243–266.

Palmer, C., Murphy, R. K., Peck, K., & Steinke, K. (2001). An international study of burnout among residence hall directors. *Journal of College and University Student Housing, 29*(2), 36–44.

Pappano, L. (2012, November 2). The year of the MOOCs. *New York Times.*

Parameswaran, A., & Bowers, J. (2014). Student residences: From housing to education. *Journal of Further and Higher Education, 38*(1), 57–74.

Parker, C. A. (1978). Introduction: A student development perspective. In C. A. Parker (Ed.), *Encouraging Development in College Students* (pp. 3–23). Minneapolis: University of Minnesota Press.

Parker, J. (2012). Does living near classmates help introductory economics students get better grades. *Journal of Economic Education, 43*(2), 149–164.

Parsons, J. T. (1982). Academic achievement of freshmen assigned to temporarily triple rooms. *Journal of College and University Student Housing, 12*(1), 34.

Pascarella, E. (1984). College environmental influences on students' educational aspiration. *Journal of Higher Education, 55,* 751–771.

Pascarella, E. T. (1996). On student development in college: Evidence from the national study of student learning. *Improve the Academy, Paper 362,* 17–29.

Pascarella, E. T. (2001). Cognitive growth in college surprising and reassuring findings from the national study of student learning. *Change: The Magazine of Higher Education, 33*(6), 20–27.

Pascarella, E. T., & Terenzini, P. T. (1991). *How college affects students.* San Francisco, CA: Jossey-Bass.

Pascarella, E. T., & Terenzini, P. T. (2005). *How college affects students: A third decade of research* (vol. 2) San Francisco, CA: Jossey-Bass.

Pascarella, E. T., Terenzini, P. T., & Blimling, G. S. (1994). How residence halls impact student learning and personal development. In C. Schroeder, P. Mable, & Associates (Eds.), *Realizing the educational potential of college residence halls* (pp. 22–55). San Francisco, CA: Jossey-Bass.

Pascarella, E. T., Terenzini, P. T., & Blimling, G. S. (1996). Students' out-of-class experiences and their influence on learning and cognitive development: A literature review. *Journal of College Student Development, 37,* 149–162.

Pascarella, E., Bohr, L., Nora, A., Zusman, B., Inman, P., & Desler, M. (1993). Cognitive impacts of living on campus versus commuting to college. *Journal of College Student Development, 34,* 210–220.

Paschall, M. J., & Saltz, R. F. (2007). Relationship between college setting and student alcohol use before, during and after events: a multi-level study. *Drug and Alcohol Review, 26,* 635–644.

Pasque, P. A., & Murphy, R. (2005). The intersection of living-learning programs and social identity as factors of academic achievement and intellectual engagement. *Journal of College Student Development, 46*(4), 429–441.

Payne, J. (2013, November 16). *Smartphone use by college students* [infographic]. *Yahoo.* Available at https://smallbusiness.yahoo.com/advisor/smartphone-college-students-infographic-153840365.html

Pelter, G. L., Laden, R., & Matranga, M. (1999). Student persistence in college: A review of the research. *Journal of College Student Retention, 1*(4), 357–375.

Perry, W. G. (1970). *Forms of intellectual and ethical development during the college years.* New York: Holt, Rinehart, & Winston.

Peterson, R. E. (1968). *The scope of organized protests in 1967–1968.* Princeton, NJ: Educational Testing Services.

Pew Research Center. (2011, August 28). The digital revolution and higher education: College presidents, public differ on value of online learning.

Available at http://www.pewsocialtrends.org/files/2011/08/online-learning
.pdf

Pew Research Center. (2014, March). Millennials in adulthood: Detached from
institutions, networked with friends. *Pew Research Center.* Available at
http://www.pewsocialtrends.org/files/2014/03/2014–03–07_generations-
report-version-for-web.pdf

Pica, J., Jones, D., & Caplinger, C. (2006). Freshman housing: Current practices,
planned construction, CHO perspectives on the future. In N. Dunkle & J.
Baumann (Eds.), *College housing: 2005 special report, 21st century project
reading compendium* (pp. 51–58). Columbus, OH: ACUHO-I Press.

Pike, G. R. (1999). The effects of residential learning communities and
traditional residential living arrangements on educational gains during the
first year of college. *Journal of College Student Development, 40,* 269–284.

Pike, G. R., Schroeder, C. C., & Berry, T. R. (1997). Enhancing the educational
impact of residence halls: The relationship between residential learning
communities and first-year college experiences and persistence. *Journal of
College Student Development, 38,* 237–249.

Pilcher, J. J., & Walters, A. S. (1997). How sleep deprivation affects
psychological variables related to college students' cognitive performance.
*Journal of American College Health, 46,* 121–126.

Pilcher, J., Ginter, S., & Sadowsky, B. (1997). Sleep quality versus sleep quantity:
Relationship between sleep and measures of health, well being and
sleepiness in college students. *Journal of Psychosomatic Research, 42,* 583–596.

Plutchik, R. (1980). *Emotion: A psychoevolutionary synthesis.* London, UK:
Longman.

Poh, M. (2013). 5 key features to expect in future smartphones. *Hongkiat.com.*
Available at http://www.hongkiat.com/blog/future-smartphone-features/

Posner, B. Z., & Brodsky, B. (1993). Leadership practices of effective RAs. *Journal
of College Student Development, 34,* 300–304.

Priest, R. F., & Sawyer, J. (1967). Proximity and peership: Bases of balance in
interpersonal attraction and behavior. *American Journal of Sociology, 72*(6),
633–649.

Proctor, R. (2008). Social structures: Gillespie, Kidd & Coia's halls of residence
at the University of Hull. *Journal of the Society of Architectural Historians,
67*(1), 106–129.

Project on Student Debt. (2013). *Student debt and the class of 2012.* Institute for
College Debt & Success.

Purcell, A., Peron, E., & Sanchez, C. (1998). Subcultural and cross-cultural
effects on the experience of detached houses: An examination of two

models of affective experience of the environment. *Environment and Behavior, 30,* 348–377.

Purdie, J. R. (2007). Examining the academic performance and retention of first year students in living-learning communities, freshmen interest groups and first year experience courses (Doctoral dissertation). ProQuest Dissertations and Theses database (UMI No. 3322736).

Purdie, J. R., & Rosser, V. J. (2011). Examining the academic performance and retention of first-year students in living-learning communities and first year experience courses. *College Student Affairs Journal, 29*(2), 95–112.

Quigley, B. M., & Leonard, K. E. (2004–2005 ). Alcohol use and violence among young adults. In *Focus on young adult drinking* (vol. 28, pp. 191–194). Washington, DC.

Rabin, L. A., Fogel, J., & Nutter-Upham, K. E. (2011). *Journal of Clinical and Experimental Neuropsychology, 33*(3), 344–357.

Ramsey, M. A., Gentzler, A. L., Morey, J. N., Oberhauser, A. M., & Westerman, D. (2013). College students' use of communication technology with parents: Comparisons between to cohorts in 2009 and 2011. *Cyberpsychology, Behavior, and Social Networking, 16*(10), 747–752.

Ratey, J. (2001). *A user's guide to the brain.* New York: Patheon Books.

Redden, E. (2013, September 23). Giving agents the ok. *Inside Higher Education.* Available at http://www.insidehighered.com/news/2013/09/23/admissions-association-lifts-ban-commissioned-agents-international-recruiting

Reich, H. (1964). *The college housemother.* Danville, IL: The Interstate Printers & Publishers, Inc.

Renn, K. A. (2003). Understanding the identities of mixed-race college students through a developmental ecology lens. *Journal of College Student Development, 44*(3), 383–403.

Renn, K. A., & Arnold, K. D. (2003). Reconceptualizing research on college student peer culture. *Journal of Higher Education, 74*(3), 261–291.

Reynolds, A. L. (2013). College student concerns: Perceptions of student affairs practitioners. *Journal of College Student Development, 54*(1), 98–104.

Rice, N. D., & Lightsey, O. R. (2001). Freshmen living learning communities: Relationship to academic success and affective development. *Journal of College and University Student Housing, 30*(1), 11–17.

Richmond, D. R. (1989). Group billing for university residence hall damages: A common but questionable practice. *Journal of Law and Education, 18*(3), 375–409.

Rietveld, C. A., Medland, S. E., Derringer, J., Yang, J., Esko, T., Martin, N. W., et al. (2013). GWAS of 126,559 individuals identifies genetic variants associated with educational attainment. *Science, 340,* 1467–1471.

Riker, H. C. (1965). *College housing as learning centers* (Vol. Student Personnel Series No. 3). Washington, DC: American College Personnel Association.

Riker, H. C., & DeCoster, D. A. (1971). The educational role in college student housing. *Journal of College and University Student Housing, 35,* 3–7.

Robinson, P. J. (1987). The relationship between favorable and unfavorable contact on the social distance attitudes of residence hall students toward residential subgroups (Doctoral dissertation). Iowa State University. Dissertation Abstracts International 49(3): 0444.

Rodger, S. C., & Johnson, A. M. (2005). The impact of residence design on freshman outcomes: Dormitories versus suite-style residences. *Canadian Journal of Higher Education, 35*(3), 83–99.

Rogers, C. (1969). *Freedom to learn: A view of what education might become.* Columbus, OH: Charles Merill.

Rogers, R. F. (1990). An integration of campus ecology and student development: The olentangy project. In D. G. Creamer (Ed.), *College student development: Theory and practice for the 1990s* (pp. 155–180). Alexandria, VA: American College Personnel Association.

Rohli, R. V., & Rogge, R. A. (2012). An empirical study of the potential for geography in university living-learning communities in the United States. *Journal of Geography in Higher Education, 36*(1), 81–95.

Ronchi, D., & Sparacino, J. (1982). Density of dormitory living and stress: Mediating effects of sex, self-monitoring, and environmental affective qualities. *Perceptual and Motor Skills, 55*(3), 759–770.

Rowan-Keyon, H., Soldner, M., & Inkelas, K. K. (2007). The contributions of living-learning programs on developing sense of civic engagement in undergraduate students. *NASPA Journal, 44*(4), 750–778.

Rudolph, F. (1962). *The American college and university.* New York: Vintage Books.

Sacerdote, B. (2001). Peer effects with random assignment: Results for Dartmouth roommates. *Quarterly Journal of Economics, 116,* 681–704.

Saenz, V. B., Hurtado, S., Barrera, D., Wolf, D., & Yeung, F. (2007). *First in my family: A profile of first-generation college students at four-year institutions since 1971.* Los Angles, CA: Higher Education Research Institute, UCLA.

Saint Louis University Housing and Residence Life. (n.d.). Saint Louis university housing and residence life residential curriculum. Available at

http://www.slu.edu/Documents/student_development/residence_life/Res%
20Curriculum%201%20pager.pdf

Salimpoor, V. R., Benovoy, M., Larcher, K., Dagher, A., & Zatorre, R. J. (2011).
Anatomically distinct dopamine release during anticipation and
experience of peak emotion to music. *Nature Neuroscience, 14,* 257–262.

Sanford, N. (1962). *The American college: A psychological and social interpretation of
the higher learning.* New York: Wiley.

Santrock, J. W. (1987). *Adolescence: An introduction* (3rd ed.). Dubuque, IA:
Wm. C. Brown.

Satel, S., & Lilienfeld, S. O. (2013). *Brainwashed: The seductive appeal of mindless
neuroscience.* New York: Basic Books.

Schacter, D. L. (2002). *The seven sins of memory: How the mind forgets and
remembers.* New York: Houghton Mifflin Harcourt.

Schein, H. K. (2005). The zen of unit one: Residential learning communities can
foster liberal learning at large universities. In N. Laff (Ed.), *Identity,
learning, and the liberal arts.* New Directions for Teaching and Learning, no.
103 (pp. 73–88). San Francisco, CA: Jossey-Bass.

Schein, H. K., & Bowers, P. M. (1992). Using living learning centers to provide
integrated campus services for freshmen. *Journal of the Freshmen Year
Experience, 4*(1), 59–77.

Scherer, J. (1969). *Students in residence: A survey of American studies* (higher
education monography series no.1). London: National Foundation for
Educational Research in England and Wales, Department of Higher
Education, University of London Institute of Education.

Scheuermann, T., & Ellet, T. (2007). A 3-D view of recruitment and retention of
entry-level housing staff: Déjà vu, deliberation, decisive action. *Journal of
College and University Housing Officers, 34*(2), 12–19.

Schudde, L. T. (2011). The casual effect of campus residency on college student
retention. *Review of Higher Education, 34*(4), 581–610.

Schuh, J. H., & Associates. (2009). *Assessment methods for student affairs.* San
Francisco, CA: Jossey-Bass.

Schuh, J. H., & Shipton, W. C. (1983). Abuses encountered by resident
assistants during an academic year. *Journal of College Student Personnel, 24,*
428–432.

Schuh, J. H., & Triponey, V. L. (1993). Fundamentals of program design. In
R. B. Winston, S. Anchors, & Associates (Eds.), *Student housing and
residential life: A handbook for professionals committed to student development*
(pp. 423–442). San Francisco, CA: Jossey-Bass.

Schuh, J. H., Shipton, W. C., & Edman, N. (1986). Counseling problems encountered by resident assistants: An update. *Journal of College Student Personnel, 27*(1), 26–33.

Schussler, D. L., & Fierros, E. G. (2008). Students' perception of their academics, relationships, and sense of belonging: Comparisons across residential learning communities. *Journal of The First-Year Experience & Students in Transition, 20*(1), 71–96.

Seaman, B. (2005). *Binge: What your college student won't tell you.* Hoboken, NJ: John Wiley & Sons, Inc.

Seifert, T. A., Pascarella, E. T., Colangelo, N., & Assouline, S. G. (2007). The effects of honors program participation on experiences of good practices and learning outcomes. *Journal of College Student Development, 48*(1), 57–74.

Selby, T. J., & Weston, D. F. (1978). Dormitory versus apartments housing for freshmen. *Journal of College Student Personnel, 16*(3), 153–157.

Selingo, J. J. (2013). *College (un)bound: The future of higher education and what it means for students.* Boston, MA: New Harvest Houghton Mifflin Harcourt.

Shay, J. E. (1964). The evolution of the campus residence hall, part 1: The decline. *Journal of the National Association of Women Deans, Administrators, and Counselors, 27*(4), 197–185.

Sherif, M., Harvey, O. J., White, B. J., Hood, W. R., & Sherif, C. W. (1961). *Intergroup cooperation and competition: The Robbers Cave experiment.* Norman, OK: University Book Exchange.

Shipton, W. C., & Schuh, J. H. (1982). Counseling problems encountered by resident assistants: A longitudinal study. *Journal of College Student Personnel, 23*(3), 246–252.

Shook, N., & Clay, R. (2012). Interracial roommate relationships: A mechanism for promoting sense of belonging at university and academic performance. *Journal of Experimental Social Psychology, 48*(5), 1168–1172.

Shook, N. J., & Fazio, R. H. (2008). Roommate relationships: A comparison of interracial and same-race living. *Group Processes & Intergroup Relations, 11*(4), 425–437.

Shushok, F. J. (2006). Student outcomes and honors programs: A longitudinal study of 172 honors students 2000–2004. *Journal of the National Collegiate Honors Council, 72*(2), 85–96.

Shushok, F. J., & Sriram, R. (2010). Exploring the effect of a residential academic affairs-student affairs partnership: The first year of an engineering and computer science living-learning center. *Journal of College and University Student Housing, 36*(2), 68–81.

Shute, V. J. (2008). Focus on formative feedback. *Review of Educational Research*, *78*(1), 153–189.

Siegel, D. J. (2012). *The developing mind: How relationships and the brain interact to shape who we are* (2nd ed.). New York: Guilford Press.

Simpson, R. (1996). Neither clear nor present: the social construction of safety and danger. *Sociological Forum*, *11*, 549–562.

Smith, A., Rainie, L., & Zickuhr, K. (2011). *College students and technology*. Pew Research Internet Project.

Soldner, M., & Szelenyi, K. (2008). A national portrait of today's living-learning programs. *Journal of College and University Student Housing*, *35*, 14–31.

Sommer, R. (1987). Crime and vandalism in university residence halls: A confirmation of the defensible space theory. *Journal of Environmental Psychology*, *7*, 1–12.

Sriram, R. R., Shushok, F., Perkins, J., & Scales, L. (2011). Students as teachers: What faculty learn by living on campus. *Journal of College and University Student Housing*, *38*(1), 40–55.

St. Onge, S. R., Ellett, T., & Nestor, E. M. (2008). Factors affecting recruitment and retention of entry-level housing and residence life staff: Perceptions of chief housing officers. *Journal of College and University Student Housing*, *35*(2), 10–23.

St. Onge, S., Nestor, E., Peter, P., & Robertson, T. (2003). Modifying RA training in support of a custom programming model. *Journal of College and University Student Housing*, *32*(2), 45–47.

Standard & Poor's Financial Services. (2014, February 6). Many factors burden the U.S. higher education sector in 2014. *Global Credit Portal*. Available at https://www.globalcreditportal.com/ratingsdirect/renderArticle.do?articleId=1256366&SctArtId=212965&from=CM&nsl_code=LIME

Stassen, L. A. (2003). Student outcomes: The impact of varying living learning community models. *Research in Higher Education*, *44*(5), 581–613.

State Higher Education Executive Officers Association (SHEEO). (2012). *State higher education finance FY 2012*. State Higher Education Executive Officers.

Stein, D. J., Newman, T. K., Savitz, J., & Ramesar, R. (2006). Warriors versus worriers: The role of COMT gene variants. *CNS Spectrus*, *11*(10), 745–748.

Steinberg, L. (2008). A social neuroscience perspective on adolescent risk-taking. *Developmental Reviews*, *28*, 78–106.

Steinberg, L. (2009). Adolescent development and juvenile justice. *Annual Review of Clinical Psychology*, *5*, 47–73.

Stern, G. (1970). *People in context: Measuring person-environmental congruence in education and industry.* New York: John Wiley & Sons.

Stinebrickner, R., & Stinebrickner, T. R. (2006). What can be learned about peer effects using college roommates? Evidence from new survey data and students from disadvantaged backgrounds. *Journal of Public Economics, 90,* 1435–1454.

Stinebrickner, R., & Stinebrickner, T. R. (2008). The causal effect of studying on academic performance. *BE Journal of Economic Analysis & Policy, 8*(1), 1–55.

Strange, C. C. (1991). Managing college environments: Theory and practice. In T. K. Miller, R. B. Winston Jr. & Associates (Eds.), *Administration and leadership in student affairs* (pp. 159–199). Muncie, IN: Accelerated Development.

Strange, C. C., & Banning, J. H. (2001). *Educating by design: Creating campus learning environments that work.* San Francisco, CA: Jossey-Bass.

Student Life Committee of the Faculty Senate. (2008). *Assessment on the curricular approach to residence life.* Newark: University of Delaware.

Sweller, J. (2010). Element interactivity and intrinsic, extraneous, and germane cognitive load. *Educational Psychology, 22,* 123–138.

Szelenyi, K., & Inkelas, K. K. (2011). The role of living-learning programs in women's plans to attend graduate school in STEM fields. *Research in Higher Education, 52*(4), 349–369.

Szelenyi, K., Denson, N., & Inkelas, K. K. (2012). Women in stem majors and professional outcomes expectations: The role of living-learning programs and other college environments. *Research in Higher Education, 54,* 851–873.

Tajfel, H. (1970). Experiments in intergroup discrimination. *Scientific American, 223,* 96–102.

Talbot, M. (1909). Moral and religious influences as related to the environment of student life: Dormitory life for college women. *Journal of the Religious Education Association, 4*(1), 41–46.

Tapert, S. F., Caldwell, L., & Burke, C. (2004–2005). Alcohol and adolescent brain—human studies. In *Focus on young adults* (vol. 28, pp. 205–212). Washington, DC: National Institute on Alcohol Abuse and Alcoholism/ National Institutes of Health.

Tatum, B. D. (2003). *Why are all the black kids sitting together in the cafeteria?: And other conversations about race.* New York: Basic Books.

Taub, J. M. (1978). Behavioral and psychophysicological correlates of irregularity in chronic sleep routines. *Biological Psychology, 7,* 37–53.

Taylor, K., Moore, W. S., MacGregor, J., & Lindblad, J. (2003). *National learning communities project monograph series*. Olympia: Washington Center, Evergreen State University.

Terenzini, P. T., Pascarella, E. T., & Blimling, G. S. (1996). Students' out-of-class experiences and their influence on learning and cognitive development: A literature review. *Journal of College Student Development, 37*, 149–162.

Thelin, J. R. (2004). *A history of higher education*. Baltimore, MD: Johns Hopkins University Press.

Thwing, C. F. (1920). Dormitory life for college men. In M. G. Fulton (Ed.), *College life: Its conditions and problems* (pp. 392–399). New York: MacMillan Company.

Tinto, V. (1993). *Leaving college: Rethinking the causes and cures of student attrition* (2nd ed.). Chicago, IL: Chicago University Press.

Townsend, B. K. (2007). Interpreting the influence of community college attendance upon baccalaureate attainment. *Community College Review, 35*, 128–136.

Trockel, M. T., Barnes, M. D., & Egget, D. L. (2000). Health-related variables and academic performance among first-year college students: Implications for sleep and other behaviors. *Journal of American College Health, 49*, 125–138.

Turner, J. C., & Reynolds, K. H. (2003). The social identity perspective in intergroup relations: Theories, themes, and controversies. In R. Brown & S. Gaertner (Eds.), *Blackwell handbook of social psychology: Intergroup processes* (pp. 133–152). Malden, MA: Blackwell Publishing.

Turner, J. C., Hogg, M. A., Oakes, P. J., Reicher, S. D., & Wetherell, M. S. (1987). *Rediscovering the social group: A self-categorization theory*. Cambridge, MA: Basil Blackwell.

Twale, D. J., & Muse, V. (1996). Resident assistant training programs at liberal arts colleges: Pre-service and inservice options and RA perceptions of training. *College Student Journal, 30*, 404–410.

Tyson, W. (2005). Roommate and residence hall racial composition effects on interracial friendships among first-year college students (Doctoral dissertation). Duke University. Dissertation Abstracts International, A: The Humanities and Social Sciences, 4738–A.

U.S. Census. (2012, December 12). U.S. census bureau projections show a slower growing, older, more diverse nation a half century from now. Available at https://www.census.gov/newsroom/releases/archives/population/cb12-243.html

U.S. Census. (2013, September). Household income 2012: American community survey briefs. Available at https://www.census.gov/prod/2013pubs/acsbr 12–02.pdf

U.S. Census. (2014, March 20). Time Series/Trend Charts. Construction spending on public education: U.S. total Jan-2004 to Dec-2014. Not seasonally adjusted. Available at http://www.census.gov/econ/currentdata/ dbsearch?program=VIP&startYear=2004&endYear=2014&categories= 05XX&dataType=P&geoLevel=US&notAdjusted=1&errorData=1& submit=GET DATA

U.S. Department of Education. (2006). *A test of leadership: Charting the future of U.S. Higher Education (A report of the commission appointed by secretary of education Margart Spellings)*. U.S. Department of Education.

U.S. Department of Education. (2014). College ratings and paying for performance. Available at http://www.ed.gov/college-affordability/college-ratings-and-paying-performance

U.S. Department of Education, Office of Civil Rights. (2011, April 4). Dear colleague letter from the office of the assistant secretary of civil rights. *ED. gov*. Available at http://www2.ed.gov/about/offices/list/ocr/letters/ colleague-201104.html

U.S. Department of Education, Office of Postsecondary Education. (2011). *The handbook for campus safety and security reporting*. Washington, DC: U.S. Government Printing Office.

U.S. Department of Health & Human Services. (2013, April 3). What is adolescence? *Office of Population Affairs, Adolescent Family Life Self-Directed Modules*. Available at http://www.hhs.gov/opa/familylife/tech_assistance/ etraining/adolescent_brain/Overview/what_is_adolescence/index.html

U.S. Department of Housing and Urban Development. (2013, April 30). HUD issues notice on assistance animals and reasonable accommodations for persons with disabilities. HUD No. 13–060A. *HUD.gov*. Available at http://portal.hud.gov/hudportal/HUD?src=/press/ press_releases_media_advisories/2013/HUDNo.13-060A

U.S. Department of Justice, Civil Rights Division. (2011, July 12). ADA requirements: Service animals. *ADA.Gov*. Available at http://www.ada .gov/service_animals_2010.htm

Upcraft, L. M. (1982). *Residence hall assistants in college: A guide to selection, training, and supervision*. San Francisco, CA: Jossey-Bass.

Upcraft, L. M., Gardner, J. N., & Associates. (1989). *The freshman year experience: Helping students survive and succeed in college*. San Francisco, CA: Jossey-Bass.

Valparaiso University Office of Residential Life. (2007). *Residential curriculum.*
Valparaiso, IN: Author. Available at http://www.glacuho.org/Default.aspx?
DN=b58b8106–7a3c-4d64-80f1-ad3edb9556df

Van Laar, C., Levin, S., Sinclair, S., & Sidanius, J. (2005). The effect of
university roommate contact on ethnic attitudes and behavior. *Journal of
Experimental Social Psychology, 41*(4), 329–345.

Vandewalle, G., Schwartz, S., Grandjean, D., Wuillaume, C., Balteau, E.,
Degueldre, C., et al. (2010). Spectral quality of light modulates emotional
brain responses in humans. *Proceedings of the National Academy of Sciences,
107*(45), 19549–19554.

Wagenaar, A. C., & Toomey, T. (2002). Effects of minimum drinking age laws:
Review and analyses of the literature from 1960 to 2000. *Journal of Studies
on Alcohol Supplement, 14,* 206–225.

Wang, Y., Arboleda, A., Shelley, M. C., & Whalen, D. F. (2003). The influence
of residence hall community success of male and female undergraduate
students. *Journal of College and University Student Housing, 32*(2), 16–22.

Ward, L. (1995). Role stress and propensity to leave among new student affairs
professionals. *NASPA Journal, 33*(1), 35–44.

Warner, M. J., & Noftsinger, J. B. (1994). Increasing student involvement
through residence hall lifestyle and developmental programming. *Journal of
the Freshman Year Experience, 6*(1), 91–114.

Washington, C. S. (1969). All-freshmen residence halls: Do they make a
difference? (unpublished manuscript). ERIC Document Reproduction
Service No. ED 123 524.

Wawrzynski, M. R., & Jessup-Anger, J. (2010). From expectations to experiences:
Using a structural typology to understand first-year student outcomes in
academically based living-learning communities. *Journal of College Student
Development, 51*(2), 201–217.

Wawrzynski, M. R., Jessup-Anger, J. E., Stolz, K., Helman, C., & Beaulieu, J.
(2009). Exploring students' perceptions of academically based living-
learning communities. *College Student Affairs Journal, 28,* 138–158.

Wawrzynski, M. R., Madden, K., & Jensen, C. (2012). The influence of the
college environment on honors students' outcomes. *Journal of College
Student Development, 53*(6), 840–845.

Way, N. (2013). Boys' friendships during adolescence: Intimacy, desire, and loss.
*Journal of Research on Adolescence, 23*(2), 201–213.

Weber, K. L., Krylow, R. B., & Zhang, Q. (2013). Does involvement really
matter? Indicators of college student success and satisfaction. *Journal of
College Student Development, 54*(6), 591–611.

Weidman, J. (1989). Undergraduate socialization: A conceptual approach. In J. Smart (Ed.), *Higher education: Handbook of theory and research* (vol. 5) (pp. 289–322). New York: Agathon.

Weidman, J. (2006). Socialization of students in higher education: Organizational perspectives. *Sage Publications.* Available at http:// www.sagepub.com/oswmedia3e/study/chapters/handbooks/handbook4.1 .pdf

Weinberger, D. R., Elvevag, B., & Giedd, J. N. (2005). *The adolescent brain: A work in process.* Washington, DC: National Campaign to Prevent Teenage Pregnancy.

Weisfeld, G. E. (1999). *Evolutionary principles of human adolescence.* New York: Basic Books.

Weisfeld, G., & Coleman, D. (2005). Further observations on adolescents. In R. Burgess & K. MacDonald (Eds.), *Evolutionary perspectives on human development* (2nd ed.) (pp. 331–357). Thousand Oaks, CA: Sage.

Weissman, J. (2013, March 20). A truly devastating graph on state higher education spending. *The Atlantic.*

West, A. F. (1907). *American liberal education.* New York: Charles Scribner's Sons.

Westbrook, T. S., Danielson, H., & Price, J. (1996). The impact of freshman residence halls of first year student adaptation and retention. *Journal of College and University Student Housing, 26*(2), 20–25.

Westcott, K. (2012, November 15). Are "geek" and "nerd" now positive terms? *BBC News Magazine.* Available at http://www.bbc.co.uk/news/magazine-20325517

Western Interstate Commission for Higher Education (WICHE). (2013, May). Demography as destiny: Policy considerations in enrollment management. *WICHE.edu.* Available at http://www.wiche.edu/pub/16709

Wetherill, R. R., & Fromme, K. (2007). Perceived awareness and caring influences alcohol use by high school and college students. *Psychology of Addictive Behaviors, 21*(2), 147–154.

Wetzel, J. (1991). The role relationship skills and self-concept play in effectiveness. *Journal of College and University Student Housing, 21*(2), 7–12.

Wheeler, L. (1985). Behavior and design. *Environment and Behavior, 17*(1), 133–144.

Widick, C., & Simpson, D. (1978). Developmental concepts in college instruction. In C. Parker (Ed.), *Encouraging development in college students* (pp. 27–23). Minneapolis, MN: Unversity of Minnesota Press.

Wilcox, B. L., & Holahan, C. J. (1976). Social ecology of the megadorm in university student housing. *Journal of Educational Psychology, 68*(4), 453–458.

Williams, D. E., & Reilley, R. (1972). The impact of residence halls on students. *Journal of College Student Personnel, 13*, 402–410.

Williams, D. E., & Reilley, R. R. (1974). The impact of residence halls on students: The research. In D. A. DeCoster & P. Mable (Eds.), *Personal education and community development in college residence halls* (pp. 211–233). Washington, DC: American College Personnel Association.

Williams, J. (2007). College student experience questionnaire assessment program. *Indiana University Center for Postsecondary Research.*

Williams, R. M. (2009, Spring). Baseball's Ph.D.s. *Amherst Magazine.* Amherst, Available at https://www.amherst.edu/aboutamherst/magazine/issues/2009spring/baseball

Williamson, E. G., & Sarbin, T. R. (1940). *Student personnel work in the University of Minnesota.* Minneapolis, MN: Burgess Publishing Co.

Willoughby, B. J., & Carroll, J. S. (2009). The impact of living in co-ed resident halls on risk-taking among college students. *Journal of American College Health, 58*(3), 241–246.

Willoughby, B. J., Carroll, J., Marshall, W., & Caitlin, C. (2009). The decline of in loco parentis and shift to co-ed housing on college campuses. *Journal of Adolescent Research, 20*(1), 21–36.

Willoughby, B. J., Larsen, J. K., & Carroll, J. S. (2012). The emergence of gender-neutral housing on American university campuses. *Journal of Adolescent Research, 27*(6), 732–750.

Wingspread Group on Higher Education. (1993). *An American imperative: Higher expectations for higher education.* Racine, WI: Johnson Foundation.

Winston, R. B., Ullom, M. S., & Werring, C. J. (1984). Student paraprofessionals in residence halls. In S. C. Ender& R. B. Winston, *Students as paraprofessional staff* (New Directions for Student Services, No. 27) (pp. 51–66). San Francisco, CA: Jossey-Bass.

Wiseman, R. (2013). *Masterminds and wingman: Helping our boys cope with schoolyard power, locker room tests, girlfriends, and the rules of the boy world.* New York: Harmony Books.

Woosley, S. A., & Johnson, N. J. (2006). A comparison of the academic and cocurricular outcomes of residence hall transfer students and nontransfer students. *Journal of College and University Student Housing, 34*(1), 25–30.

Wright, R. (1994). *The moral animal.* New York: Vintage Books.

Yan, L., McCoy, E., Shelly, M. C., & Whalen, D. F. (2005). Contributions to student satisfaction with special program (fresh start) residence halls. *Journal of College Student Development, 46*(2), 176–192.

Yao, C. W., & Wawrzynski, M. R. (2013). Influence of academically based living-learning communities on men's awareness of and appreciation for diversity. *Journal of College and University Student Housing, 39*(2), 32–47.

Zatorre, R. J. (2012). Beyond auditory cortex: Working with musical thoughts. *Annals of the New York Academy of Sciences, 1252*, 222–228.

Zatorre, R. J., & Salimpoor, V. N. (2013, June 7). Why music makes our brain sing. *New York Times.*

Zeller, W., James, L., & Klippenstein, S. (2002). *The residential nexus: A focus on student learning.* Columbus, OH: Association of College and University Housing Officers International.

Zuckerman, M., Schmitz, M., & Yosha, A. (1977). Effects of crowding in a student environment. *Journal of Applied Social Psychology, 7*(1), 67–72.

# Name Index

# Subject Index

# If you enjoyed this book, you may also like these:

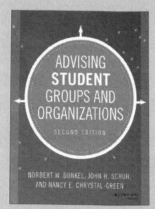

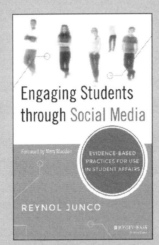

**Advising Student Groups and Organizations, 2nd ed.
by Norbert W. Dunkel,
John H. Schuh,
and Nancy E. Chrystal-Green**
ISBN: 9781118784648

**Engaging Students through Social Media,
by Reynol Junco,**
ISBN: 9781118647455

**Students Helping Students,
by Fred B. Newton, 2nd ed.
Steven C. Ender**
ISBN: 9780470452097

WILEY

# Want to connect?

Like us on Facebook
http://www.facebook.com/JBHigherEd

Join us on LinkedIn

Subscribe to our newsletter
www.josseybass.com/go/higheredemail

Follow us on Twitter
http://twitter.com/JBHigherEd

Watch us on YouTube

Go to our Website
www.josseybass.com/highereducation

WILEY